Claire

12-30-17

May this, your friends
version of "the most
beautiful Story since
The birth of Christ
be for you a source
of increased happiness
& hope.

Ed

p 268 email address

1969
2012
2017

A WALK TO GARABANDAL

TO

GARABANDAL

A JOURNEY OF HAPPINESS AND HOPE

ED KELLY

A Walk to Garabandal
A Journey of Happiness and Hope

ISBN-13: 978-1544281650
ISBN-10: 154428165X

Santos Gutierrez Gonzalez, SDB and The Workers of Our Lady of Mt. Carmel helped with the translation of Appendix III. All of the other translations are by the author unless otherwise noted.

The man on the cover, returning to the village from work in the hills, is David Torribio, a long time Garabandal resident.

GOODBOOKS MEDIA
3453 ARANSAS
CORPUS CHRISTI, TEXAS, 73411
goodbooksmedia.com

DEDICATION

Receive, most merciful Mother, this small labor, done with the intention of contributing in some way, to the propagation of devotion to you among your beloved children.

And since I have been until today a prodigal who inopportunely abandoned the father's house, obtain for me, my Mother, from your divine Son and my Brother, that henceforth I might never be separated from the house of my Father in Heaven, and that I might serve Him grateful for so many favors and through your powerful intercession.

May all my abilities and all my senses be employed in the service of your Son and my God…

Ed Kelly

(Borrowed from Ramiro Fernandez)

TABLE OF CONTENTS

CHRONOLOGICAL HISTORY 1

FORWARD 3

PREFACE 5

ACKNOWLEDGEMENT 7

PROLOGUE 9

CHAPTER ONE: GARABANDAL JULY 1969. 15

CHAPTER TWO : A SECOND VISIT. 23

CHAPTER THREE: THE VILLAGERS TALK. 37

CHAPTER FOUR: SPANISH SUMMER. 51

CHAPTER FIVE: THREE BROTHERS. 69

CHAPTER SIX: THE GENEROUS POOR. 81

CHAPTER SEVEN: NEIGHBORS. 95

CHAPTER EIGHT: A FATHERLY BROTHER. 105

CHAPTER NINE: CIRIACO. 115

CHAPTER TEN: AFTER THE VISIONS. 123

CHAPTER ELEVEN: THE DIFFERENCE. 135

CHAPTER TWELVE: REPORTERS. 143

CHAPTER THIRTEEN: RAMON'S MICROPHONE 155

CHAPTER FOURTEEN: FOREIGN INVASION. 167

CHAPTER FIFTEEN: PEPE'S THREE MIRACLES. 179

CHAPTER SIXTEEN: INVITATION. 189

CHAPTER SEVENTEEN: BEAUTIFUL BILBAO. 195

CHAPTER EIGHTEEN: MARÍA 211

CHAPTER NINETEEN: FORTY YEARS. 225

EPILOGUE: RETURN VISIT 2017 247

APPENDIX ONE
Two Long Interviews of Bishop del Val Gallo   277

APPENDIX TWO
A Lesson in Charity   289

APPENDIX. THREE
Twice Cured   293

APPENDIX FOUR
Catholic Church Authorities Look Favorably on Garabandal   301

SOURCES CONSULTED   325

PHOTO ACKNOWLEDGMENTS   327

CHRONOLOGICAL HISTORY

June 18, 1961: An angel appears in Garabandal.

June 19 to June 30: The angel appears eight more times. Visitors grow in number every day and witness the girls in ecstatic trances.

July 1, 1961: The angel tells the four girls that they will see the Blessed Virgin Mary the next day.

July 2, 1961: The young girls, separated immediately after their ecstatic trance by examining doctors and priests, coincide perfectly in their detailed descriptions of an extremely beautiful young lady.

August 8, 1961: Conchita reports that the lady, who said she was Our Lady of Mount Carmel, told them that a great miracle would happen in their village.

October 18, 1961: The girls read the first of two formal messages. It ends, "if we do not change, a very great punishment will come upon us."

June 20, 1962: The girls draw away from the crowd. Their long horrifying cries terrify everyone. All remain praying until six in the morning. Everyone in the village goes to confession the next day.

July 3: Conchita announces that on July 18, the angel will give her communion and the host will be visible. She writes this in letters to the bishop and others.

July 18, 1962: Thirty people sign and swear seeing the host appear mysteriously on Conchita's tongue. A man from Barcelona films the end of this with his movie camera.

June, 1963: Conchita is told, and reveals when the end times will begin.

January 1, 1965: Conchita says that everyone in the world will experience a divine warning that will frighten us a thousand times more than an earthquake and that we would rather experience the pains of death.

June 19, 1965: Conchita reveals the second message. "…Many priests, bishops and cardinals are on the way to perdition and with them they are taking many souls."

November 13, 1965: The Blessed Virgin appears for the last time in Garabandal

FORWARD

A Walk to Garabandal is lyrical. It is a walk back in time that also touches eternity. It begins shortly after the Virgin Mary's last visit, makes a final stop in 2017, and shows the way forward. Ed Kelly tells a traveler's tale full of wonderment, full of his personal impressions of the faces and places, local dances and cafes, old busses and taxi cab drivers that he came to know personally. His story forms, as Wordsworth described, a poem from the "spontaneous overflow of emotion recollected in tranquility."

What this book does that most other books on the subject do not, is combine devotion with humor, youthful emotion with mature reflection. As an American high school Spanish teacher, a young bachelor in 1969 on summer vacation in Spain, Kelly is lured by seeming chance to pay a visit to this remote mountain village. Despite a thought-provoking encounter at the bar, he tells his British companions that he has heard and seen enough, and that he won't be back. But life's plans change. He returns to live in the area and blends in and becomes trusted by the villagers. He knows them on a first name basis. They go fishing in the trout streams that flow by the village. Ed shares with us his intimate accounts of what he heard and discussed with all the young visionaries, including his dinner conversations with the main visionary, Conchita.

For those who believe in Garabandal, this book provides a fresh account of familiar details seen from new angles. For those who would like to hear a first telling of the story, and who may be skeptical about the reported apparitions, this book is a must read. Mr. Kelly's off-the-cuff, wry comments about phony visionaries and overly sentimental sensation seekers, sparkle with wit and discernment. However, the author assures us that you might as well doubt that Americans walked on the moon as deny that Our Lady visited every street of the mountain village of Garabandal.

Garabandal changed my life a long time ago. This book brought it all back again, the grace and wonder. It would seem providential that Ed Kelly has finally told his tale to help us prepare before the long-foretold heavenly events come to pass. Like walking the Camino de Santiago or joining the pilgrims in Chaucer's Canterbury Tales, in reading *A Walk to Garabandal* you meet unforgettable characters with whom you laugh and cry. More importantly, you experience lived faith and conversion which are the best evidence of the authenticity of the message of Garabandal.

D. Brian Scarnecchia, M.Div., J.D.

Associate Professor of Law,

Ave Maria School of Law,

Naples, FL

PREFACE

I travelled to Spain for the first time in 1969, seeking adventure in the land of the people whose language I taught. In a bar close to the country's North Coast, a man greeted me. He said I was late, that a few years earlier, people had flocked to the area to watch what doctors termed "unexplainable reactions" of four little girls who claimed visits with an angel and the Blessed Virgin in a nearby hamlet called Garabandal.

I sampled the good food and wine and headed for Pamplona, where avoiding being gored by the bulls chased away thoughts of little levitated, Spanish girls.

An experience back home in California prompted a return, but the long journey back to the foothills of the Cantabrian Mountains challenged my less than determined resolve. Even if an angel and the Virgin Mary had visited, they were long gone. But despite taking a step back for every two forward, I plodded on to find a quaint, quiet place with rows of rock houses pasted together with gobs of cement.

Josefa, the bread seller, rented me a tiny room for two dollars a night, three meals a day included. One night she described the mysterious way the girls crossed the little foot bridge in front of the church. I decided to stay to hear more.

During the next ten days, my new housemother and others relived for me, as if the events had occurred the night before, what they had seen, heard and felt almost daily for a year and a half. Photos and movies reveal observers intently watching the little girls in ecstatic trances and walks.

Despite the local Catholic Church's attempt to prevent the events from becoming widely known, there is now more interest in the happenings than in 1961 when the events, according to the locals, "turned the capital city, Santander on its head."

For some there might be too much "me" in the story. At first I took notes on getting served pigs feet when ordering ox tail stew, on how to find an affordable guest house in towns crowded with tourists, and on how to have a good time in the bars for fifteen U.S. cents. Only later, while at dinner with the fascinating girl who knows and will announce the date of a great miracle at which the sick will be cured and unbelievers believe, did I decide that everyone should know about this.

Here is happiness. God is still in charge of our troubled world and sent help. Luís Padilla writes that the divine warning foretold at Garabandal "is a happening of such great magnitude and transcendence, that it will be the definitive parting of the waters in the history of humanity . . . that modern history will be divided into a 'before' and 'after.' "[1]

In the award-winning BBC documentary, *Garabandal: After the Visions*, Conchita says that if all of the supernatural events [the Chastisement] prophesied in her visions come to pass, it would be better that her children had never been born.

To help us avoid this terrifying punishment, in his great mercy, within a calendar year of the worldwide warning, God will perform at Garabandal the greatest miracle in history and leave a permanent sign at the Pines as a reminder. We are living in the end times.

After learning all this, I wrote little or nothing about walking across Spain to Santiago de Compostela, playing in the 1972 Oviedo International Invitational Tennis Tournament, or falling in love and getting married. I focused on telling "the most beautiful human story since the birth of Christ."[2]

---

1 *El Gran Aviso De Dios*, (Mexico, Gráficos Amatl, 2007)
2 Pope Paul VI to Father Escalada

ACKNOWLEDGEMENTS

For providing manuscript reader feedback, and pointing out errors and weaknesses, thank you: Tom Anderson, Al Bernhard, Joe Donahue, Carolyn Furlong, Dina Grossman, Skip Howard, Melanie Howie, Dean Kenyon, Angel Lemieux, Jeff Moynihan, Mary Oxendine, Harry Roberts, Rebecca Streaker, Tom Windfelder, Horst Wolfe and Tom Zeitvogel.

For the hours of typing early drafts and help cutting and pasting, thank you, Susie Lantz.

For designing the word processor, thank you. Please accept my offer of stacks of old Scotch-taped chapters.

For your e-mails from Garabandal helping keep me up to date on your special village, thank you, Fatima Gonzalez Cuenca.

For letting me play basketball, baseball and football, and helping me feel valuable, thank you: Ed Nokes, Woody Mize, Brother Lackie, Brother Finch, Andy Slatt and Eddie O'Brien.

For organizing thousands of photos, scanning slides, keeping my laptop tuned up, and encouraging me, thank you Ira Tozer.

For helping revise this work during your pilgrimage to the village, thank you, Beth Anne Tuiton.

For not charging a dime for those five hundred commas and for being my supportive big sister forever, thank you, Maureen.

For inviting me to accompany you and your son to hear Tina, Pepe, and Maximina, for the tapes of those unforgettable meetings and those of your interviews with Serafín, Padre de la Riva and Ciriaco with whom I had spoken previously, *gracias, merci,* thank you, Ramón Pérez.

For prodding and pushing me into second gear, thank you, Peter Joyce. Only you and God know how much longer this work might have taken without your valuable help.

For your fatherly patience, kindness and generosity spending three hours with me, thank you, Your Excellency Bishop Antonio del Val Gallo.

For the courage to say, "I'll publish your book," and for your persistent patience and encouragement, thank you, Jim Ridley.

For relating what took place in your little hamlet, thank you: Pepe and Tina, Serafín and Paquita, Ben, Maximina, Josefa, Lucía, Gabino, Cencio, Angel, Cándida, Ciriaco, Mercedes, Vitoria, Clara, Milagros,

David, Antonia, and others. Thank you also visiting eye-witnesses: Manolo, Mary Loli Villar, Placido Ruiloba, Lucio Rodrigo S.J, Ramón Andreu S.J, Father Ramón de la Riva, María Saraco and Joey Lomangino. I will be eternally grateful to you, and trust that those who read the story you told will be grateful also.

For risking your good name by writing it under your recommendation that others read *A Walk*, thank you: Dr. Ronda Chervin, Dr. Rosalie Turton, Doctor of Law Brian Scarnecchia, Lt. Colonel USN retd Al Hughes, Todd Nichols, Bruce Campion, Tom Anderson, Tom Windfelder, and Bishop Emeritus of Corpus Christi, René Gracida.

PROLOGUE

For much of my early life I played baseball, basketball and tennis, or in college sat on the bench watching others. I tried coaching, but the high school principals weren't impressed, so I switched to teaching (and learning) Spanish. Spending two summers in Mexico working as a *bracero* and two more there taking classes, helped prepare me for a longer trip to Spain. Although baptized early as a Catholic, I was never much interested in apparitions — until July 1969. Chapter I starts there for me.

The *A Walk* story started before my arrival, in a little hamlet some fifteen miles inland from Spain's North Coast at an elevation of 1800 feet with the 6,000 foot Peña Sagra Ridge rising above it to the west.

Serious hikers walk on the remains of a Roman road high above the village, and marvel at, and take photos of, mysterious monoliths in the area. When the locals smell oil burning in the hills they remark, "The lamps of Jerusalem are lighted." The French Dominican Father François Turner speculated that this might signal the coming of the end times.

People in the surrounding area considered Garabandal villagers good, and said that the women there never offended God seriously. With no residing priest, the residents kept up religious practices meeting in the church to pray daily. The men, who spent days and nights in the hills, had time to talk with the Lord. During the horrible Civil War (1936-39), the villagers hid the priests from the enemy, and the first bread out of the oven was for them. Their saintly bishop, Don José Eguino y Trecu (RIP May, 1961) recognized the little village as special. He said that the people of San Sebastian were so faithful in their religious lives, and so devoted to the Blessed Virgin Mary, that something very great was going to happen there in the future.[1]

Until then, nothing exciting had ever happened there — nothing to merit mention in the local papers. The hamlet lost in the mountains didn't show up on maps. Many people in that area, Santander Province, didn't know where it was, and some had never even heard of it — until

---

1 www.virgendegarabandal.net, chapter 121

July 2, 1961. By the end of the month it would have been difficult to find anyone in the region who hadn't heard of San Sebastián de Garabandal.

With a small suitcase under one arm and a tennis racquet under the other, classroom polished Mexican style Spanish in my head, and years of playing and coaching sports as the only other preparation, I wandered into the area on the same day eight years later.

"They don't believe in you or in your conversations with the Lady in White, but they will believe when it is too late."

Saint Pio.
In a letter to the four children—March 3, 1962

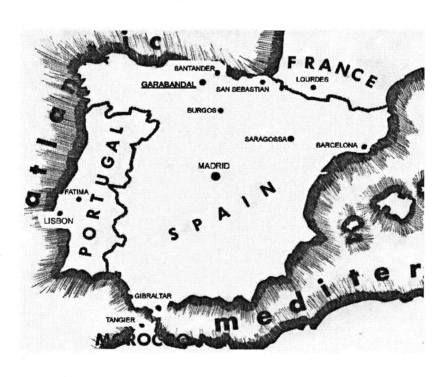

Garabandal is actually closer to the coast and further from Santander than the map shows.

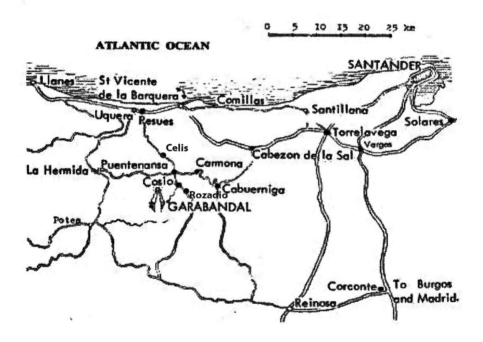

Puentenansa to Cosío 3 k.   Puentenansa to Celis 5.5 k.   Cosío to Garabandal 5 k.
Cosío to Roazadío 1.9 K.   Pesués to Puentenansa 23 k.

Kilometers to miles: 1 kilometer = .62 mile

Pesués Train Station 1969

CHAPTER ONE

GARABANDAL JULY 1969

he four-car narrow gauge train swayed back and forth heading west along northern Spain's Cantabrian Coast. Rain splashed against the windows. Station masters waved us past Treceño and Roiz before, minutes out of bigger San Vicente de la Barquera, the train slowed and then stopped. "Everybody out; track repair ahead," the conductor shouted. We crowded into the train station at tiny Pesués to wait.

"BAR" stood out in large black letters against a white house across the tracks. One wouldn't die of thirst if they never got those tracks repaired. I headed for the place, and, inside, joined a man standing at the bar holding a small glass of white wine. I greeted him.

Pesués bar.

"*Americano*," he replied, "you should have been here a few years ago. People poured through here by the thousands. We don't know if it was due to God or the devil, but something unexplainable happened up there in the mountains."

While the stranger ordered another *blanco*, I settled against the bar with my own glass, my mind wandering. In one week during this, my first visit to Spain looking for adventure in the land of the people whose

language I taught, I had chatted with Basque fishermen, imbibed a lot of good red wine and watched too much of it wasted in a gun-type fight with *bota* bags at a wine festival at Haro, used rolls of film on the picturesque ten-century-old Gothic cathedral at Burgos, and perhaps permanently damaged my right knee, dancing at a café in the same city.

The train and I were headed for Galicia in Spain's northwest corner with Portugal to the south. But pleasantly surprised to have someone with whom to talk in this "we don't mix readily with outsiders" area, I let the train leave without me and listened to the middle-aged fellow beside me:

> Day after day, up there in the village of San Sebastián, we watched four young girls crash to their knees onto the rocks and gaze motionless into the sky. Doctors came from Santander to test them. They poked them with sharp objects, touched them with hot items and shined bright lights into their eyes. The girls weren't bothered by anything. They claimed they saw an angel and later the *Santísima Virgen*.

Although skeptical, three hours later I crowded into a rusty old bus which then labored up the Nansa River Valley toward San Sebastián. After less than twenty kilometers in well over an hour, we stopped at the first place that looked like a town since leaving the coast, Puentenansa. Our driver drank a glass of wine in the corner bar while giving the bus a much-needed rest. I also rested in the same bar, store, restaurant and guesthouse. The bill for a three course meal with all the fresh bread and wine I wanted, plus a night's stay in a spacious, immaculately clean room? One dollar and fifty cents. I slept well.

Puentenansa bar, el Sindicato.
Now closed. 2012 photo.

The next morning I awoke unable to bend my knee for the second day in a row. Had my three-month summer vacation in Europe come to an untimely end? It was only the second of July! I joined a line in front of the town doctor's house. Two women behind me chatted, and I overheard one of them say, "I was this close to Conchita and saw the host appear on her tongue. It seemed to grow bigger while I watched." Hearing this second mention in as many days of the unusual events at San Sebastián made me think there might be something to this story.

It felt good to be able to follow the ladies' mountain version Spanish, but inside, the doctor's *"menisco"* and other unfamiliar medical terms were a different story! Cartilage damage? I understood that I might not die and should have the knee looked at upon returning home. The doctor prescribed a liniment, some pills and an ace bandage. No, it wouldn't hurt to walk on it.

Back outside, the morning haze had lifted to reveal jagged gray mountains against a clear blue sky. I filled my lungs with the pure, cool morning air. A woman walked down the road carrying a fresh loaf of bread. In town along the valley road, I counted three banks, two grocery stores, at least two bars and an oversized cement drinking fountain.

Although it wasn't my style to burst into that hamlet asking to see their Blessed Virgin, I decided to continue on, and at least try out my bad knee.

The morning bus took me three kilometers further up the valley to Cosío, a cluster of some twenty-five houses where nobody knew the distance to San Sebastián.

"*No, Señor*," I pleaded, "not how many hours but how far?"

The cowhand looked at my long legs and calculated, "an hour if you walk fast."

Stupid! Didn't he understand good Spanish? I wondered where this adventure would lead. Following directions, at the mountain side of Cosío I found a road, or at least a wide burro path, and started up. Blackberries provided a mid-morning snack. The way seemed endless. In an hour and a half I hadn't seen a soul, and not one car had passed me heading up or down. Did the "road" turn busy at rush hour? Hmm, those who always travel on foot would measure by time rather than by distance, no? The American teacher was a slow learner.

The hot sun had now risen high overhead. I had walked far enough. I peeled off my shirt and sat down on a rock to rest before heading back down. Far below, two dots inched up along the trail. I had climbed farther than I thought. Who would want to live way up here? I would see and test their Spanish before heading down.

Some time later, the man in the twosome said, "Jim is my name. This is my wife, Anne. We're from Liverpool. Is this your first time here? Is it well-known in America?"

"I don't know. I don't know anything about it."

"This is our third visit to the village. We've never seen the girls though. We don't speak Spanish and can't ask for them. People say they're beautiful now."

It was good to hear my native language (albeit British style) for the first time in ten days. Three times to this place? Maybe I'd walk along with them awhile just for the company.

San Sebastián, which Jim called Garabandal, wasn't much. No sidewalks or pavement. Residences, made of rocks pasted together with uneven patches of cement, were attached to each other in rows. A black-haired fellow, with bushy eyebrows and mustache to match, opened a shed door, glanced at us, and then led a cow up the street and through a little dirt square. The center of town? Women leaned over rails on second story balconies and smiled. Chickens scampered away in front of us. Dirt paths, rather than streets, separated the rows of houses. To walk through the whole village took ten minutes. No stores, no restaurants, nothing.

Ceferino's home/bar is to the right of the town square behind the man

To the west, a mountain ridge rose thousands of feet above the village. A cluster of nine pines stood on a bluff a few hundred yards above us. We started up toward them over large rocks left from a long dried-up stream.

Rocky lane at edge of village

"Here on this rocky lane is where the girls first saw the angel," Jim said. "It all started in June of 1961 while they were playing. One of the girls, Conchita, fell into a trance. Before her frightened playmates could run to get her mother, the same thing happened to them. At first only the villagers witnessed the girls in ecstasy, but soon people came from the surrounding villages, then from the cities and even from foreign countries. We've seen slides and movies and heard tapes."

We continued up the steep way to the pine trees. Below us, farm land, separated into parcels by rock walls, spread out like wide airplane wings on either side of seventy or so houses. Beyond narrow canyons on either side of the flat area, patches of light-green cultivated land broke the darker green of the predominant scrubland on the mountainsides. Below the village, the dirt road, up which we had hiked three miles from Cosío, snaked around as far as we could see.

Later, back down in the village, we entered the only establishment that looked like it might serve food. A big, rough looking fellow stood behind the bar. No one sat at three unfinished wooden tables.

"Shall we have a drink?" Jim asked. "Find out what they serve."

"*Un tinto, por favor*," I ordered, and the proprietor placed a small glass of red wine in front of me without speaking. My English companions preferred soda.

"I think he's Conchita's uncle," Anne said. "Ask him if he is."

"No, Ma'am! I can't do that!" But at her pleading, I relented.

The barman shook his head. "*Soy el padre de Loli.*"

"Loli's uncle?"

"No, Ma'am, her father." The English woman lit up like a child at Christmas.

"Oh, ask him for a medal or anything kissed by the Virgin!"

"Really Ma'am, I don't want to bother the poor guy."

"Oh please! You speak Spanish and we don't. Please ask him."

I didn't want any part of it. These poor villagers must be fed up with curiosity seekers, I thought, and headed for the protection of one of the

Loli and her father, Ceferino

tables while Anne insisted on her kissed object. How she asked without speaking Spanish, I don't know. It embarrassed me to watch.

"Loli," the bartender called. And a round-faced, slightly plump girl of about twenty came out from the back room. The English lady reached out to touch her or kiss her. I would have crawled under the table if it had been big enough. The girl didn't laugh.

"How are you, dear?" Anne asked. The Spanish girl didn't understand so the two of them just stood there looking at each other. Jim, still at the bar, and the father standing behind it, watched the two women. I ordered another *tinto*.

Then to my surprise, the father held out a religious medal. *"Joven"* ("young man"), he nodded over to me, "tell the lady that this was kissed by the Virgin." The woman grasped the medal, smiled at Loli, and then cradled the precious gift in her left hand. No one spoke.

Finally Jim muttered, "I wonder if we can get something to eat here".

"I hope so," I answered, and asked the Spaniard, *"¿Se sirven comidas aquí, señor?"*

He nodded, and then spoke to the girl, whereupon she retired to the kitchen. The couple joined me at the table. "That's Mari Loli," Anne started in. "She's one of the girls who saw the angel and talked with the Blessed Virgin."

Lady, I gathered that, I thought.

"Oh look!" she whispered. "Here she is!"

Unsmiling, Loli set plates, bowls, silverware and fresh bread on the wooden table. Next she brought out a large dish of soup, ladled out spoonfuls for each of us then left the big serving dish of steaming soup on the table. Fried fish and french fries followed.

"¿Quieres vino?" the father asked from behind the bar from where he oversaw the whole operation.

"Do you want wine?" I asked my companions.

I thought about all I had seen and heard the last two days. If anything ever did come of it all, someday I might want to tell people that I had talked with one of the "visionaries". And so since I was here, and would never come back, when Loli approached with the wine, I asked, *"¿Eres la cocinera?"* ("Are you the cook?")

"No, mi madre." She smiled while pouring our red wine from the typical copper-colored clay pitcher and then returned to the kitchen where we could hear her singing.

After dinner while his wife went to visit the church, Jim and I sat and worked on the generous jug of wine and wondered why it tasted better up in the mountains. *"Lo bautizan en las ciudades,"*[1] Loli's father explained.

We discussed the possibility of heaven meeting earth here or anywhere. We didn't know, but agreed that if the Blessed Virgin had come to earth for a visit, this was the kind of place she might choose.

Anne returned all excited. "I ran into Conchita! She is the most beautiful girl I have ever seen!"

Yeah, I thought. She probably smiled and said hello and that makes her beautiful.

We paid our bill, and hiked down the mountain.

Garabandal 1969

---

1 "They baptize it [add water to it] in the [restaurants of the] cities."

CHAPTER TWO
A SECOND VISIT

In July 1970 I was back in Spain for the second straight summer, this time touring the country in a Volkswagen van with four young California companions. In our four days together we had visited Montserrat, crossed the Pyrenees Mountains to Lourdes, crossed them again south to watch the bulls chase, gore and kill people in the streets of Pamplona, and then driven west along Spain's northern coast. Our plan now was to detour to Garabandal for a day or two before continuing westward towards Galicia and Portugal.

Pamplona during feast of San Fermín

The old VW labored up the recently widened but still challenging burro path from Cosío. To preserve the van as much as to sacrifice as on a pilgrimage, we got out and walked the last of the five kilometers from the valley road to the village.

Josefa's house

In less than an hour, my companions informed me that there was nothing of interest in the place and were leaving. I felt betrayed. Back in San José they had asked if they could join me and if I would show them around Spain. Now the four would seek other adventures leaving me alone on the mountain. I nursed my hurt with a shot of cognac and then slept the night in a cubbyhole of a room in the village bread distributor, Josefa's house.

Monday morning broke dreary and rainy. "The girls have denied having seen the Virgin and none of the villagers will talk about it," a disgusted English speaking visitor complained. "The local bishop has denounced the apparitions as a fraud."

The young men and boys stood out of the rain under the doorways and stared as if to ask what I was doing in their village. The little kids threw rocks at me. I retreated to the bar where solemn, unsmiling Loli set a *tinto* in front of me.

What a disappointment! I had traveled ten thousand kilometers and parted with my companions for this? The rain continued its incessant drizzle, the kind that lasts for months in my native Seattle. Alone at the table, I hunched over my glass of red wine bemoaning the loss of a summer of tennis back home in sunny San José, California. What was I doing back in this place anyway!

Joey Lomangino on Cosío to Garabandal path

The past winter at Santa Clara University, I had heard a lecture by Joey Lomangino, who had spoken with the accent of a second-generation Italian from New York. Blinded in an accident twenty-three years previous, the forty-year-old speaker traveled the world telling audiences:

We don't know how others will receive these words, but we'll tell it how it is for us. Some facts on Garabandal: In that little village, starting in 1961, the Blessed Virgin appeared to four little mountain girls: Conchita, Jacinta, Mari Loli and Mari Cruz some two thousand times. She gave the following message for the whole world, "We must make many sacrifices, perform much penance, and visit the Blessed Sacrament frequently. But first we must lead good lives. If we do not, a punishment will come upon us."

It sounded strange, more like a Mafia ultimatum than a sermon. Joey fired on, never varying his matter-of-fact, historical approach— no pauses—like a machine. He might not win any speech contests, but standing, facing out unseeing at the large crowd, his confidence, his certainty, and his story hushed his listeners.

The Blessed Virgin also announced a horrible warning that will be experienced by believers and non-believers alike. Conchita said, "It will be a thousand times worse than an earthquake.

Dying is preferable to a mere five minutes of what is awaiting us.

Joey neither embellished his account for the gullible nor attempted to make it more palatable for the skeptic:

> After the Warning there will be a Miracle. It will happen on a Thursday, at 8:30 in the evening. It will coincide with the feast of a young martyr of the Eucharist. It will be visible for all who are in the village and in the surrounding mountains. The sick who go there will be cured and the unbelievers will believe. It will be the greatest miracle that God has ever worked for the world. There won't be the least doubt that it is of God and for the good of humanity. Conchita knows the date and will announce it to the world eight days beforehand. After the Miracle a sign will be left forever in Garabandal for all to see.

Hmm. That "visionary" was leaving herself open to refutation by prophesying! Joey was something else. Perhaps, if you're blind, you don't sense the reaction of the listeners and you just barrel on. I liked the guy more and more. He added, "Now the girls are twenty, and although they don't like the attention this has brought, they graciously receive all visitors."

The visionaries didn't mind us going up to their village? I would go and listen to anything they would tell me.

And so when classes ended in June 1970 at Fremont, California's Mission San José High, I had again packed my one small suitcase and tennis racquet and returned to Spain. But now I sat dejected and alone keeping out of the rain in the small café-bar. That blind man might not have anything better to do, but I wondered what I was doing here. Loli watched, silent behind the bar. A visionary? I finished the wine and stood in the doorway. The rain had slowed, but water ran through the rocky paths. The smell confirmed that cows shared the village paths with people.

Outside, teenager Marielena, a visitor from the province's capital and its biggest city, Santander, sympathized, "A dreary place, no?"

"Yeah, I'm going to Burgos for some sunshine, and to enjoy their juicy roast lamb." One day in this primitive place was enough.

"Why don't you return on Saturday for the fiesta? Many visitors come up. Everybody dances. And it's lots of fun. Conchita will probably be in town."

Here was at least one friendly person. "Well, perhaps. *Adios*."

I soon tired of Burgos and its succulent roast lamb three days in a row. I wandered aimlessly, thinking more about what Joey had said back in Santa Clara:

Villagers and visitors saw the girls drop to their knees onto the rocks and heard their bones crack, but they didn't seem to feel anything. They walked at times backwards and at times on their knees faster than the onlookers could keep up with them. Everyone who visited the village witnessed the ecstasies

Loli and Jacinta walk backwards on rocky path.

and the actions of the "visionaries." Many people were drawn into the act. The girls gave religious articles to the Virgin to kiss, and then, with their eyes still focused on their heavenly visitor, handed them back unerringly to the correct owners. One day Conchita announced that St. Michael would come and give her Holy Communion and that it would be visible. This prophecy was fulfilled.

If that girl had announced with certainty about the visible host, it lent credibility to her announcement of a future warning and miracle. "Those who go to Garabandal experience an increase in faith, hope and charity," Joey had said.

I could use some of that, I thought, and wondered if it had stopped raining there yet. In Burgos the sun shone against the pale blue sky. Awesome! Residents said that directors came from Hollywood to shoot movies here in Burgos because of the picturesque sky.

Return to Garabandal? That young visitor from Santander had been friendly—and cute.

The five-hour bus trip north tested my resolve, but I arrived on time for the fiesta—and for the most significant adventure of my life.

After the noon Mass, we followed arrow-pierced Saint Sebastián in procession from the church to the rectangular ten pins bowling field where a dozen village youths, accompanied by the primitive tambourine, danced *Picayos*[2] in their patron's honor.

The long dance looked simple. The boys, in white shirts and pants, separated at the waist by a red sash, jumped back and forth. Their partners wore red skirts and white blouses with black vests.

Village youth celebrate the feast day of St. Sebastián.

A few dozen people of all ages stood along three sides of the rectangular dirt bowling area to watch the performance. "Jacinta is shaking a tambourine," Manolo, a curly-haired bachelor from Pamplona pointed out. "She's the one in the pink polka dot dress. She's one of the visionaries."

Light brown hair falling almost to her shoulders, fair complexion, attractive. She was taller than Mari Loli who stood next to her. The seriousness of both Loli and Jacinta contrasted with the festive joviality of the others. If they were twelve in 1961, now, nine years later, they would be twenty-one, I calculated.

"Have you seen Conchita, Eduardo?" Manolo asked. "Look. There she is in the corner behind her mother, the girl in the white coat."

Tall, long black hair, lovely dark complexion, dark eyes, serious but happy. Yes, she was beautiful! That English lady the year before knew

---

2 A folk dance typical of the region.

what she was talking about.

"Let's see if we can talk to her," Manolo suggested.

Talk to her? What do you say to someone like Conchita, to someone who talked two thousand times with the Mother of God and held the Infant Jesus in her arms? Talk to someone like that, and in a foreign language? I have never had a witty opening line even for ordinary girls, and in English. But as I stood wondering, she approached, smiled and greeted, "*Hola.* (Hi)"

I don't know whether I answered in English, Spanish, or just grunted. How would I ever explain the attractiveness of Conchita? I would try to find out, but first the fiesta.

Early Saturday evening we danced in the dirt bowling area and celebrated. There I met Lolita, a Cuban then residing in Santander. She, like Manolo, had been to Garabandal during the apparitions (1961–1965) and was well received by the villagers, especially, it seemed, by Jacinta. She danced well, and some village women soon spoke of my *novia* (girlfriend).

The dance, which started about six, was a family affair. Old widow Doña Vitoria refused my invitation and insisted that I dance with the *chabalas* (young girls). Jacinta and Loli danced often. Conchita always chose a girl as a partner. Mary Cruz looked happy dancing with Ignacio, her husband of a couple of months. I once found myself in her small group trying the regional dance. The band played every tune to the same rhythm.

By 10:00 P.M. suppertime I was beat. My new housemother, clearing the dishes from the table in her small kitchen, also looked tired. Gray-haired, with one front tooth missing, Josefa Cosío, like many village widows, dressed always in black. The day had been no holiday for her. She had cows to milk and bread to fetch five miles away in Puentenansa even on St. Sebastian's day. Now while she washed the dishes, her son, Loi, and her two sons-in-law, Cecilio and Domingo, talked about the *verbena* (night session). I thought they joked.

"Come on, Eduardo" they urged. "We'll stop for a cognac and another coffee and you'll feel fine." Pleased at this first sign of acceptance by the village men, I fought sleep and weariness and joined them.

A strong combination, their syrupy-thick coffee with a generous shot of cognac! And then out in the cool night mountain air, I woke up and warmed to the festivity. The children from the earlier session were now in bed, but more teenagers and couples from the surrounding villages filled the dirt dance area. Even the music sounded better. When I complimented the drummer in the combo, he held up the reason— an almost empty tequila bottle—saying, "My Mexican friend in the mountains gave this to me."

The next morning after 8:00 A.M. Sunday Mass, I strolled through the village. Young Marielena had been right; visitors seemed to outnumber the some three hundred village residents.

In the afternoon, Lolita Villar invited me to pray with a group from Santander at the Pines.[3] When I arrived, three or four men and about a dozen women and girls gathered together listening to a tape recording. Three young boys warmed themselves over a small fire under the trees thirty feet away. We sang a couple of hymns then knelt to pray the rosary. I reluctantly joined in—at a distance.

On kneeling down I heard, "*Acérquense*" ("Draw near"), and turned to see a man fall over in an apparent faint and the others crowd around him. The middle-aged man immediately knelt up with his head thrown back and arms outstretched. People put their rosaries in his hands. I tried to concentrate on prayer but didn't want to miss anything behind me. At the third mystery a man approached me.

"Clemente wants your rosary. The Virgin is asking for it." Hogwash, I thought, but not wanting to cause a scene, gave it up. So this man who had fallen over was Clemente, the "seer" from Seville. A mist rolled in and chased away the sun.

An old-timer hiking down the mountain stopped for a moment to observe the scene and then moved on. Was it because, after the 1961 drama of ecstatic trances and marches, he saw nothing of interest now? The young boys still hovered around their fire paying us no attention.

After the rosary, a fellow with white, wavy hair and dressed in a suit arranged his tape recorder and repeated into it phrase by phrase what Clemente was saying. Clemente paused, waiting for each phrase to be

---

3 A cluster of nine pine trees that stands on a "shelf" some three hundred feet up a rocky lane west of the village. Because a number of the apparitions took place there, many visitors go there to pray and to look out over the village.

recorded. Some of the women cried. What I could hear (from a distance) of the slow, repetitious Spanish words bored me. I shivered and wished for a sweater. The hypnotist at our June high school assembly had put on ten times the show. Finally Clemente got up. Two men embraced him before the three of them walked away. Pat, an Irish girl, and a couple of Americans, rushed over to me. "Did you understand that? Did you get every word of the message, Ed?"

I tried not to laugh at Pat in her seriousness. Someone asked me to identify and claim my rosary. A businesslike Frenchman climbed to investigate the commotion. I heard him ask a woman, "Was it the same as with the girls' ecstasies?"

"No, very different," she answered.

"Ah, sure." And that satisfied the Frenchman's inquiry about Clemente. He took a brief look at us, then turned and headed back down the mountain.

Interesting! Clemente's "ecstasy" moved to tears the more sophisticated Spaniards from the cities and the few foreigners present. Yet nobody in the little farming village stopped work to watch "the show." Backward mountain people prone to deception? From what I had just seen, it seemed the opposite. The villagers were too busy earning their daily bread to be curious about hypnotics and fakers. It was the outsiders with their leisure and "learning" that had trouble distinguishing the true from the trite and the false.

Conchita at her window.

Down below in the village, my new Cuban friend strolled with Manolo. "You've been favored," she called out to me, "The Virgin asked for your rosary because you were praying with such attention."

Balderdash! That wasn't the way I had seen it. I continued to Conchita's house hoping to see her and even talk. I stood outside her window and listened to a familiar Argentine tango. She leaned out.

"Hello. Practicing for the dance tonight?" I asked.

"No. That's my favorite record. I play it all the time."

How beautiful she was, and friendly! I told her about my coming to Garabandal the summer before and about meeting blind Joey (Lomangino) and her brother Miguel in Santa Clara. No, all the tourists coming here didn't bother her.

"I studied the last two years in Burgos," she said (September 1968 till June 1970). "*Pero mi madre no quiere que mi secretaria.*"[4] It was cute the way she talked, leaving out the verb. Did she do so to make it easier for foreigners to understand her? "I will study nursing next fall," she added.

I racked my brain for something profound to say so she would stay and talk. She and her three young companions had felt the same way ten years previous when the Blessed Mother visited them. "Conchita," one of the three had pleaded, "you know some funny stories. Tell the Virgin one so she won't go away."

It was not as I had feared. I felt at ease in her presence. And better yet, she seemed content to stay at the window and chat with me.

Later I strolled through the festive village alone with my happy thoughts. Loli smiled and her sixteen-year-old sister, Sari, even waved at me.

Monday morning I rose early and accompanied Lolita halfway down the mountain towards Cosío. There had been little chance to talk in the celebrating village. Her priest brother worked summers in Huandacareo, Mexico. Huandacareo? That sounded familiar. But I had visited so many places these past years. Ah yes, 1966, and I had met Father Villar there. We laughed and parted.

Back up near the village, a young man was cutting grass. He looked up and smiled.

"Looks like hard work," I greeted him.

"Some." He stopped cutting to sharpen the scythe.

"How many cuttings do you get per year?"

"Oh, it depends." He leaned on the scythe to rest and talk. "Two, and sometimes one extra green cutting from the fields close to town."

A smiling pregnant woman approached and handed him something to drink. She raked the hay that the man cut. Some days later I learned

---

4 "My mother doesn't want me (to be) a secretary."

the man was Serafín, the oldest of Conchita's three brothers. The woman was his wife, Paquita.

I entered the village puffing. Doña Vitoria invited me in for lunch. *"Coma, coma. Más. Coma más."* [5] Great woman! She served me homemade *chorizo*, fresh bread and wine. Her son, Angel, ate stale french fries and a cold fried egg. They argued whether he was thirty-four or thirty-five. "No Angel," she insisted in her shrill voice, "You're the same age as María's son. You go ask."

She had given up on getting her son married and started to work on me. "Do you like the Spanish girls? *¿Muy bonitas, no?*" The older women were by far the friendliest in the village. Some seemed happy to have visitors in Garabandal. The aloofness of the men and boys still disturbed me.

Manolo, the visitor from Pamplona, and I spent much of the day together. Walking through the village, he related what he had seen during his visit in 1961 and what eyewitnesses had told him.

"There used to be a bridge here in front of the church," he said. "I saw the girls cross it four abreast but there was only room for two. The others floated across to the sides."

He questioned the villagers about the apparitions, as if trying to relive them as well as to learn more. "Did you get all that, Eduardo?" he would ask after each session with a villager.

"Not all of it." The language of some of the old-timers was challenging, but I easily understood Manolo's retelling the villagers' accounts in his educated Spanish and valued his help. Too timid to confront the villagers myself, but anxious to hear anything they had to say about what they had seen and heard and felt *"cuando las apariciones"* ("at the time of the apparitions"), I happily tagged along behind pushy Manolo on this, his last day in the village.

"Angel," he blurted out without introduction, "What impressed you most?"

"The crashing to their knees onto the rocks. We could hear their bones crack, yet the little girls never paid the slightest attention."

"Did you ever get tired following the visionaries?" Manolo continued.

<hr />

5 "Eat, eat. More. Eat more."

"No, never. We would follow them all over the village, sometimes for hours, three or four times a day and often at night."

"What else impressed you?"

"Well, one day I gave my watch to an acquaintance from the Province of Leon and told him to give it to Mari Loli for the Virgin to kiss. Then I went into the bar and forgot about it. A long time later, Loli entered the bar in a trance gazing into the air as always. She walked straight to me, opened my hand, and gave me my watch." Angel pulled out his big pocket watch with A.H. printed in black on it and told us, "It didn't have my (identifying) initials on it then."

"You don't believe in the apparitions, do you, Angel?" Manolo probed for reasons, but Angel just shrugged. By "don't believe" Manolo meant that Angel was not convinced that all that he, his neighbors, and countless visitors had observed and experienced was of supernatural origin. Angel and others remember what they saw, and recount their experiences with a certainty and confidence that surprised and impressed me. But many of these eye-witnesses were uncertain of the cause and meaning of the happenings.

That night Manolo and I walked to the church and then up the dark street into which thousands had crammed on July 18, 1962, where those close enough had seen the host on Conchita's tongue. "A man from Barcelona captured some of it with his movie camera," Manolo explained. One weak porch light broke the darkness. Had the light been there during the apparitions? Even in 1970 there were few street-lights in the village.

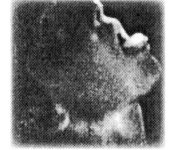

"Shall we climb to the Pines, Eduardo?"

We were grateful for each other's company that dark, moonless night. Manolo's small flashlight lent little help, and we stumbled climbing up over the large stones in the lane. I had heard a villager say that the girls in ecstasy ascended and descended this rocky path with such ease and speed that it seemed as if their feet didn't touch the rocks, and that they moved three times as fast as normal, day or night.

Manolo interrupted my thoughts, "Conchita used to go up there to pray at 6:00 A.M. In winter that is night. I saw the girls, gazing into the

33

sky, come down that part of the hill—backwards. Imagine that!" And he pointed to the very steep brush covered area off to the left of our rocky path.

Later, after leaving Manolo, I wandered through the dark village, careful not to stumble. The gate leading out to the cemetery creaked and I quickly changed direction. I didn't know whether it was God or the devil but didn't stick around to find out.

In the morning, Mari Nati invited Manolo and me for *almuerzo*.[6] Nati was a talkative young woman from Bilbao who stayed with her mother[7] in a dollhouse-sized two-room addition built onto the front of important eye-witness Ben Gómez' place. She didn't stop the chatter while serving us cognac and coffee. I hoped her thick glasses would stay on straight while she poured the steaming drink. We talked about the United States and Spain, of the Kennedys and Francisco Franco, the Spanish general and dictator from 1939 to 1975, and about the apparitions.

"We have tapes of the girls saying the rosary in ecstasy. Come and hear them sometime." Nati went out to invite Conchita to join us but returned saying she didn't visit the homes.

Later outside, Manolo and I saw Conchita heading toward the church. He tried to say a proper good-bye. The Virgin Mary had some competition in the village. People came to learn about her visits to Garabandal and to pray, but ended up intrigued by Conchita.

Loli holding up religious articles for the Virgin to kiss

After Manolo left, I wrote six or eight postcards, and then knelt alone in the old stone church. I prayed poorly. Thoughts of girls floating across the stream and about the serene and beautiful Conchita chased away prayer.

It was Tuesday already. Four days in this place? I had only planned on a couple and should have been on my way along the coast toward

---

6　A snack usually around 10:00 or 11:00 A.M.

7　They are among the dozen or so outsiders who own or rent dwellings in Garabandal.

Galicia and Portugal. But I still wanted to see Walter's slides of the girls in their ecstatic trances. Maybe another day would do it.

Walter stood out among other visitors—and the villagers. Tall, partially bald, a stately business type, dressed always in a suit jacket and unbuttoned white shirt, Walter Kushion exchanged "hellos" and more with many of the villagers. A retired Savings-and-Loan investigator from Michigan, by this summer of 1970 he had been in Garabandal about six months. To use as an office and for emergency guest lodging, he rented the three story new house that borders the village square, but he stayed at Conchita's Aunt Maximina's house.

I found him talking with Loli at her father's bar. He offered me a *tinto*. Surprisingly, Loli seemed interested in talking.

"Loli," I kidded, "with all these foreigners coming here, you should speak five or six languages by now."

"*No soy inteligente,*" she smiled. "I don't have the brain for languages." She talked about prices, rich Americans, travel in Spain. I wanted to remain to talk more, but she got busy with customers in the family's combination home, bar, restaurant and store, so Walter and I left to see the slides.

A borrowed antique projector challenged our ingenuity. But there they were, the happenings of the four little girls of San Sebastián de Garabandal on film: in ecstatic trances, walking down the stairs without looking, walking backwards, returning religious articles to their owners, levitated, posed in statue-like positions, and Conchita with the host on her tongue. After forty or fifty slides, Walter and I attended the rosary in church, after which we met Father Burns and some women from New York who were there to see the church and Conchita. I thought these were the strangest of tourists—those who come to "see" Garabandal. They could see it on a map. It would be easier and cheaper.

After *cena,*[8] I was anxious to get down to the bar for coffee and to

---

8 Supper, served in the area from 9:00 p.m. to about 10:30 p.m. in summer and earlier in the winter.

show off my Spanish in front of the newly arrived Americans when Josefa exploded in anger. I had been reading a Catholic periodical and asked if they ever wrote about Garabandal. "Yes," Josefa bellowed. "All against."

Her outrage surprised me. Although still reluctant to broach the subject of the apparitions with the villagers, when Josefa provided the opening, I asked, "How does that make you feel?"

"We don't like it," she fumed. "Why do the priests say that what we witnessed was nothing, when we saw it with our own eyes? From the pulpit they tell us to forget it and say it can all be explained naturally, but out on the street some won't say that. We don't understand this."

Josefa's married daughter, Ofelia, nodded in agreement. She and her family, visiting for the festival days, lived in Celis some five miles farther down toward the coast from Puentenansa. I explained that this negativism was the typical attitude of the Church on apparitions in order that unbelievers couldn't later claim that they were fabrications of the Church. "Have the priests ever said this? Do you ask them why they say it was nothing or to explain the naturally unexplainable happenings that you witnessed?"

"No. We are not educated. We respect them." They talked to my heart's content—a great conversation until almost midnight. Their outbursts of anger and eagerness to talk about what they had seen and heard and felt during the apparitions that had started some nine years previous (1961) sharpened into focus for me the drama of Garabandal.

Although I had been awake since 4:30 a.m., I scribbled these remembrances of an eventful day, the first notes I wrote in the village. I almost overlooked the ten-minute conversation with Conchita when she came to buy bread at our place.

Maybe I should stay awhile, I thought, content to be somewhere, and fell asleep.

 THE VILLAGERS TALK

elevision was a novelty in Garabandal. In the mid sixties, the bishop removed Pastor Father Valentín Marichalar and forbad him to return to the village. The new young pastor had a community center built and a television set installed in order to get the people's minds off of the dramatic happenings there. Now, Friday morning at breakfast, Josefa's oldest, but childlike son, Loi discussed his favorite program.

"We like *Bonanza*. And the Indians, very bad people, no? They wanted to govern—rebels—but oh how they died. Pum, pum."

Hearing about heaven's possible visit to earth in this little hamlet hidden in the Cantabrian Mountains interested me. Bonanza and our Indians excited Loi more.

I didn't linger over my bowl of hot coffee with rich, fresh milk and fresh bread and butter. I hurried to catch Father Burns to say good-bye to him and his American tour group starting down the mountain.

It was a treat to speak and hear "American," so on that bright, sunny morning I decided to finish the five kilometers to Cosío with them and then walk another mile to Puentenansa to buy razor blades, soap, postage stamps, and a notebook. I didn't know how long I would be in Garabandal now.

The priest treated the women like children, pulling out a surprise for all—medals kissed by the Virgin. They gathered around him and he explained, "The girls reported that the Blessed Virgin promised that through articles she kissed, her Son would work prodigies and miracles. Would you like one, Ed?" I felt happy that Father considered me one of his children.

Down below in Puentenansa, two sisters running the inn where I had stayed were happy to see me. Yes, they would keep my extra baggage longer so I wouldn't have to lug it up the hill. They seemed interested that I would stay so long in Garabandal.

I sang as I shopped, reflecting on Josefa's outburst the night before: "What do the priests mean by telling us these children are sick, that they are playing games? These are our own nieces!" Would others reveal their feelings? I looked forward to learning more up on the mountain.

I walked by and looked in the windows of six or eight shops in Puentenansa, the commercial hub of the Nansa River Valley. At a hardware store I bought anise with which to cure my new *bota* bag.[9] The owner of the store spoke up. "If you had only seen what went on up there in Garabandal. At first all believed. I went up many times. Now if we talk about it, people laugh. That fiasco Sunday [Clemente's show] will wreck Garabandal."

Another woman entered the shop and joined our conversation. "I heard that Clemente was a good man. Who is to blame, he or someone else?" she asked.

"Another. A man from Santander who takes Clemente there," the woman behind the counter answered.

She sounded sure of herself and added that bad priests reacted against the 1965 message about priests leading people to hell. Since she seemed willing to talk, I probed, "Are politics involved?"

"Yes. These new young priests are anti-Franco, Carlists or whatever you call them."

The clerk who had a niece in nearby Celis would look for a wife for me—whether I wanted one or not. I said my good-byes.

Later that afternoon, fortified by a three course meal and sufficient wine for a whole day's walk, I headed up the narrow valley with the Nansa running in the opposite direction on the right. Would it get to its new home in the Atlantic twenty-two kilometers away before I walked a third that far to my new home?

Out of Cosío, climbing at a fast pace, and with the Vendul cascading down in the opposite direction hundreds of yards below, I soon caught up with two señoras each with a large woven basket on her back. The forty

---

9 A small leather bag used to carry wine.

and forty-three year old sisters also wanted to know about Clemente. I offered to carry one of the baskets but they protested, "No, it's too heavy for you. We're accustomed to it."

I smiled down at the short, stout women. "Well, at least let me try it awhile. We'll trade off."

Large jars of cooking oil, bottles of wine, canned goods. Supplies for the whole winter? I shouldn't have insisted.

"Oh, if we could only have those happy times back again," they sighed. "How we prayed and how we sang. We would come down from the *prao*[10] very tired and yet follow the girls all over."

"How would you know there would be an ecstasy?"

"There would be something all the time. From our fields we saw the girls and people gathering at the *cuadro*.[11] What most impressed us was their falling down onto the rocks without flinching. We'd hear their bones crack right in front of us, but the girls didn't seem to notice. They were in a different world."

One of the women, Clara, stopped and stared up at me and said:

> But God punished me. I didn't believe it could happen. I didn't believe the angel could give Conchita Holy Communion and that we would all see it. But at the last minute it struck me [that it would happen] and I jumped out of bed and ran to the alley where the others gathered. But I arrived too late. When my sister here,

Author with Clara, 1999

Milagros, and my friends told me how the host appeared and grew bigger on Conchita's tongue, I wept because I knew that God was punishing me for my lack of faith.

◦•◆•◦

10 Badly pronounced "*prado*" meaning parcel of workable land, where some people pastured their cows. Many rural people don't pronounce the Spanish intervocalic "d".

11 To protect the visionaries from the crowd, the village men cordoned off a square (*cuadro*) area where many of the first apparitions took place.

I stood spellbound. Again the emotional outburst impressed me most. Just recalling having missed the "miracle" of the host eight years previous so troubled this woman that she stopped on the trail unable to hike on. I was ready to carry that heavy pack up and down the five-kilometer mountain trail in order to hear more. It seemed that all had not stopped believing in the divine source of the ecstasies, but only needed an invitation to discuss them in public. I had yet to find anyone who denied the happenings.

Ouch! The darned entryway to my home was about four inches shorter than I. My room was small, furnished only with a bed, a wooden chest and a small table. The one window faced the house next door. Through it I had seen the rain fall part of every day since the fiesta.

The old house, with one floor of living space above the ground level cellar,[12] was quiet now. Ofelia and her children, except Rosamaría who stayed to help grandmother take care of the cows and me, had left for their home in Celis in a cart pulled by the faithful burro. They had been with *abuela* since the feast day and I suspected that grandma had moved them out of the small bedroom to make room for me.

Josefa, hard-working and ambitious, was one of two village bread sellers who walked the fourteen-kilometer round trip to Puentenansa for fresh bread every day. She also sold milk by the cupful to a couple

Josefa ready to work in the fields   *Josefa's grandchildren with their Uncle Loi*

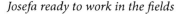

12 Most of the village houses were two stories. They didn't have basements but had dirt or cement on the bottom floor which was not usually inhabited but used for storage. A few kept cattle on the first floor during the winter.

of neighbors. I had seen her come in from the fields with hay piled high on her head and feared that if I offered to help, I couldn't handle the load. Besides me, she fed seven or eight house construction workers and prepared their rooms nearby.

I didn't go hungry in her house during my stay, but at times longed for a lettuce and tomato salad. We ate a lot of potatoes. Potatoes for lunch, for dinner, potato soup, potato omelet. She also served tasty *merluza a la romana* (breaded fried hake) a couple of times. There was a fifty gallon wooden barrel of good red wine underneath the stairs so we had plenty to drink with the daily supply of fresh bread. Breakfast consisted of bread and a large bowl of café con leche, the typical breakfast drink in Spain. The percentage of milk to coffee depends upon the server. In Josefa's house it was about three-to-one, with the plentiful milk coming from the cow to the pail to the stove to the table. They gave this American butter with his bread.

A dreary, boring place in which to spend a couple of weeks? On the contrary. Although my life soon settled into a routine, the days proved fast and fulfilling. After that frugal breakfast I would walk twenty yards to pray in the church where for generations the people of Garabandal have prayed to *La Virgen bien aparecida en las montañas*.[13] Then I would stroll through town until meeting up with a fellow visitor or one of the townspeople. If that failed, I would often find someone with whom to exchange stories and impressions at Ceferino's bar. Almost everyday a handful of new visitors trickled in for a day or two. Some stayed longer.

The main meal was served soon after 1:00 P.M. or when the bread arrived. Afterwards I undertook some project: studying the slides taken during the ecstasies, talking with Walter, or listening to the little gray-haired Filipino lady, Eloisa, talk about Padre Pio and the Garabandal visions. Sometimes I snuck down to fish in the streams cascading on both sides of the Garabandal bluff. At eight o'clock in the evening Jacinta or her mother walked through the streets clanging a bell to remind us to pray for the souls in purgatory. Shortly afterwards, the first of three bells called us to church for the rosary.

---

13 The Virgin truly seen in the mountains. The patroness of the Diocese is honored under the name, La Bien Aparecida. This title has nothing to do with the reported apparitions in the Village.

*Jacinta's mother, María calling
people to prayer*

Dinner, followed by a quick cognac and coffee at one of the village's three bars, completed the day. Sometimes I returned to my cubicle too tired to jot down the day's highlights, but on this July Friday of 1970 I wrote:

> These are turning into busier days than I wished, but crazy, wonderful days when one outdoes the other. Today, for example, when I left the house in the morning for Walter's office to see more of the slides, women hurried to spread the wash out to dry on the bushes under the bashful sun. I ate the midday meal at Ceferino's—the lamb butchered yesterday because it had a broken hip. Friendly Loli seemed willing to stand around and talk. I had asked her if the dinner would be good, and then kidded her saying that the lamb she served wasn't as tender as the lamb in Burgos.

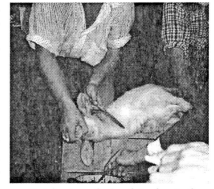

*Butchering of a lamb in front of
Ceferino's establishment*

The next morning, a large, gray-haired woman in her late fifties, dressed in "outside-the-village" clothes, greeted me. Madame Pelletier from France or Belgium, I'm not sure which, asked if I had seen Father Laffineur yet.

"Who?"

"Father Laffineur, the author of the Garabandal book, *The Star on the*

Mountain. Everyone visits him, but you must make an appointment. He works every morning and receives people only in the afternoon."

Sounded like a prima donna. What kind of person here required an appointment?

The following day a little before 2:00 P.M., I arrived at Father's door for my "appointment." A note hung on the door latch:

> For the young American,
> I'm sorry I don't remember your name. Can you come back at 4:30? Father is busy.
>
> Madame Pelletier

That was too much. Who'd the guy think he was—the bishop?

Later that afternoon, Madame Pelletier ushered me into a comfortable, modern sitting room in one of a half-dozen or so new houses scattered throughout the village.

"The owner from Barcelona lets Father stay in this place." Madame smiled all the time and it gave me the creeps. "He'll be right down."

A stately, white-haired man descended the stairs holding onto the rail. He was old enough to be a bishop. He extended his hand and greeted, *"Parlez-vous francais?"* His voice was deep and melodious.

"No, Padre."

"Oh, ¿pero hablas español?" ("Oh, but you speak Spanish?")

"Sí. Me defiendo, como dicen los españoles." ("Yes. I get by, as the Spanish say.")

"Pues entonces hablamos español o la Madame puede interpretar." ("Well then we will speak Spanish or Madame can interpret.")

His Spanish was slow with a marked accent but grammatically close, much better than the dictionary (infinitive only) Spanish of many tourists.

He shot out something rapidly in French that indicated the conversation would turn serious. Sure enough, Madame Pelletier repeated his request: "Father wants you to tell him all about what you saw up at the Pines on Sunday—about Clemente."

I told him that the "ecstasy" hadn't impressed me, that I had seen a much better show when a hypnotist came to perform at our California high school a few months previous.

His expressive eyes opened wide. He smiled and nodded in agreement, "*Oui*."

He seemed impressed by my not having been duped by Clemente, a new "visionary" brought to Garabandal to see visions and who, in father's opinion, was doing damage to Garabandal. Father asked about my background and education and then about what else I had heard.

"Father, I came here to listen to you."

"No. Tell me what the people have told you."

He must have had sufficient contact with the visionaries and townspeople to enable him to write *The Star on the Mountain*, I thought. Why this insistence on hearing my report now?

"It's more value to listen to you now than to spend hours with Conchita," he continued. "The villagers won't tell me anything now. I'm a priest. Tell me what the people have told you, and then come back anytime and I'll answer your questions."

So I told him about Josefa's anger at the priests telling them from the pulpit that all that they had seen was natural, and about the women stopping in their tracks on the path to relive the miracle of the host. Father nodded. Yes, this confirmed his suspicions that more villagers than would admit among themselves or to the priests still maintained a firm conviction that the ecstasies and prodigies they had witnessed were the work of God, or at least extremely serious.

"You are unique in that the people express their feelings to you," Father said.

The people, I had reasoned, must be fed-up with foreigners coming up to their village jabbering in strange tongues. Thus, so they wouldn't suspect me of disparaging them, their humble village, or their four chosen children, I always spoke Spanish when they were present. And because I looked and sounded (at least a little) foreign, neither would they suspect me of being a Spanish spy for the Santander Bishop's Commission.

"Why do the bishops oppose the apparitions, Padre?"

Again, the deep melodious, measured answer. He enunciated each word: "The bishops are opposed to Garabandal because they don't believe in it."

Jacinta, Conchita, Loli

"Really?" I asked. "I don't see how anyone with intelligence could doubt. It's impossible that these girls could concoct and maintain a hoax of this magnitude for ten years. All the happenings here were open to investigation and close scrutiny by all who wished to come. No?"

"Not all are given the grace to believe in the apparitions. Many bishops are above this [Marian apparitions].[14] The French and other Europeans are too old and too proud."

I recalled that, "The things of God are, above all, a pure and simple matter of faith."

Father continued, "You Americans are younger and more open to look at new things." Tears came to my eyes, and I swelled with pride in my countrymen. This compliment on our religious bent was a first in my travels to Catholic countries where some people doubt that faith exists at all in the United States. He went on to say:

> Visit Father de la Riva, the pastor of a church out on the coast. He was present during many of the ecstasies and is one Spanish priest who will talk openly about what he saw. Many priests here want to stay on the good side of the new bishop, José María Cirarda, who, we hear, has taken it as a principal objective of his episcopate to stamp out Garabandal. These priests tell people that nothing of importance happened here.

---

14   In May 2010, the editor of the Santander daily, *El Diario Montañés*, told me that Bishops Puchol (1965–1967) and Cirarda (1968-1971) felt that apparitions were out of style and that giving them importance would work against their ecumenical and evangelizing efforts.

Father said that the preceding bishop, Puchol Montis, took formal testimonies from the girls who stated that they weren't certain that they had seen the Virgin. He explained saying, "The visions and attending phenomena have taken place. The girls' present uncertainty about what they saw is now unimportant. It is part of their sanctifying process. The doubts are the sign that they are now being taught to believe, unaided by the presence of Our Lady."

This seemed reasonable. Being chosen by God to be his intermediaries didn't guarantee salvation. They, like us, must earn it by faith and good works.

"Once Conchita asked me, 'Father, will you also someday doubt the apparitions?' 'No,' I told her, 'I remember what I saw, and if someday my memory fails, I will just look at the slides to remind me.'"

Conchita with Fr. Laffineur, c 1965

"Another time when I was baffled in trying to allay Conchita's doubts about God's love for her, I pulled out a photo of a stigmatized nun and told her, 'One day you will have it.' She looked at the bleeding feet and hands and replied, 'I hope so, because then I will be sure God loves me.' The visionaries must be completely humbled, even to the extent of doubting God's love for them."

"Does Conchita still want people to spread the Garabandal messages, Father?" I asked.

He threw his arms up and switched to Spanish. "*Ni hablar.*" ("Such a question.") Madame Pelletier got a rest. In fact, so expressive were his face and gestures that I forgot we had been communicating with Madame translating his French into Spanish. He spoke with authority!

"You should have been a bishop, Father," I said.

His smile broadened. With two short phrases in French, he sent Madame Pelletier off. She returned in a minute and handed him a red and black paperback with the picture of three ecstatic visionaries on the cover. "I don't have any more of the English copies but here is my book in Spanish."

"All the better, Father, no? Since the Blessed Mother spoke that language with the girls."

"I will write a note in it for you." He then handed the book to me and I read, *Con recuerdo cariñoso de mi corazón, Padre Laffineur, Garabandal 23-7-70* (With affectionate heartfelt regards).

Smoke swirled above his cigar. It was 7:30 P.M. It would be difficult to record all I learned and felt in those three hours. How I loved that man for making my comments on Clemente and about Josefa's feelings seem important. His deep, melodious French moved me to consider tackling another foreign language. *"Merci, Padre. Y au revoir."*

The next morning I spent time sitting in the sun on the side of the mountain reading in his book *The Star on the Mountain*:

> Conchita Gonzalez. Daughter of the sun, of the wind, of the mountain's storms!
> Pure beauty of Spanish youth. Downcast eyes hiding the reflection of the living image of Our Lady of Carmel.
> Composure similar to that of the Mother of the Word who was keeping the mysteries within her heart, even when near the Cross.
> Miraculous modesty, pleased only when playing with children, especially with the youngest.
> Reflection of the woman who is the Dawn arising on a world much in need of a new Pentecost.
> Prophet of Good Friday, preceding the joy of Easter.
> A star lost amongst the splendor of all the stars twinkling above the luminous diadem of her vision.[15]

In the afternoon I returned with my questions for Father Laffineur.

"Father would like to read your notes," Madame Pelletier informed me. "Can you bring them up?" Father entered the room. We exchanged greetings in Spanish but again relied on Madame le Pelletier to translate my questions and Father's answers. What a wise man.

"What does Conchita think about the praise you shower upon her in

---

15   M. Laffineur & M.T. le Pelletier, *Star on the Mountain*, (New York: Our Lady of Mount Carmel of Garabandal, Inc., 1968), p. 136.

your book, Father?"

"She hasn't read the book." He smiled, as if to say, "She is the book; she is the star."

Conchita

"I noticed how well-dressed she is. She's so fashionable, so stylish. She would attract attention anywhere. Do others comment on this?"

"She wears nice clothes so that people will think badly of her, so they will think she is vain. She used to change two or three times a day, but I advised her against that. Friends take her to the store and buy her fancy clothes and keep the old ones for relics. They have been unfair doing so much for Conchita and so little for the other three."

Father lit a cigar and settled back into his chair for the next question. How different are the ways of those who strive for perfection, I thought. Patient, charitable and humble, Conchita tries to camouflage her virtues; I, cancerous with vice, work to disguise or excuse my faults.

"She is different, padre. Instead of drawing attention to herself, she focuses the attention on others. She makes you feel important, as if she

Conchita at her door

sees goodness in you that others miss. One observer told me, 'When I stood in a large group, I felt she always paid special attention to me even when she was looking at the others.' How does she remain humble and selfless when throngs of people flock to her door and idolize her?"

Father chose his words carefully. "Seminary professor Father Retenaga said, 'Her vivid realization that all that she is and all that has been done to her are gifts from God, is the best explanation for her profound humility.'"

Back out on the street that evening, I spotted a newcomer in the town square where the men gather. He stood up as I approached.

Big, around 6'4", red hair and glasses, an American for sure. Who else would sit on a log in the center of town studying a Spanish-English dictionary?

"Oh. Thank goodness you speak English," he answered to my greeting. "I've wandered around for two hours wondering how I would eat or find a place to sleep."

An ex-marine from Pasadena, California, Chuck Robinson had left his brother and a friend on the beach near Barcelona and ridden eight hundred kilometers across Spain on a motorcycle to Garabandal. We spent time together and became friends.

Chuck Robinson with newlyweds Domingo and Nati, Josefa's daughter.

A few days after that first meeting, Chuck came running up out of breath, "Ed, I just talked with Conchita." "Now slow down. What do you mean you talked with her?"

"I did," he panted. "I talked with her for ten minutes." Here was another who journeyed to Garabandal out of interest in the Blessed Mother's reported visits here, enchanted now by this fascinating Spanish girl to the point of instant language acquisition.

On Saturday Chuck and I decided to hike out of the hills to the dance in a nearby village. Starting down to Cosío, we stopped to chat with a group of girls gathered at the edge of the village. Yes, they would attend the dance. Chuck watched and couldn't even muster an intelligible *"Buenas tardes."* Only upon leaving did we notice Jacinta looking on over a girlfriend's shoulder from the back of the group.

A kilometer up the valley road out of Cosío, the crowd gathered, swelling the population of little Rozadío. The Garabandal teenagers huddled together as did the young people from Cosío. The band warmed up—a high class group compared to the combo that had played in Garabandal.

"Ed, how do you say 'dance' in Spanish? How do I invite a girl to dance?

What? You talked to Conchita for ten minutes. You shouldn't have any trouble here, I thought. But I swallowed that jibe and modeled,

"*¿Quisiera bailar? ¿Quisiera bailar, señorita?*"

"*¿Key she ara by lar?*"

"'*Ra*', Chuck. Not like the English 'r' with your tongue dangling loose. Make it tap the roof of your mouth."

"*Key she ara.*"

"No, not 'she', but 'see' as in 'I see'. Oh ... Just say, '*¿baile?*' or easier and safer yet, just extend your hand and smile."

Friendly, kind and patient, the girls from Rozadío, Cosío, Puentenansa, and Garabandal danced with us two awkward Americans struggling with the regional steps in the dusty, crowded town square.

We didn't stay for the *verbena*, the second dance session that starts in the early morning hours after a late supper. "Come on. Let's catch up with the kids from Garabandal," Chuck suggested.

We stocked up on peanuts and chocolate bars in Cosío a little before midnight, and then hurried to join the others hiking up the mountain in the dark. What are these Garabandal teenagers like? What do they say about the apparitions and about the countless thousands of visitors? How have the apparitions and the resultant popularity of their little village affected them?

Mostly we sang during the brisk hour's walk, and I didn't find all the answers then or that summer of 1970. I didn't sit again at Father Laffineur's feet or ask Loli, Conchita or Jacinta what the Virgin was like or even what they called her. I would be back.

———◦•◆•◦———

Editor's Note:

Perceptive readers may by now have detected a casual alternation between the author's use of metric and imperial units of measurement (miles here, kilometers there, etc.). The author begs your indulgent leniency in faulting his random inconsistencies. He says that he would buy chicken at 238 pesetas a kilo and had to figure how much of real money (dollars and cents) each six ounce portion cost.

CHAPTER FOUR
SPANISH SUMMER

antander is a bustling modern city of some 170,000. The port on the Atlantic Ocean has three magnificent beaches, a busy harbor, a modern downtown, good food and wine and stylishly dressed women. Spaniards flock there to escape the scorching Madrid summers, and the locals dare you not to move aside as they walk towards you two or three abreast on the crowded sidewalks.

Santander, 1971.

On arriving back there in July 1971, I first hunted for a decent restaurant and a good meal with which to fortify myself for the summer's seclusion in the mountains.

While I ate, a familiar looking man in workman's clothes walked up the steps and stared at me. It was Loli's father, Ceferino. He returned my greeting, no doubt recognizing me as one of the thousands of pilgrims who in the past ten years had come into his bar for food, a drink, or just to catch a glimpse of his celebrity daughter.

51

He and his two companions ate at a nearby table, and when I passed by on the way out, they invited me for coffee. To avoid walking the five kilometers from where the bus drops off passengers, Ceferino suggested we share a taxi up the hill from Cosío the next evening.

Activity in the Port of Santander

After lunch I walked a half-mile to the busy port and watched the dock workers unload grain. The chaff fluttered in the salt sea breeze. "*Soja de Chipre*," the sailor yelled. Soy beans grown in Cyprus, transported in an American ship to be made into oil here on the Northern Coast of Spain. I strolled over to the next ship. The crane hoisted giant mouthfuls of salt to the waiting trucks. Since my boyhood days in Seattle, ports have fascinated me. I watched the ship rise ever so slowly and could have watched for a week, but then I would never get back to Garabandal.

There were errands to run and supplies to be bought. I dropped off exposed film, visited a tourist office, checked the price of tailor-made pants, and called to ask Lolita Villar to join me for dinner. She accepted and also invited me to fish in her brother-in-law's boat in Santander Bay the next day. Lolita, whom I had befriended the summer before in Garabandal, knew the visionaries, had been present during the apparitions, and liked to talk.

Coming out of the tailor shop, I again ran into Ceferino.

"*¿Adónde va Usted?*" I greeted him.

"To the clinic. My wife is sick and I need advice." I had to run every third step to match his mountain-stretched strides. At the hospital desk he didn't claim "visionary father's" status to gain preferential treatment from the attendant nun but waited two hours for the doctor. Did anyone know he was Mari Loli's father? I waited with him and we talked about his family, the low price he got for his cows and the increasing number of pilgrims who come up to the village.

After a brief medical consultation, we retraced the mile between the clinic and the center of town. Deep lines creased his strong, determined face. I imagined he worried about his land, the hard work, and his wife needing an expensive operation. If Ceferino has grown rich from the tourist trade at his bar (and I doubt it), he still had the habits and tastes of the owner of a few cows.

"*Hasta mañana, Ceferino.*"

At the bus stop I sought directions. A new friend gave more than bus route information. He paid my fare. We sat down together.

"Do you like Spain?" he asked.

"Yes, a lot."

"What parts have you seen?"

"Most of it." And then trying, as I often did, to learn the extent of the Spaniards' knowledge of, and interest in Garabandal added, "Last year I spent most of the time in San Sebastián de Garabandal. Have you heard of that place?"

"Sure. Ten years ago it turned Santander on its head. That's all we talked about. I went up there many times. But now the priests have prohibited us from going there. The Church doesn't want it to become a tourist scandal, another Lourdes." That was a new wrinkle on the purpose of the local church authorities dissuading people from interest in the apparitions.

"The happiness and obvious sanity of the four visionaries impressed me," I told my new friend. "It's impossible that they could maintain a hoax of such magnitude for ten years and still be so open and happy. Nobody can pretend to be what he is not for very long without it disturbing and unbalancing him."

"Then it's a miracle," he concluded, and I realized that not all Spaniards were stubborn, opinionated, and thickheaded as I had read about those from Aragon. "Oh. There's my ice cream wagon," he said and dashed off.

I needed to find an economical hotel or guest house (*pensión*). My method without paying a huge cab fare or dragging luggage all over town? Check your bags at the bus or train station for a few *pesetas* while you look for lodging. If you sit and rest from the effort at an outdoor café and drink a beer or glass of wine, the task turns pleasant; if you sit long enough, the guest house might even find you.

This time in a Santander bulging with summer tourists, luck helped. Although one proprietor wouldn't change the sheets for just one night's lodging, the doorman in the building offered a room. Spotlessly clean like most Spanish homes, Señor Santos Gutierrez' small, seventh story flat featured hot water, a view of the bay and an attractive daughter.

Already late for dinner with Lolita, I washed up quickly. But reflecting that we often pass up more opportunities than we ever catch up with, I accepted the daughter's offer of a rum and coke in their sitting room.

What sane people are the Spaniards! Attractive, friendly Manoli, or Manolita to her father, was in her early twenties. Her brother Antonio appeared a year or two younger. He was a seminarian home for summer vacation; she, a student, a nanny, a seamstress—a woman. At ease and comfortable in their presence, it would be easy to get sidetracked here from my Garabandal mission. "She is *una buena pájara*" (a good person), her brother said. I couldn't disagree, but reluctantly left and ran to Lolita's apartment.

After I said "hello" and "good-bye" to her parents, who had fled with their young family to Spain from Cuba at the time of the Castro rebellion, Lolita led the way walking through town. She chose a typical and popular place with large wine barrels stacked along one wall. Legs of *serrano* ham and garlands of garlic hung from the ceiling in the bar. The aroma of food cooking in olive oil and garlic quickened my hearty appetite. We sat in the dining room in the back.

"Do you like fish, Eduardo? Why don't you try *lubina*?" Delicious fried fish, a generous lettuce, tomato and onion salad with olive oil and vinegar, fresh bread and *sangria*[16] welcomed me back to Santander dining.

Typical Santander bar

"My brother is in the United States doing his army duty in Fort Mead in Maryland. Is that near California? I'll give you his address so you can

---

16 *Sangría* - a cool drink made of wine, sugar, soda water, fruit and sometimes brandy.

meet him. Jacinta stayed in our house for a month between October and November (1970). She also lived for two months in my sister's house helping with the children. She's a saint."

Lolita talked fast about more than I could remember in a lifetime. Her animated facial expressions and gestures communicated. She said, "Watch Father Odriozola, a member of the commission that investigated Garabandal. He's a key figure determining the Bishop's stand on the apparitions."

She continued, "This priest (Odriozola) stopped Jacinta on the street recently, spoke to her, and asked her forgiveness for anything that he had done in his work on the Bishop's Commission that might have offended her. He also requested that she ask forgiveness for him from the other three girls." Walking home after dinner, we ducked in and out of doorways to dodge the rain.

Early the next afternoon, Lolita, her sister Corita and Corita's husband, Ignacio and I carried full picnic baskets to the thirty-foot pleasure boat. Ignacio owns a paint factory and two cargo ships. Corita told me, "My husband lets me send books and pamphlets all over the world." I had noticed that even the one-year-old baby wore her medal kissed by the Virgin at Garabandal. These Cuban sisters were zealous Garabandal fans.

We swam, sunbathed, ate, and fished while sailing on Santander Bay all afternoon. At sundown, as we approached the harbor, flag-draped boats sailed past us in procession celebrating the eve of the feast of the "*Virgen del Carmen*," the patroness of fishermen. Before parting, Lolita arranged for me to meet with Doctor Policromio at 9:30 that evening. "He will tell you about the Garabandal chastisement."

I ran home, showered, and without stopping for a bite to eat, hurried to the Monoco Café on the crowded main boulevard, Calle Castellar. People out for their pre-supper wine and *tapas* (snacks) filled the tables along the sidewalk. A tall, thin, bespectacled man about fifty and dressed in a gray suit spotted me. "Mr. Kelly? I'm Doctor Policromio. Shall we go downstairs where we can talk?"

He allowed me only a word or two about myself and my interest in the local apparitions before he started in.

"The Warning prophesied at Garabandal is unique in mystical

phenomena. But the Warning, the Miracle and the Punishment are all one. I've made a thirty-year study of the apocalyptic gospels and the writings of the saints, especially St. Peter Nero and St Vincent Ferrer. Back in the sixteenth century St. Vincent Ferrer predicted that the Chastisement would befall us when we can't distinguish the dress of women from men."

The more he got into this theory, the faster and softer he spoke. He didn't pause while we moved to the inside room to get away from noisy children. I was hungry, drowsy and bored.

"The Chastisement is connected with flying saucers! Men from space not contaminated by original sin and therefore with unclouded intellects will come and be amazed at our degradation. They will approach the earth in space ships or asteroids, and the heat created will endanger the nuclear stockpile." And the heat in this closed off back room is endangering my brain, I thought.

The guy wouldn't stop. Perspiration stuck the clothes to my body in the suffocating room, and roast chicken and cool *sangria* interested me much more than spacemen free from original sin.

"They will depart shortly, leaving us terribly frightened, and in that moment we will have a realization of Christ. That is the Miracle."

By now he was whispering, "The Punishment will consist in babies of the next generation being so terribly deformed that people will refrain from procreation. Beware of next year."

I couldn't listen any longer. "Doctor, I have to leave."

"OK," but he talked all the way up the stairs and down the street. I was starved sick. Would he try to accompany me to supper?

It was almost midnight when I sat down in a small restaurant and settled for the only item left—fish soup. The waiter swept the floor around me while outside the rain poured down.

After "dinner" I sipped a Drambuie while waiting for the downpour to subside. When it let up, I dodged puddles to the pensión for a good night's sleep—if I didn't dream of heat-creating asteroids damaging nuclear stockpiles.

How trusting and honest are the people of Northern Spain! In the morning, Señor Gutierrez left his full cash box on the chair in the little cubbyhole of an office beside the elevator while he went upstairs for a

El Mercado de la Esperanza

train schedule for me. Will they lose this trust dealing with some foreigners with their "Do whatever you can get away with" code? I paid seventy-five *pesetas*, or just under $1.10 at the 1971 exchange rate, for the room. I would always be welcome to stay there. With such an attractive, friendly daughter, sir, I'll remember that.

Later in the day, I wandered through the colorful town market. An itinerant clothes vender smiled and asked, "*De dónde es Ud?*"

"América."

"*Sud América?*"

"*No, los Estados Unidos.*"

"Ah, but they don't speak Spanish there."

"*Algunos, sí. Muchos latinoamericanos viven en mi estado, California.*"

"Ah, California! That is in Los Angeles, no?"

"Yes, more or less."

"Would you like to buy a shirt or a bathing suit?"

"No thanks."

"Do you have any American money? I like to have money from all over the world. I'll give you this bathing suit for one dollar. Look. It says right here, 350 pesetas."

"That's a fair price but I don't need a bathing suit."

"Where did you learn to speak Spanish?

"In school." His complimenting my book-learned language flattered me. Come to think of it, my ten or twelve-year-old suit had a couple of holes in it and lacked a cord in the waist. I rummaged through his pile

Fruit and vegetable section of market

57

of shirts, shorts and bathing suits. "How much did you say? They look small. Are you sure they're for men?"

"*Sí*. Here. Try this one."

The friendly Gypsy gloated over his American dollar. And I wandered over past the attractive, colorful display of oranges, lemons, melons, and grapes to the poultry section where an old woman purchased two eggs. The butcher weighed and wrapped the entrails of a chicken for another.

"*Señor. Señor.*" It was my Gypsy buddy. "If the suit doesn't fit bring it back. This afternoon I'll be at the *Mercado de Santa Teresa*."

"*Gracias*, but I'll be on my way to the mountains and Garabandal."

I headed for the train station. The Santander business area runs only about a couple of kilometers parallel to the bay, and much less than that from the bay to the hills so people walk everywhere. But busses (some of them the double-long second car attached in the middle type) come by so often, especially on the main streets, Castellar and Avenida Pareda, that it seems like they are looking for you rather than you waiting for them. Before I could decide whether to ride or walk, Walter Kushion, the American whom I had met in the village the year before, greeted me. He had just been at the library.

"Ed, I'll bet you haven't seen these five articles written by a member of the Bishop's commission investigating Garabandal. They were

published in the local papers here before Bishop Fernandez released the first official notice on the reported apparitions. They're great. I'll make you copies if you like. There is a copy machine outside the train station."

A half hour later, after thanking and taking leave of Walter, I was comfortably seated on the train out of Santander. For a narrow-gauge railroad, the Cantabrian Line train chugged and swayed right along heading west, paralleling the coast. I looked at Padre Saiz' first article:

Apariciones y Revelaciones Privadas

Por JOSÉ MARÍA SAIZ
Profesor de Teología del Seminario de Corbán [Santander]

> When one of these presumed preternatural happenings bursts onto the scene, few are able to remain on an even keel. Those who possess the perfection of equilibrium are limited in number. The majority fall into one of two extremes, skepticism or facile acceptance. The Church speaks with relative ease when the absence of the supernatural is manifest. On the other hand, for positive affirmation, its reserve is much greater than those unfamiliar [with the Church's manner] would imagine. We would do well, when confronted with a presumed supernatural phenomenon. . . to imbue our attitude with the same caution and prudence which the official conduct of the Magisterium reflects when it intervenes in cases of this type.

It seems like he was preparing people not to be discouraged when they read the "wait and see" advice of the first "Official Notice" about Garabandal published a month later by Bishop Fernandez. I would finish reading later but first the tailor shop at the train's next stop, Torrelavega, the second largest city in the Province of Santander.

While he measured me for four pairs of pants at eight hundred *pesetas* each, the owner, Manuel, talked about going up to see the ecstasies in the early 60's. "Everybody talked about Garabandal then."

At 6:00 P.M., commuters and I crowded onto the train. Strange, the pushing and shoving didn't bother me like it had on my first visit. The four blue cars swayed from side to side along the narrow tracks the forty-five minutes to Pesués. Now familiar with the operation, I got off and ran with the others to cram into the waiting bus. Did the regulars resent visitors occupying many seats? The driver squeezed most of

Puentenansa bridge

us in, and the leftovers hung onto the back of the old bus that labored up the hill under the load. I didn't see Ceferino.

The festive weekend passengers chatted and sang. Were all headed for the celebration of the patron saint's day at San Sebastián, and would there be a room for me on this, my third visit?

At 8:30 we crossed the narrow bridge over the Nansa and stopped in front of the big corner bar, guesthouse, store, and main local gathering place. Twelve miles in an hour and a half. Right on time.

Puentenansa (Nansa river bridge), is the halfway stop on the bus route from Pesués on the coast up the valley to Polaciones. Every time I've stopped there or passed through, it seemed that many of its two hundred or so inhabitants have been in, outside of, or in view of the corner bar. Was there no other place in town to gather?

"Sorry, we're full," the lady behind the counter informed me. "Try across the street."

It surprised me to find a second *pensión*, but one might even dig up one or two more. I didn't see any signs on the buildings, but I was learning that in towns and villages you just nose around and ask in order to find a guesthouse.

And what a great find this second mansion was—less than two dollars for room, supper, and breakfast! Only visiting Frenchman René, his wife or girlfriend, Katrina, and I ate a late tasty supper in the large, fashionable dining room.

In the morning, the clear blue sky that had greeted me on my first visit two summers previous welcomed me back. Sitting on the bench outside their bar-restaurant-guesthouse where I had spend my first night in the Rionansa area, the two red-headed sisters gave me a "wonder why he is back here again" look. This was a town most visitors passed through. "*Cuando las apariciones*" at Garabandal, they saw thousands of *foresteros* (outsiders,) but the ones who stopped were those who had to ask how to get to where the crowds were headed.

"*Hola, Eduardo.*" The funny, fast talking taxi driver for the area, Gabino, knew my name.

Later, while I was looking for razor blades in the more popular of the town's two grocery stores, a young woman greeted, "*Hola.* I'm Lupe. I see that you know my Aunt Mercedes. She loves to talk, especially with

60

Cosío bridge over the Vendul

visitors. She watches for them, and then steps outside to invite them—or bribe them with a treat—to stop and visit."

And I had thought it was only me that charmed the elderly, but vivacious, sparkling blue-eyed grandmother. Because her house is on the path leading to the church, everyone walking to or from Mass has to pass right in front of it on the village side of the Vendul River Bridge. Friendly and talkative, like someone else in her family, Lupe continued:

> I've seen you before—last year also. You must like Garabandal. Everybody used to go up there during the apparitions but now nobody talks about it. Conchita and I were friends. We are the same age. One day our teacher asked for a volunteer to carry a doctor's bags and I offered. On the way up I heard the big doctor tell his companion that those girls probably got into some drugs and that he would take care of it. The other man didn't say much, but Doctor Morales said he couldn't understand why everyone was so excited, that this was nothing, that he had dealt with many children who showed the same symptoms and on and on about his vast experience with this sort of mass hysteria over nothing and that he would soon put an end to it all. During the hour walk back down the hill the doctor was silent.

Doctors Morales and Piñal observing (LtoR) Mari Cruz, Jacinta, Conchita and Mari Loli.

I had read and heard about Dr. Morales, one of the two leaders (Father Odriozola was the other) of the five-man commission appointed by Santander Bishop Fernandez to study the happenings. Acquaintances in the area told me that Morales was a good psychiatrist, but that it was commonly held that he was crazier than his patients.[17]

"My aunt is a kick," Lupe continued. "She gets excited at times, but she is a good person. Her husband fought in the War (1936-39) on the side of the republicans so that sets them apart in their own village and even in this whole area."

I said good-bye, paid for the razor blades, and then walked to a bar for a second *café con leche*. Inside, René and his partner invited me to join them. Yes, in France people promoted Garabandal, but they hadn't been interested. But now, with no definite immediate plans, they offered to drive me up to the village. With a suitcase and back pack to lug more than four miles mostly up hill, I accepted.

Welcome to Garabandal! What a contrast with the previous year when the children had thrown rocks at me! Now all seemed friendly. Some men extended their hands. Loli's father, Ceferino, back from Santander, said hello. Above all, I heard, "*Hola.*" Who could forget that shrill soprano voice? Old Doña Vitoria almost fell down the steps coming to hug me.

"Where's your *novia*?" (girlfriend).

"Who?" I asked.

"Lolita. *La cubana*, the one you danced with last year during the fiesta. Don't you remember?"

Oh, I danced with her three times, so now I have a girlfriend?

My ex-house-mother also afforded me a warm smile and greeting.

"*Hola, Josefa.* I see that my room is taken. All the family is in town. No?"

"Yes, for a few days."

Where would I stay? I hoped everyone didn't have as many relatives as Josefa Cosío. At the far side of the village, near the lane that led a hundred yards up to the cluster of pines, I stopped at the steps of the smaller of two imposing new stone buildings. The workmen who ate at Josefa's place last summer built the bigger one for the large family from

---

17 Twelve years later, Morales had a change of heart. To a packed house in Santander's main meeting place, he stated that he now believed in the supernatural authenticity of the happenings that he had studied back in 1961.

Seville but what was this other place?

"Are you staying here?" I asked a paunchy, balding fellow who stood on the porch.

"Yes. It's the best place in town."

"Do they have room for me?"

"I think so. Here's the owner, Serafín."

I recognized the man I had met the year before cutting grass near the entrance to the village—Conchita's brother. "*Buenos días. ¿Tienes habitación?*"

Paquita and daughter María Conchita hanging clothes (August 1971)

"*Sí*. My wife, Paquita, is washing the sheets. It will be ready after dinner."

I set my suitcase, knapsack, and tennis racquet inside the door and headed toward the church. After noon Mass, villagers and visitors processed behind a life-size statue of the village patron to the *bolera*[18] where, as the year before, and for many previous years, four or five young couples danced *picayos* to honor Saint Sebastian who looked on from the end of the bowling field. He didn't seem too sad for a guy with arrows sticking through his chest, stomach, and legs.

"*Te traemos música con nuestros instrumentos de la región.*"[19] Jacinta again shook a tambourine. Another girl clapped castanets.

Haven't they heard of the guitar up here yet?

"Eduardo, how's it going?" I turned around. It was my pushy but helpful buddy from last year.

---

18 A small dirt plot where the villagers gather to attempt to knock over bowling pins with rough wooden balls the size of a swollen soft ball.

19 "We bring you music with our instruments of the region."

"Manolo! What a surprise!"

"I'm here on business trying to sell some Bibles. Conchita's mother, Aniceta, doesn't understand the Bible and prefers the lives of the saints. Conchita works in Barcelona now and won't be back until August."

Poor Manolo looked dejected. Conchita wasn't the only attraction in Garabandal, but kind old Doña Vitoria and widowed grandmother, Josefa, with a front tooth missing, looked faded by comparison. Could be a long summer here in the village!

I spotted Mari Nati from Bilbao with some girlfriends. She would be some thirty years younger but jabbered more about less than the two above-mentioned old widows combined. Without her thick glasses she didn't see me, so after the performance I ducked right back to my new home.

Just completed in April 1971, the house was as bare as a jail, but at 165 *pesetas*[20] a day for room and board, a bargain. My second story, seven by nine foot cell faced the *calleja*[21] and the Pines. A single bed, a lamp stand with no lamp, and one twenty-five watt light bulb hanging from the wall were its only accouterments.

There were four similar rooms and two bathrooms on that floor. The Serafín Gonzalez family of three crowded into one bedroom in the basement and rented a couple of other rooms there. The little kitchen where Serafín's wife, Paquita, spent much of her long day preparing our meals, was too narrow for two people to pass each other. A dining area and small bathroom took up the rest of the space on the first floor. Four plain unpainted four-legged stools stood around each of four square tables standing on the red painted cement floor. Nine-month-old María Conchita sat and played in a playpen behind a long red tile bar which ran from the kitchen door out into the dining room almost to the entry door. A single picture of Conchita graced the mantle over the dining room fireplace.

It was in this dining hall that strangers met and expressed in different languages their common interest, *La Virgen del Carmen*, and became

---

20 About $2.40 at the 1971 exchange rate.
21 Lane leading from village to the Pines. The first apparitions of the angel took place on this lane some fifty feet from the front door.

friends.

At dinner that first evening, cook and waitress Paquita seated me with the helpful guest from the porch. The retired Portuguese policeman and his new Dutch schoolteacher wife live in Holland. With thin strands of hair slicked back over his bald head, the paunchy, past his prime policeman tried to communicate with everyone—in broken Spanish, horrible French, and worse English.

Two familiar looking men sat by the window speaking Spanish. Two other middle aged men sat at a third table. They looked like English speakers so I asked, "Where are you from?"

"From Belfast, Ireland."

"Do you know much about this place?"

"No, not much. We just heard one talk given by a blind fellow, an American, I believe."

"Do you believe in the apparitions?" the Portuguese asked me, and when I hesitated, pointed an accusing finger saying, "Ah, very little."

"What do you mean by believe? Believe in what? Nobody denies that the four girls fell into ecstatic trances, fell heavily to their knees onto the jagged rocks, and walked backward down that mountain at night faster than the onlookers could keep up with them." And I turned to the Spaniards by the window for affirmation.

They agreed. The shorter one added, "The girls prayed with their hands folded and their heads thrown way back like this." He gazed at the ceiling to demonstrate.

The Belfast men stopped eating and put down their wine. "Ask those Spanish guys if they saw the ecstasies."

I again became an interpreter.

"Yes, we came up to play for the fiestas then also. We've been coming up for twenty years."

"I thought I recognized you [the bad musicians]. How are you?"

The Belfast men wondered who, if anyone, was trying to commercialize the village. Some people point out Ceferino, with his centrally located bar, store, and tiny restaurant where his visionary daughter Loli pours the wine and waits on table, as being the biggest financial gainer.

Or the cab driver, Gabino. Has he made a fortune shuttling pilgrims up and down the mountain the three miles between Cosío and Garabandal? He won't admit it, but he keeps busy; and I wondered what he did before June 18, 1961. What does he think of us Garabandal followers? Does he think he's profiting from our gullibility and facile credulity? I will ask him. I've heard he charges ten dollars for the difficult climb over sharp switchbacks but I'm not sure. In all the times I traveled to or from Cosío, I either walked or was given a free ride—mostly by Gabino.

Some have profited, yet many villagers are moving out. "Now there are only twelve boys in the school. Last year more—twenty," a bright eyed, blond third grader informed me. "*Se van saliendo del pueblo.*" (They are leaving the village).

María outside her house

Both Spaniards from outside the village and foreigners have purchased property here because of the belief that the site will draw an increasing number of pilgrims. Property values have shot up. Thus, to sell for enough to set up elsewhere would be the biggest gain for many. Some villagers with an extra room or two to rent, earn enough to live a little better. A few have started to fix up their old houses.

Lose or gain, the villagers provide services for which most pilgrims are grateful. But one, in an American group, who hadn't been happy was big Father "Carbuncles." Garabandal hadn't shown him much. "My feet are killing me. I suffer horribly. What's Cosío like, Ed? Is it a fairly good size place?"

He must have been asleep when his group passed through it, I thought. "Cosío, two hundred six inhabitants. Noted for its big, manorial houses," reports the Santander daily *El Diario Montañés* (2007 figures).

"Has it got any good hotels? I've got to get out of this damn place and get a decent night's sleep."

"I haven't seen any, Padre." I don't know if he toughed it out for the week the Americans stayed in the village, or if he took a taxi out to find a proper hotel in Santander.

The two Irishmen paid Paquita sixty *pesetas* each for dinner that included all the wine they wanted, plus their before-dinner drinks. At the 1971 exchange rate of 68.7 *pesetas* to the dollar, money went a long way. Two *pesetas* for a glass of wine, white or red. "*Blanco* o *tinto?*" they ask you. Seven for a liqueur: cognac, Benedictine or Triple Sec. Lugging the bottles up the mountain inflates the price of beer and Coca-Cola to a costly nine.

The going rate for a room was fifty *pesetas*. For this you got clean sheets (hand-washed) and individual care and attention unrivaled in the tourist world. I don't know what discount they'd grant for washing your own sheets in the frigid water that plunges straight from the mountains into the large community tub.

Village lavadero (washing place)

"When we were poor farmers," they might think, "nobody cared about us. Nobody bothered to come way up here even to say 'hello' or ask how we were. But now that God and his mother visited us, everyone else wants to crowd into our little village also."

May God, through the intercession of his Virgin mother, shower his choicest blessings on the people here.

CHAPTER FIVE
THREE BROTHERS

round 10:30 Saturday evening, the young villagers headed for the Community Center in twos and threes for the dance. I hadn't danced much during the day so I returned to see if the night session would be better. Perhaps the band would play in tune this time.

Author at Ceferino's with Loli's brother Gustavo 1970

Jacinta was there in style wearing a blue pantsuit. She danced with her girlfriend, Alicia, and with the boys. I danced twice then headed for home.

As I turned the corner, I noticed a group still in Ceferino's place. They would be the foreigners who couldn't understand enough Spanish to hear about the dance or perhaps considered themselves too old.

Most of the villagers patronized the other two bars in town. Whether they preferred not to mingle with visitors or envied Ceferino's increased tourist trade, I'm not sure.

"*Buenas tardes, Loli,*" I said, stepping to the bar. "You're not at the dance."

"No. I have to serve your countrymen here. They want something, but I can't understand them." She smiled, unruffled. I glanced back and saw three men in tweed jackets drinking beer. "They don't look like Americans, Loli."

"They're not French. They must be speaking English. Where are they from?" We eavesdropped a minute.

"Loli," I kidded, "can't you tell Englishmen from Americans yet?"

"No. I can't."

I didn't like to speak English in front of the villagers. Last year, by avoiding it to a fault, I might have offended some English speaking visitors. But now, since Loli provided the opening, I would see how her customers were faring. I turned to the young men and greeted them.

"Oh, you speak English," one said.

"Yes. Some."

"Then maybe you can help us," the fellow who looked the oldest continued. All three smiled at their predicament.

"We've been sitting here drinking beer and trying to order a snack. How do you say cheese?"

"*Queso.*"

"*Que i so,*" they repeated. "We'll have to learn Spanish. We left our dictionary back in the suitcase. And bread? How do you say that?"

Oh that all my high school Spanish students back in California were so eager to learn! "*Pan,*" I modeled, content to be back in the teacher role.

"*Pan. Pan y queso.* We want some *pan* and *queso*," they practiced. "No, you ask her for us."

I turned to Loli, alone behind the bar. How difficult it must be for her to serve people she can't understand. "They would like to know if it's too late to get some cheese and bread."

"Do they want sandwiches?"

"Loli," I smiled, "I deserve a percentage of the profits for all my translating." And to the young men, "Do you want sandwiches?"

"No, nothing fancy. Just cheese on bread."

"Don't worry. You won't find anything fancy in Garabandal." Loli disappeared into the kitchen, and I pulled over a four-legged wooden stool and sat down beside the men.

"I'm Ed from Santa Clara, California."

"I'm Tony Warren. These are my brothers Phil and Mick. We're from Birmingham, England."

"Loli thought you were Americans."

"That's Mari Loli, one of the visionaries?" They lost interest in their beer. "We didn't know that. We just came in looking for something to eat. We only heard about Garabandal last year. How long have you been here?"

"A couple of days. I also came last year and the year before."

"And you were talking to Mari Loli! Did she tell you anything about the apparitions?"

"Actually, we were talking about you." The Englishmen sat in wonder of it all.

"This place is interesting," one commented. "I wish we could talk to her. We'll just have to learn Spanish."

I had considered Americans weak at speaking other languages, but maybe the English and the Irish are worse.

"Would you like a beer?" Tony offered.

"No thanks. I've got a glass of wine on the counter, and I'm about to head for bed."

Loli set the plate of bread and cheese on the table. My new English friends seemed more interested in her than in their snack. But feeling too tired to start another translation job at this late hour, I extended a "*Gracias*," to Loli without further comment.

"Wow!" I sure wish I knew how to speak Spanish. How long did it take you to learn?"

"Oh, I've been working on it about ten years."

They turned to their bread and cheese. One said, "We found a comfortable place to sleep. That surprised us way up here. Where are you staying?"

"At Serafín's new guest house. We're probably at the same place."

"Do you eat there also?"

"Yes, three meals a day." Loli looked on in silence from behind the bar.

"Will you be in the village a while?" I asked.

"We plan to stay a week."

"I'll see you around then. I'm falling asleep."

Back at the bar I sympathized with Loli, *"Difícil de estar aquí tan tarde, no?"*[22] I swallowed the rest of the wine, said, *"Buenas noches,"* to Loli and the Englishmen, and then stepped out into the dark.

I walked up the rocky lane thinking how difficult for her and the other bar proprietors to have to stand for hours waiting for one or two customers to finish. The locals often tarried as long as the visitors—at times spending only a few *pesetas* nursing one glass of wine.

Sure enough, the three Warrens showed up in our dining room the next morning for breakfast. Tony, in his early thirties, did most of the talking. Phil was twenty-seven and Mick a couple years younger.

Three young monolingual English brothers spending a week here? There wasn't much to do in the village if you didn't speak Spanish. Was this just a religious pilgrimage for them? What strong faith those brothers must have.

"My brother Phil was away from the Church for seventeen years. We prayed to the Virgin of Garabandal for him, and in April he received the sacraments," Tony said. "Then my father came back to the Church. He had been away from the sacraments for five years. We are still praying for my mother."

"That's hard to believe. Serafín just remarked what strong Catholic parents you must have."

"Mick and I were undecided about entering the religious life. But Garabandal confirmed our decisions. He intends to become a religious brother, and I, a priest."

In the afternoon Nati, her mother, the Portuguese couple, Nati's friends—the four "nuns" from Bilbao and I prayed at the Pines. They really weren't nuns, but they looked a little like nuns, most of them with dresses down to their ankles.

"You're an American male. Do you think our dresses are too long?" one asked.

Nati was a scream, like a mother hen to the others. "Come on, Eduardo. Give us your opinion. Carmen's skirt is too short, no? That's a temptation to a man, right?"

--------◦•◆•◦--------

22 Difficult to be here so late, no?

That one wouldn't distract anybody no matter what she wore, I thought. But they really weren't so bad, just different. Actually the tallest one with glasses was attractive. She seemed amused by her companions' preoccupation with their appearance.

They talked about the newly reported apparitions at Ledeira, Portugal (that were never considered by scholars as even possibly authentic), and what we ought to do according to the latest scuttlebutt from there. What we ought to do, I thought, was heed St. John of the Cross' warning that running after rumors of miracles and prodigies is dangerous to faith and a sign of weak faith. However, that Doctor of the Church couldn't accuse me. I hadn't run around looking for apparitions; they found me. And anyway, he has been dead for over four hundred years.

We prayed the rosary—all fifteen decades. Nati's idea. After a short time attempting to pray, my mind wandered. Ledeira, Palmar de Troya, Clemente[23] and more. I recalled that around each true apparition there often arise many false ones that distract believers and scandalize others.

After the rosary, Nati caught up with me descending from the Pines. "Eduardo, you're a good man, very impressive. When can we talk?"

"Later. This afternoon I'm going fishing."

While I dug worms below, one of Nati's "nuns" came by. "What are you looking for?"

"Worms."

"What for?"

"To eat."

"What? You don't eat worms!"

"Sure." And I picked up a big one, put my cupped hand to my mouth, licked my fingers and smacked my lips. With two beautiful trout streams, the Sebrando to the north and the Vendul to the southeast, both within a thirty minute walk from the village, anyone asking what worms were for deserved that response. The two streams join about a quarter of a mile below the village and the wider stream flows down into the Nansa River at Cosío.

---

23 Clemente was the false visionary that I had seen at the Pines the previous year. He later declared himself Pope. Ledeira, Portugal and Palmar de Troya, Spain are places of recent false apparitions.

"Aye! This *americano* eats worms," she screamed to her friends.

I spent the late afternoon and evening down on the beautiful tree-lined Vendul. With the winter and spring rains the stream swells to a raging river. But in July it runs clear and low enough to allow one to step on the dry stones in the middle.

The stream abounds with small trout. I watched many dart away in the crystalline water as I approached the fishing holes. Some of the

Gabino fishing in the Nansa River

villagers use a ten or twelve-foot pole with a long leader tied to the end. They hide behind the rocks and drop the bait into the pools. I fashioned a pole from a willow branch but had neither pole, patience, nor practice to deceive the easily spooked fish. After some three hours climbing (and falling) over rocks and stumps, I limped back up to the village with two, six inch trout. I might as well have eaten the worms.

"Is the food all gone?" I asked, pushing open the *pensión* door. Eight guests filled three square wooden tables.

"No, there is still some left." Serafín stood by the door shifting his weight to his other foot. "The English boys were ready to eat, and we now have two from your country."

Just when I had adapted to the 9:00 P.M. Spanish mealtime, the inn now accommodated the Americans and the English with 7:30 suppers.

"Where are the fish?" Serafín smiled his lack of confidence.

"I left them outside."

"I bet you didn't catch any. Walter (the American who has been living in Garabandal) never catches any. He bought all the equipment too. These fish are intelligent. You have to fool them.

Walter Kushion with Jacinta and her mother

Bring in the fish. Paquita will cook them for you. Put them in the sink and she will clean them."

Trout, tasting of the bay and alder trees that line their pantry, plus plenty of bread baked in the morning, provided a succulent first course. For dessert I enjoyed fresh fruit, more wine and a long enjoyable evening with delightful dining room company. Much of the fun came at the expense of the Portuguese/Dutch couple who had entertained us throughout the week. We considered them the antithesis of romantic newlyweds and questioned the wisdom of Gilberto's marrying at his age. He laughed too, understanding just enough English to know that he was the center of attention.

And now the Americans, Katy and Evelyn, both on the fat side of fifty, compounded the merriment. Even Serafín laughed, and he couldn't understand a word.

"What did they say, Eduardo? They're having a good time. They're easily pleased. They say, '*sí*' to everything. Paquita just asked them if they would prefer canned peaches or fresh fruit for dessert, and the big one said '*sí*.' Ask them what they would like."

I turned towards the women, "Hello. You're from the United States?"

"Yes, from Monterey, California," one answered.

"Really? We are neighbors. I'm from Santa Clara and fish in Monterrey Bay."

"We were told you had to stay in private homes. This is quite a guest house."

"It just opened. They want to know what you would prefer for dessert."

"Anything. They've been so nice to us. She, what's her name?"

"Paquita."

"Yes, Paquita. She's so friendly, but of course we don't speak Spanish. I'd love to talk to her. In a place like this they should learn English." And also German, Korean and Dutch, lady?

Why Garabandal enchanted them and so many other visitors, I don't know. But these two were experts.

"We've been to all of the shrines in Europe. That was Evy's idea. But it's been fun."

Yes, Garabandal was different from other popular pilgrimage spots. Here there are no extra public religious ceremonies. The three hundred villagers and maybe a fifth that many visitors a day go their separate ways with minimum interaction.

Even in the homes that accept guests, some owners go about many of their daily tasks almost as if guests weren't present. I always ate breakfast at Josefa's place last year, but she prepared it on her way to or from milking the cow. Ceferino's bar is a main hangout for many tourists, but the other two bars, bigger and much better supplied with food and dry goods, go mostly undisturbed by visitors. Mesón Serafín is the one exception when it is occupied by guests. Even then, like the other men of the village, Serafín spends much of his time cutting, raking, stacking, and storing the grass for the winter; cleaning his barns; fertilizing the fields; and tending his cows.

Fields and winter barns to the south of the village

Tourism appears to be the main industry, but it is not. Cows, pastured in the hills out of sight, outnumber us, and bring in more village revenue.

Katy and Evy complained about having to leave. "We have to be in Santander tomorrow. We left our luggage there in our hotel room. I wonder if it will be all right. We came up by taxi and didn't know it would take so long. The man will drive us back tomorrow noon. Do you think he understood us, Katy?"

"I hope so and also hope they don't charge too much for this place."

I smiled and assured her, "You can probably afford it."

"I spent all my traveler's checks. You pay him, Evy."

Serafín studied the unfamiliar check and asked me the exchange rate.

Katy rambled on to me about their pilgrimages, "We went to San Damiano and St. Michael's in Italy and, oh, have you ever been to the shrine of

Our Lady of Loreto? It's just beautiful and so peaceful there. I wanted to stay a month. Oh, and the shrine to St. Anthony at Padua. You would love that place, Ed. He

San Giovani Rotundo, Italy

still performs miracles there all the time. People told us . . ."

Evy rejoined us at the table. "I gave Serafín a twenty and told him to keep the change."

Wow, twenty dollars for their five dollars room and board for two! I hoped Serafín wouldn't expect such a generous tip from all Californians. I calculated: twenty dollars for one day stay here; thirty dollars to Gabino to drive them the sixty miles to Santander; probably fifteen dollars to store their luggage in the hotel (Some of us put it in the left-luggage room at the train station for seven cents a bag); and a return by taxi across Spain to the Lisbon airport for their flight to Amsterdam. No wonder they worried about running out of money.

"Do you want to come with me, Katy?" her friend asked. "I'm going to visit the church."

"No. I'm staying right here. I've seen enough."

Evy left but Katy didn't budge. I think she sat at that table her whole stay in Garabandal. She didn't go anywhere—not to the church nor to St. Michael's Chapel nor to the Pines.

"How about hiking down to the river to go fishing with me tomorrow, Katy?" I kidded.

"I'm not going anywhere. Evy has dragged me all over Europe, and I'm not moving any more."

She would have rambled on all day if we had let her. Maybe she did, but I excused myself to attempt to get "in" with the villagers and learn more. I headed for Ceferino's place.

The dark, handsome, Manolo from Pamplona stood at the bar. Loli stood behind it.

"Hola, Eduardo. How's it going? I'm showing Loli these Bibles. She should buy one. How much do you weigh, Loli?" He was his old, inquisitive, pushy self.

"Sixty-five kilos. I want to lose ten. I've always had a complex about being overweight."

"No," Manolo flattered, "you're not too heavy."

Sari, Loli, their mother, Julia

The twenty-two-year old Loli was so friendly, natural and approachable that it was easy to forget she was one of the four favored visionaries. Although she hid behind a solemn expression, she was quick to smile when engaged in conversation.

"You're happier than last year, Loli," I said. "Why"?

Her younger sister, Sari, poked her head out from the kitchen and called out, "Because she's in love."

Loli's face turned scarlet. "Sari," she admonished. Her sister would answer later for that comment, and Loli changed the subject. "Your hair is longer this year, Eduardo. I don't like it. Aye, in Barcelona! What a sight! They frighten me, those guys with long hair."

While we talked about styles and comparative customs, a couple local fellows dropped in for a quick drink. Around 10:00 p.m. we closed shop. At times the night spots died down early in the village. Had I lived here a week already?

The next morning, Serafín woke me at 6:00 so I could attend Mass in an unfurnished shack that Ceferino owns. When I arrived, a young man was spreading a white cloth on a card table for the priest putting on a white alb, stole, and maniple.

I didn't understand a word of French but followed the familiar Mass prayers that ended with their version of "St. Michael, defend us in battle. Be our safeguard against the wickedness and snares of the devil . . ."

People told me that the Blessed Virgin hadn't visited this house because no one lived there during the apparitions. But this morning her Son came to visit it, the French priest, his travelling companion, and me.

"We don't have much but will you join us for breakfast?" Father asked while he divested. His broad, welcoming smile prompted me to accept. He boiled water over a small portable gas stove. True campers those two. He was right. We ate frugally—hot chocolate and biscuits without butter.

But they didn't need butter. Father and I didn't speak a word in common, and Pierre was making his first attempts at English. But they were pleasant, hospitable hosts.

After breakfast they rinsed off the dishes, and then threw their camping equipment into a small overloaded station wagon.

"*Adieu.* We're off for Toulouse. We'll see you for the Miracle."

"*Adieu, Padre. Adieu, Pierre.*" And two more reasons to study French drove down the mountain.

Carmona with Puentenansa area in the distance,

CHAPTER SIX
THE GENEROUS POOR

he village ran like clockwork. Pierre and the French priest had left, but a forty-plus-year-old Ukrainian rite priest arrived the next day. Born in Canada, Father introduced a hundred different topics: bad clergy, false visionaries, and our weak economy. He spoke with authority but bounced from one topic to the next, never allowing us time to comment. He traveled with two women. Was the younger one his wife or can those priests have wives?

The Portuguese/Dutch couple left Friday morning. To take their place, Mike Kelly, his wife, and three young sons arrived from Scotland. Mike was a Spanish teacher.

Saturday morning we celebrated Mass "a la Ukraine" in the basement hallway. I don't understand Ukrainian but heard, "María" many times. Serafín held María Conchita. Mike's one-year-old son sang the foreign music as well as any of us.

The Kelly family only stayed one night in our "hotel." After Mass, I begged a ride out of the mountains with them on my way to attempt to find, and seek an interview with, Garabandal author Father Ramón García de la Riva. Before I finished my *café con leche* and biscuits with butter, Gabino backed the taxi up to the porch. On the trip down, Gabino talked about his prices and business.

"This year the people started coming in January."

Twenty minutes later, at the bottom of the hill in Cosío, we changed to Mike's car. The generous Scotchman wouldn't let me help with the cab fare.

The day broke beautiful with the sun searing the morning mist. We marveled at the scenery over Carmona Pass between Puentenansa and Cabuerniga and then enjoyed the drive through the valley along the Saja River to Cabezón where I bought the men drinks while Mrs. Kelly shopped.

The city of Cabezón de la Sal bustled with festival preparations. But neither street dances nor carnivals interested me now. The previous summer Father Laffineur had suggested that I talk with Father de la Riva who had been present at many ecstasies and would talk openly about what he saw. He would be a rare find—if I could locate him.

After our drinks and shopping and then a ten mile drive to busy Torrelavega, we parted.

"*Adios, Sr. Kelly.*"

"*Igualmente.*" (Same to you). They were off to pick up their trailer on the coast, and I, to pick up pants from the tailor before doubling back west to Barro-Llanes and, hopefully, find Father de la Riva at home.

Frustration! If you visit the area, stick to Garabandal. Investigating apparitions is less complicated than buying tailor-made pants. I walked out of the fitting room holding up the first of four pair. My face flushed in anger.

"What's wrong? Don't they fit?" Don Manuel grabbed the waist and pondered the extra four inches. "Don't worry. They'll come out O.K. They'll be ready by Monday."

"Monday? I want to leave this afternoon. Besides, they'll look funny in the seat if you take them in. How could you miss by so much?"

"Oh. They'll look nice. You'll see."

"That's what you promised before." Did he just take them off the shelf and try to make them my size? Trying to cheat me because I was a foreigner? "*Caramba*" was the strongest expletive I knew in Spanish. It would take long enough to get to Barro-Llanes and find Father de la Riva. I worried about finding him at all and whether he would agree to talk.

"*Señor*, let's forget the whole deal. You keep the pants and I, my money. Can you sell them?"

"I suppose. But I want you to have the pants. Look, this is good material, and we'll fix them so they'll be perfect."

"OK," I relented. "Monday afternoon and they had better fit!"

That meant another delay in getting back to Garabandal. No advantage now to start off for Barro in the afternoon. Less than resigned, I checked into a second-class hotel a few blocks from the center of town.

Maybe it was third class, but clean and comfortable. I ate dinner in its crowded dining room, and then headed out to look for a movie theater. Learning about apparitions couldn't be my only interest in Spain. Furthermore, as we tell our students, watching foreign movies improves your language ability. As I walked through the plaza a band boomed away playing a familiar piece.

Wow! *Los Valientes de Kelly.* I enjoyed Brian Hutton's *Kelly's Heroes* with Clint Eastwood, Telly Savalas and Don Rickles, but a day later, writing my notes, couldn't remember a thing about it. Was that because this other adventure was so much more real, so much more significant?

Sunday after Mass I boarded the 11:15 Cantabrian Special heading west for Llanes, Oviedo, and intermediate points. Crowded with beach-goers, the train was suffocatingly hot and smelly. If it didn't speed up, it would be hard to stand the heat and the stench of perspiring bodies.

A strange looking couple sat across the aisle. They wore the typical ill-fitting old clothes of the Gypsies. He criticized her loudly and tears trickled down her cheeks. She was young but already looked old. Poor people! From Spain's northwest corner, Galicia?

That couple and many more got off at San Vicente and then the train sped up. Not knowing if it would stop at tiny Barro, I hopped off at Llanes where tourists mingled with celebrating townspeople. I selected a corner restaurant. Inside, four college-age boys struggled with the menu.

"Having trouble with the language?"

"We don't know what she said. We want this but want some soup also."

Englishmen! "Why don't you order the tourist menu? That way you get soup, a main dish, bread, wine and dessert all for eighty-five *pesetas.*"

"Sounds good. We're camping out on the beach and don't eat in restaurants much."

After dinner I found out there was no evening bus or train to Barro, seven kilometers away. The next morning bright

Main course of the meal in Llanes $1.20 in 1971

and early, I got into a taxi without haggling over the fare. I didn't mind paying for a worthwhile journey, but one's sense of values gets distorted at seventy *pesetas* to the dollar. I sure hoped to catch Father at home.

Ten minutes later we turned off the highway into the beach village of Barro. "Señor, do you know where the priest lives?"

The driver pointed off in the distance. "That's the church over there, but I think the priest stays here on the corner with his mother."

"How much do I owe you?"

"Seventy-five."

It was almost 10:00 A.M. when I approached the white stucco house partially hidden amidst trees and a big badly overgrown flower garden. A middle-aged balding man in a black cassock finished talking with a couple in the garden. What luck! I hoped he wasn't busy.

"Good morning, Father. I'm from the United States. They tell me you know about Garabandal and won't mind talking about it."

"Well, what do you already know?"

"I spent two weeks in the village last summer and am staying there now. I have read the books including yours and the 1970 booklet, *Declaraciones Oficiales*, published by the Santander Chancery. There are lots of contradictions in that."

"Well, you already know the history. Sit down. I'll get my scrapbooks."

Settling into the straw garden chair, the frustration of uncertainty faded. The soft-spoken priest sat down beside me saying, "I took these when I visited the village." We looked through one scrapbook full of photographs of Conchita and a second of Loli, Mari Cruz, and Jacinta. A third contained letters, notes, and autographed cards from the four girls.

Fr. José Ramón García de la Riva

Loli, Jacinta, Mari Cruz, Conchita.

"Here is a recent letter from my archbishop which I consider important."

Oviedo
11 de junio, 1971

Rev. Sr. Don José Ramón García de la Riva,
Párroco de Barro, Llanes

Muy estimado José Ramón en Nuestro Señor,

I have received your kind letter of the first of this month, the tape recording, and the two copies of your book in French about Garabandal. One of these I have sent to the Apostolic Nuncio in Spain. I remain very grateful for this documentation that you have sent me and esteem very much your reiterated affirmation of filial submission of judgment to the magisterium of the Church. I recommend myself to your prayers and pray for you to Our Lord and to the Most Holy Virgin.

Tu afectísimo seguro
Servidor en Jesús,

Gabino, Arzobispo de Oviedo

Father de la Riva went on to say:

> We were on a retreat for priests on May 21, 1971. At recess the Archbishop asked what I knew about Garabandal. The Holy See was asking him for information, and he said he didn't know anything. That wasn't correct because he had the reports from the Santander bishops that were, of course, negative. Although he had allowed us fifteen minutes for a break, we spoke much longer. The Archbishop was most interested. This was the first time that the Church officially asked me for my eyewitness account.

This was news. The Archbishop of the area was involved. I had recently read in *Declaraciones* (the above-mentioned booklet) the seven public communications on the apparitions from the Santander bishops. The last of the seven was a letter dated April 25, 1970 (the year before archbishop Gabino's meeting with Father Ramón) to all the bishops of the world. In it, Santander Bishop Cirarda wrote that his predecessor had closed the file on the supposed apparitions with a judgment that they were not supernatural. Now Father Ramón showed evidence that the Vatican didn't consider it a closed issue.

In his letter, Bishop Cirarda quotes and paraphrases the salient points of his predecessors' five official *Notes*. He wasn't careful! Canon Julio Poro, writing under the pseudonym José María de Dios, points out nine significant discrepancies between the predecessors' *Notes* and what Cirarda wrote about them.[24]

Kelly with Ben Gómez and American women

Father de la Riva explained more about his meeting with the Archbishop:

> I had sent him my book, a tape of Fr. Ramón Andreu's conference, the testimony of Ben Gómez describing the visible communion, and the four girls saying the Our Father and other prayers while in ecstasy. This letter dated June 11 was to thank me

---

24 José María de Dios. *Dios en la Sombra*, (Zaragoza: Editorial Círculo, 1967)

for this documentation. You can see here that it is signed in his handwriting, Gabino, Arzobispo de Oviedo.

So I could see it better, Father pulled the letter out of the plastic folder, and handed it to me saying, "I believe this to be important because it demonstrates that, contrary to what some think and promulgate, the Holy See's official portfolio on the Garabandal apparitions and prophecies for the whole world isn't closed."

I had read articles in the Catholic press that stated or implied that the case had been definitively decided as not being supernatural. Father Ramón's material would be valuable in refuting these. He continued, "Useful documents pro and con will be accepted so that one day the Holy See can issue its judgment. To which future judgment I submit myself."

This guy was all right. Has the Spanish hierarchy given him any guff? He didn't seem to worry and added:

> In regard to the possibility that the four girls played games and fooled so many people, that is something that nobody with any common sense can think. It would have been easy for people of different social classes, religions, cultures, and education to spot any deceit that lasted four years.

Father said that, at times, thousands of people were present. I have heard estimates of some 5,000 being in the village on October 18, 1961, the day the first message was given—and that on a horrible rainy day.

"As some final words, I will tell you that I am certain that the Garabandal events are of supernatural origin."

He then repeated what he had said earlier, that he knew that the final judgment on the authenticity of the reported apparitions belonged to the Church. He wanted to make it clear that his certainty was personal, and he wasn't representing the Church.

> We must comply with the Messages. They are the most important. The prophecies of the Warning and of the Miracle will come to pass, as have the previous ones. Conchita has never been wrong.

I believe that they are not far away from this date.[25] I'm sorry I'll have to leave shortly. I have an appointment at 12:00.

Questions flooded my mind. How could I crowd them in before Father left? "What do the people here in Spain think about the apparitions, Father?"

"The press is censored and the local bishops have said not to print anything. The people, in general, follow the bishops."

"Anyone who studies the happenings can see their importance. In my country," I told him, "someone would investigate, even if the local clergy were opposed or not interested." But I dropped that argument. "In America" comparisons don't go over well abroad. "Why are the bishops, the present Santander bishop and his predecessor, against the apparitions?"

"The devil is involved here."

I waited for a clarification but none followed. That was his full explanation for the opposition of the Santander Bishops, "The devil is involved." I recalled Fr. Laffineur's answer to the same question a year earlier. "The Bishops are against these apparitions because they don't believe in them."

"Do you know the story of Father Luis Andreu?" he asked.

Father Luis Andreu walking to Garabandal, 1961.

---

25 The tapes which Ramón Pérez gave me were used to compliment and corroborate what I heard in separate, private interviews with Father de la Riva, Ciriaco and Serafín, and from accompanying Pérez when he interviewed Maximina, Pepe and Clementina.

"Yes. He was the healthy, thirty-six-year-old Jesuit priest who died of no apparent cause the night he visited Garabandal in August 1961. The visionaries claimed that after his death he spoke with them and taught them English, French and German words and some prayers in Greek."

Father added, "The girls also say that on the day after the great Miracle to come, his body will be found incorrupt."[26]

"Did Conchita go to Rome, Father?"

"Yes. She was called there and spent two hours with Cardinal Ottaviani."

Father rose. "Excuse me while I get ready. You may look at these if you wish."

"May I take notes from this article, Father?"

"Sure."

All of a sudden there was so much to write down and so little time, and it had taken so long to find him. I wrote furiously, trying to copy the important points before Father returned.

Here was a recently published booklet. *Garabandal 10 Años 18 de junio 1961 – 18 junio 1971.* In it I read:

> Hasn't this affair [Garabandal] ended yet? . . . Ten years are a lot of years. . . . In 1965 the apparitions ended and [then]: the contradictions and negations of the protagonists, the [negative sounding] Episcopal note, Conchita's trips to the Vatican, and the intervention of the Sacred Congregation for the Doctrine of Faith. The girls denied [having seen the Virgin] and Father Pio died, yet the good news of Garabandal, contrary to all human logic, goes around the world. And when all ought to be ended, we realize that in June 1971, the faith in all that encompasses Garabandal is more alive, more widespread, and more solid than it was during the apparitions themselves nine or ten years ago.[27]

---

26 Fifteen years later, when the Jesuits transferred his remains from Oña to Loyola, only bones remained. If this prophesy comes true, it will be the first of that nature.

27 *Garabandal 10 Años,* (Barcelona: Centro Difusor de Garabandal, 1971), p. 2.

The "good timers" have been chased away. I had surmised this from talking to many Spaniards. "Yes," they say, "we used to follow Garabandal. But now it's all over." My fingers ached from writing as I continued copying from the *Garabandal 10 Años* booklet.

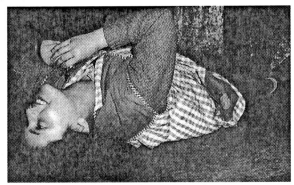

Loli levitated. Dress in place

The pruning has taken place. We have been pruned of human enthusiasms, of sentimental effusiveness. In a word, the advice has been heeded, that Garabandal must be purified of all that savors of the human, even of enthusiasm, in order that only the mark of God remain.[28]

I wrote fast. The Spanish Bishops aren't unanimous in their opposition to Garabandal.

As recently as the last Spanish Episcopal Conference (1971), at the insistence that that Body officially condemn Garabandal, the ordinary of a diocese distant from Santander affirmed that he would oppose the approval of such a motion, since he personally believed in the supernatural origin of the Garabandal Apparitions.[29]

Father came out dressed in the traditional black suit and Roman collar and said,

"I have to go now."

———◁·◆·▷———

28 Ibid.
29 Ibid.

"May I continue to copy some of this material?"

"Yes. Leave the notebook with my mother when you finish. Good-bye." As his old white Renault putted down the road, Father's white haired mother turned to me.

"It's a miracle that you caught him here." She combed her stringy hair, wet from a washing. "He's meeting some French people for lunch, and then he's going to the deaf and dumb hospital run by the nuns in Oviedo. They operated on him for cataracts last month. If he didn't have to leave, he would talk with you all afternoon. People come here all the time, especially the French. Some other priest, or somebody, sends them here. What's his name?"

"Señor Courteville?"

"Yes, I think that's it. My son sits here for hours talking to them. He never gets tired. That's his whole life. It's too bad he had to leave today."

The *señora*, with her hair now up in curlers, sat on the couch tying up a small package while I wrote. Conchita has announced that the Bishop will lift the prohibition against the priests going to Garabandal. "He will do it moved by a personal proof that he will receive from heaven. It will take place before the warning."[30]

"You say you are from the United States?" Señora de la Riva interrupted. She didn't demonstrate any interest in Garabandal, only in me.

"Yes, from California."

"How did you get here?" She stopped her work on the little box.

"I walked."

"All the way?" she asked.

I continued with my hurried reading and copying. Hmm. Conchita knows the nature of the conditional prophesied Chastisement:

> I know in what it will consist, but I can't say it. Furthermore, I have seen it and can guarantee that if it comes, it will be worse than if we were enveloped in fire, worse than if we had flames above and below us. I don't know the time that will elapse for

---

30 Ibid.

God to send it after the Miracle.[31]

This reminded me of a saint's statement on purgatory, "One hour of punishment there will be worse than a hundred years of the most severe suffering here."

"You are taking a lot of notes. My son could tell you so much. He saw things in Garabandal every time he went. It wasn't because of him, but because things happened all the time. He accompanied Conchita when she went to live in the Carmelite convent in Pamplona when she was sixteen."

This turned out to be a profitable visit after all the difficulties. I had met a man who had witnessed hundreds of ecstasies. His telling about them in a slow, clearly-enunciated Spanish was a delightful relief from the challenge of the mountain dialect of some of the villagers. His widowed mother vouched for the character of the soft-spoken man and now mothered me.

"Here. This is for you, something for your journey."

Glory be! She didn't believe that I had walked, did she? I was in no hurry to leave the delightful old house with its overgrown plants and ill-kept garden. But because it was about lunchtime, I didn't want to keep the *señora* from preparing her meal. She showed me through the spacious garden.

"You have a beautiful place."

"It's too hard for me to keep up. Father used to work in the garden but his eyes have been bad in recent years."

"Can I walk to the center of town?"

"Sure. It's not much of a town. Just a motel, a restaurant and a couple of campgrounds and, of course, the beaches. Just turn to your right at the end of the road. Open that package when you get hungry."

One service Padre Ramon's mother hadn't offered was the use of the bathroom. Thus I was relieved to get out to the bush-lined dirt lane. An approaching car interrupted me, and to my embarrassment, stopped. One of the four college-aged boys leaned out of the old wood-paneled station wagon and yelled, "Hello." It was my young English friends from

—————◦•◆•◦—————

31 Ibid., p.4

92

the restaurant in Llanes.

"What are you doing here?" I yelled.

"Our tent is pitched at the campgrounds. We're on our way to make lunch. Will you join us for coffee?"

"Sure. What a surprise to run into someone I know!"

"Here. Get in. I'll walk," one of them offered.

We continued down the dusty road that narrowed into a path as it approached the tent-filled campground. We hurried to beat the rain.

"You've got a fancy place. How long have you been camping here?"

"About a week. We've taken a few side trips up to Covadonga and to Panes. It's beautiful up there. Get the water, Jeff."

"We don't have much to eat. We've been living on a tight budget. We've got sardines, soup, tomatoes, bread and butter, and coffee."

"I don't know what's in this package." I unwrapped a can of tuna, a hunk of the prized *jamón serrano* (mountain cured ham), half of a *chorizo* and eight or nine cookies. How generous are the poor! I recalled James Russell Lowell's "The Vision of Sir Launfal" in which Christ appeared to the generous knight and told him,

> Not what you give but what you share,
>
> For the gift without the giver is bare.
>
> Who gives himself with his gift feeds three
>
> Himself, the hungering beggar, and Me.[32]

We sat down on the ground to a sumptuous lunch while the rain drizzled against the canvas tent.

"What do you all do?"

"We're in school, the university. Brian studies biology; Jeff, history; Gerald, mathematics; and I, sociology."

The rain hit harder. "Man, this thing leaks bad in here," Brian warned as he stood up to avoid getting wet.

---

32 www.lib.rochester/camelot/launfal.htlm

"Throw the clothes onto the cot," directed another.

A third yelled, "Let's get out of here before we get soaked. We can make a dash for the restaurant if it lets up a bit."

It did; and we sprinted, some with shoes in hand, to the restaurant crowded with rained-out campers. I treated my English buddies to cognac and coffee, and then with an extra drink, bribed Brian to drive me to the train station.

CHAPTER SEVEN
NEIGHBORS

he train didn't go far. Seven kilometers along at Llanes, the porter called, "Washout ahead. Everybody out." Again? Was I a jinx on this narrow gauge train that runs along the Cantabrian Coast from Irun near the French border to La Coruña in Spain's northwest corner in the region of Galicia?

In the lobby we milled around like restless cattle. The rain poured down. At 6:00 P.M. it was black as night. When the bus arrived, about eighty of us squeezed in for forty seats. Water leaked onto many of them, but in just a few minutes the bus stopped, and the word passed through the crowd, "Up and off the bus. Back to the train." We had passed the damaged track.

I hoped so. Water poured out of the black Cantabrian sky and lapped against the windows as the train swayed along the narrow tracks east towards Torrelavega. I got off there to look for a place to sleep and, hopefully, pick up my pants.

Washed out tracks, a leaky bus, and now, with the Spaniards flocking north to escape the July heat of the central plateau, I had to walk all over town in the rain looking for a room in bustling Torrelavega. All I needed now were cockroaches in my bed, if I could find a bed.

Yes, finally there was a room for me. And to my question about the number of Gypsies in the area, the woman proprietor said that they were more trustworthy than the people from the region of Andalucía in southern Spain.

She added, "My husband buys *caracoles* from them along the north coast from Bilbao to Asturias. We ship the shells all over."

Caracoles

Cockroaches! He buys cockroaches? No, *caracoles* are snails. It had been a long, but fruitful day. I slept soundly in the guesthouse two doors from the railroad station.

But the next day more trouble with those darn tailored pants. "*Señorita*, they still don't fit. Look! They've done nothing but shorten the waist. They look horrible in the back, and this gray pair doesn't button properly. I don't want them."

A second young lady apologized and agreed that somebody had messed up. "Yes, they are bad. Here, we'll take them up to the tailor ourselves. When does your train leave?"

"At 6:30. But I have other errands. I've already wasted too much time here."

"Ah, you tourists have a lot of time," she smiled.

"I'm not a tourist. I'm. . . ." Oh they would never understand about investigating apparitions and how Americans get fidgety when away from work. I had spent three nights away from Garabandal already.

"We'll have them ready for sure this afternoon."

What could I do? The Spanish salesgirls were so agreeable and courteous I couldn't swear at them even if I knew some swear words in Spanish.

After waiting out a cloudburst at the tailor's, I couldn't find a suitable guitar but bought eighteen cognac glasses for Serafín and a cheap telescope fishing pole for myself. They were sold out of fish eggs (that are illegal in the two Garabandal streams anyway).

Even lunch was a mistake. Remembering the delicious oxtail stew I had eaten in the outdoor restaurant in Seville during my first visit two years previous, I was pleased to see it now offered on the *menú del día* and ordered it with *vino tinto*.

After a passable *ensalada rusa*

(potato salad), the waiter served me something that looked like an old misshapen rubber glove resting on a bed of green peas. What was this? I checked the menu. *Pie de cerdo.* Pig's feet! I ate the bread and the peas and drank the wine then headed for Manuel's.

"Your pants will be ready in a few minutes. She's gone upstairs to press them."

"To press them?" I yelled. "That won't do any good. You're going to send them to Madrid anyway. I told him that." How frustrating it must be for those who only speak Chinese or German or English in Spain. The hand-tailored pants still didn't fit any better than ones off the shelf. Now to worry about them arriving in Madrid.

"Will you have a drink with us?" the tailor, Manuel, invited.

That's a businessman for you, botch the job and then invite you for a drink and small talk. But that's why I had come to Spain, to learn (sometimes painfully) the customs. We walked a couple of blocks, and then entered Café Medina. As in many bars shortly before the 4:00 return to work hour, men stood two deep with a *cortado* (espresso coffee with milk) or a small glass of wine in their hand or on the counter in front of them.

Manuel introduced a short, dark young man sporting a well-trimmed mustache. "Eduardo, this is Gabriel. He's Cuban. Many Cubans live in Spain because it's easier to get papers to come here than to the United States. From Spain, many then arrange to live in America."

They talked about the high cost of food. "How do people live? What percentage of their salary do people pay for food?" I asked.

"About sixty percent," Manuel answered.

"I had expected it was high, but not more than half their income. Most Spaniards don't spend as much as Americans do on transportation, right?"

"Correct. But many now buy cars they can't afford."

Gabriel related how he had worked two years cutting sugar cane to get the money to buy permission papers to emigrate. His wife and child were still there waiting to get out of Castro's Cuba.

Manuel finished his drink and rose. "Well, let's go. I've got an appointment this evening."

"Don't forget the pants," I reminded. "Send them on August 5th."

"Don't worry. They'll be there."

I wondered. He hadn't fulfilled his promise to make them fit. Now I feared I'd be chasing them all over Spain.

I picked up my knapsack at the *pensión* and hurried to the train. Commuters crowded the small depot. I pushed through the gate and jumped onto the train as it pulled out heading west toward Puente San Miguel. Standing room only again. The rain splattered against the train windows. Dark and cold outside, it was muggy and sweaty in our crowded compartment. Three women across the aisle chatted away. Traveling far next to them, one's Spanish comprehension would soon improve. Many Spaniards talk loudly in public and, mostly it seems, about matters of little importance. Often in a group, one does all or most of the talking. The others are just there, backboards for the tennis ball.

This time, one hadn't stopped talking since we boarded. "And there was Josefina carrying on in front of the church in a skirt barely to her knees. You'd think she had no parents. Why, if she were my daughter. . . ."

"Cabezón de la Sal," the train conductor yelled. "Next stop Treceño." A patch of blue shone through the dark evening sky. The hour walk up the hill from Cosío would be muddy. The woman blabbered away, but one companion got off at Roiz leaving only one listener and me for the chatterbox.

"San Vicente de la Barquera." My stop was next, and then the change to the bus to carry us twelve miles up along the Nansa River to Puentenansa. I felt happy to be getting back.

"Pesués." A dozen or so of us, including a few who looked familiar, got off and headed for the bus.

An hour and a half later we pulled across the Nansa River bridge and stopped at the corner in front of the restaurant-bar-guesthouse.

Although right on schedule, it was already night, and too late for me to continue the other mile on the bus to Cosío and then trek the three miles up the mountain. But if the talkative owner of that second *pensión* was home, this unplanned additional night away from Garabandal might turn out interesting. I knocked, and then pushed open the big,

Pensión Fidel on the left

iron fortified wooden door built to keep intruders out. "Anybody here?"

The middle-aged woman leaned down over the stair rail. "Oh. It's you."

"Do you have room for me tonight?"

"*Claro.* I had a full house the night before last, but you're the only one here now. You can have your pick, here or up on the third floor."

What a mansion, one in which you could escape and hide from bothersome siblings, and for which you'd pay a fortune in the San Francisco Bay Area.

"Do you want dinner right away?"

"Anytime. Don't bother setting up in the dining room. The kitchen is fine" and it would provide a better opportunity to talk. So accustomed are the Spanish to do it "the way it's done," it is difficult to receive different or special treatment. Don't waste your breath, for example, telling the maid not to worry about your room. One must have an orderly room. This proprietor, though, was different and I loved it.

She wiped her hands on her apron, looked at me, and frowned. "What? You'll eat in the kitchen? Well, you're an odd one! Do you like fish?" It crackled in the frying pan and the smell of hot olive oil piqued my appetite.

"Garabandal will never die out now," she started. "It will only get stronger—but because of you foreigners. You believe in it. We, who saw everything, don't believe." She looked at me to see how that struck. "Some of you are interested because you believe; others because of the money."

"Because of the money? Who's in it for the money?"

"Some Catalans. [People from Spain's region of Cataluña where Barcelona is the chief city]."

"Who?" I probed.

"Oh, a writer from Barcelona. She gave Serafín the money for that house. Where would a poor farmer like Conchita's brother get money for a place like that? It's hers. She just put him in there to run it. Serafín doesn't have the head for such a project by himself. More wine?"

She continued, "Why would God send his mother to a little place like that? They are bad people just like us. The father of one of the girls even owns a bar." I didn't comment on the closed down bar on the ground floor of her own guest house.

My hunch was right. The friendly *señora* was wound up and ready to sing. "The wine is delicious here."

"The higher up you go, the better it tastes and the more potent. Better yet up in San Sebastián."

There it was again—San Sebastián instead of Garabandal from a local. And the hearty red wine chased away the frustration of washed out train tracks and a leaky bus, of ill-fitting pants and pigs feet. I hadn't made it back to Garabandal, but who cared? I sat back and soaked up the impression the Garabandal happenings had made on this *pensión* owner from neighboring Puentenansa. And at no extra charge! She picked up my soup bowl and set a plate of fried fish fillets and french fries in front of me. I recognized the smell, a local favorite—*merluza* (hake). The Spanish señora watched me enjoy it, poured herself another

Conchita at 19 or 20

glass of wine and sat down. The cook drink with a guest? Was that proper? I laughed to myself and beamed at her willingness to talk and confide in me.

"Just imagine" she said, Conchita going off like she did to live in the city and running around with some American! We even heard he is divorced. Why, if the Virgin had appeared to me, I'd put myself in a convent so fast and wait for God to call me to Him."

Watch that wine, lady! This fish frying frau was not alone in wondering why none of the girls had become nuns. Should I remind her that Conchita entered the Carmelite Convent in Pamplona on her 17th birthday, but reported that a week later Jesus spoke to her and said that he wanted her to remain in the world and tell people about his love for them, that she would always have much to suffer because before the Miracle few would believe her? No, even if this were a history class, it was dinner break time. So I just said, "Come on. What do you mean, 'put herself in a convent'? If she had done that, people wouldn't have had the chance to be edified by her."

She laughed, appearing to enjoy the good-natured banter as much as I. "I don't care I tell you. She should lock herself up in a convent." She stepped back and looked at me. Her mouth dropped and her eyes opened wider. She slapped her hand to her forehead. "Ah, it's you! You're probably the boyfriend sitting here listening to me like this."

"See, you've got to be careful to whom you say such things," I kidded, pleased to be able to tease and joke in a second language. They should serve wine before every oral foreign language exam.

"No. It can't be you. Is it?"

The next morning the sun broke through the window of the spacious room and woke me early. I leaned out and watched the previous day's rain float up and over the mountains in fluffy, snow-white clouds. I dashed cold water on my face, paid the hundred and fifty *pesetas* (less than $3 U.S.) for the room and supper, and hiked up the road the mile to Cosío. There a lady informed me, "Mass isn't here this morning. It's a kilometer up the road in Rozadío. If you hurry, you can make it. Better run along though. Our priest, Don Valentín prays fast. He mumbles too so you can't understand a word."

I hiked on, getting my exercise early for the day. A couple of boys cut hay in a field along the road. Chiming bells signaled the way to the church. Mass did go fast. Afterwards, I followed Conchita's mother, Aniceta, up the path out of Rozadío to the valley road. She was stepping it off for home at a wicked pace and I ran to catch up with her.

"Ah. It's you, Eduardo. I brought a letter up to the house for you yesterday."

She knew my name! The overbearing protective guardian had disappeared. I felt happy to talk with, and to get to know, the mother of the most popular visionary. "What a fast Mass," I started and hoped the Spanish would roll out right this early in the morning.

Aniceta, c.1966

101

"Yes, Father speaks very fast, and you don't understand anything, but Don Valentín has been with us for twenty years. We love him. They have made him suffer though." She looked younger than I had thought. Maybe she was less worried now with Conchita in Barcelona away from curious pilgrims. It delighted me that she talked freely.

> Previously, we didn't know anything about apparitions. We were very isolated up there in the mountains. But now I understand that the church has to be careful to find out the truth. There are many false visionaries. The bishops have the right to intervene but not to the extent of damaging the religion of the people. Why don't they permit Mass up in our village?

"I don't know, Aniceta."

> This last bishop, [Cirarda, the fourth since 1961] they said he was smart, but he hasn't done anything good [in regard to Garabandal]. He doesn't know anything about the truth. I know that there are many false apparitions, but in my house there is no falsehood!

A powerful statement from a strong woman who often walks six miles up and down a mountain to Mass, and who gets up at 5:00 A.M. to pray. "In my house there is no falsehood!"

I hoped to spend more time with her on our walks up the mountain but this morning she stopped to buy meat in Cosío. I continued on alone, but when *doña* Mercedes called out her greeting to me and extended her invitation to talk—this time a couple of apples—I also stopped. Looking through her open door, I spotted a guitar on the table inside. "Señora, you know what other favor you could do for me? Let me play your guitar."

"It belongs to the boy who stays here but he won't mind." *Cielito Lindo* and other Mexican songs rehearsed for ten years in my high school Spanish classes so delighted her that she served me *chorizo* on fresh bread so I would continue the serenade.

I arrived back in Garabandal after getting a lift the last mile in the road construction foreman's jeep. Work had started this morning on the road up to the Peña Sagra ridge above Garabandal where the government planned on putting in a winter resort. I asked around to find out if this was connected with developments at Garabandal. No, they had talked

New road

about a resort for years, and the new road bypasses the village. Just past the new bridge, about three-quarters of a mile below the village, it separates from the Cosío-Garabandal road and parallels El Sebrando River to the north of the village. The bypass disappointed some villagers.

A crowd gathered in front of Ceferino's place. Loli was among them but saying nothing (indicating that the visitors were foreigners). A woman turned to me. "You speak Spanish. Will you ask her if she saw the Virgin and if she will pray for this woman who has a bad knee?"

"No." I would feel terrible asking Loli something I already knew. Then a man in the group addressed her in Italian.

"Are you the girl who saw the Madonna?"

How stupid! Loli's answer was clear and decisive but without rancor or annoyance, "I can't tell you."

I took it in the sense of "I am not sure and don't want to be wrong," not that "someone has prohibited me from answering." The question infuriated me. Imagine going up to the girl without any introduction or even a "hello" and confronting her with a question about the most profound experience of her life. Loli's composure amazed me. I walked away to avoid further embarrassment.

Once again back at Mesón Serafín, three women from Florida waiting for the 1:00 P.M. meal chatted away. "A priest said the Holy Father has condemned Garabandal." I recognized the woman who had been out front talking to Mary Loli and she recognized me.

"I only asked you because that poor woman has been suffering from a bad knee for years, and she walked all the way up here. Her companions who don't believe in this place made fun of her. When Mari Loli said 'no,' that she had not seen the Virgin, her friends left, disgusted."

"I don't think Mari Loli said that she didn't see the Virgin."

"Oh yes she did, and lying is wrong no matter what. I wouldn't lie no matter who told me to, or what the people would think."

"What would you expect her to answer in such circumstances?"

"I would tell the truth. If I had seen the Virgin, I would admit it no matter what the bishop or the priests told me to say. Black is black and white is white and there is no in between."

Here was another who knew exactly how she would act if God had chosen her to be his intermediary between heaven and earth. Was this how the rumors and contradictions started? "Ma'am, I think Loli answered, 'No les puedo decir.' Do you know what that means?"

"I heard the 'no.' That means, 'no, I didn't see the Blessed Mother.'"

"I don't think so. I heard, 'I can't tell you.' That is a lot different."

"You ought to tell that woman with the bad knee. She was embarrassed and that would make her feel good."

Why Loli's answer? I don't know. But it's tempting to speculate about God's plans. Besides being intermediaries between God and us, the four visionaries of Garabandal are also our models and examples. And if they are to be models, then is it not logical that the memory of the apparitions fade in order that they might strengthen their faith and trust in God in the normal way? If the memory of the visions of Jesus and of his Mother were always present to them, no act of faith would be necessary on their part, for there would be no gap between the evidence and the certainty of God's existence.

But no, now I can hold Loli up as one to emulate. I cannot say, "Oh, she saw and talked to God's Mother. That's why it's so easy for her to be good. If I had seen . . ."

These four daughters of Garabandal must strive courageously, humbly, patiently "to be perfect as their Heavenly Father is perfect," working under the same cloud of uncertainty as the rest of us.

And the San Sebastián residents? What are they like? How many believe in the divine authorship of the extraordinary happenings in their village?

CHAPTER EIGHT

A FATHERLY BROTHER

onchita's brother, Serafín, is the one I got to know best. Slightly under six feet tall, balding, strong, browned by the sun, he looks you straight in the eye inviting confidence and a desire to be his friend. Unassuming and humble, he didn't often initiate conversation with the visitors at Mesón Serafín. He seemed content with letting his friendly wife, Paquita, greet the guests and make them feel at home.

Serafín and María Conchita, 1971

I had met him the year before (1970) cutting hay near the village. But not until later did I learn he was the oldest of Conchita's three brothers. Thirty-seven years old, he married three years younger Paquita in 1969. "We went together for twelve years," they told me.

Father Laffineur had talked about him. "He is the wisest young man in the village." Father attached great importance to his building and running the new guesthouse. "A wise young man like that wouldn't invest the time and money in such a project unless he was sure that Garabandal would continue." Such confidence would be based in large part on his knowing the veracity of his sister and her companions. Who better than Serafín, brother and protector of the most favored visionary, could confirm Conchita's truthfulness or discern deceit?

This summer of 1971, I had planned on again boarding with Señora Josefa Cosío, the bread distributor, but finding her house filled with family, I moved into the Serafín Gonzalez family's new guesthouse.

He, a bachelor until age thirty-four, and I, still one at that age, became friends. Serafín seldom talked about the girls' apparitions or the ecstasies that he had witnessed from 1961 through 1965. (Many of his guests had a difficult time asking for a glass of water). However, when he did discuss the apparitions, he, like all the other eyewitnesses, spoke with certainty and enthusiasm.

One day while we sat on his front porch digesting dinner, I caught him in a reminiscent mood.

Miguel, Aniceto, Aniceta, Conchita, Serafín, 1965

When the apparitions began I was working in Leon. I remember my brother and I were on our way home and arrived in the train station at Torrelavega [some thirty miles east of Garabandal], the Estación del Norte. There I met a guy who had been with me in the military. We talked awhile and soon he asked, "Say, what's going on in your village?" I didn't know what he was talking about. Then he said, "Well, I believe that the Virgin is appearing and a lot of people are going there." I didn't know what to think. I started to laugh. I didn't believe it.

Serafín related how later, when they stopped at a bar, and the owner also talked of the apparitions, half jokingly he asked, "What can it be and who can it be?"

They told me that they were four little girls, one of whom was the daughter of a barman who lives in our village. Later that night at a party, all that the people talked about were the apparitions, and when they told me my sister was involved, I became so uneasy I couldn't enjoy myself. I had to get back to the village.

People, crowding the lane from the village to the Pines,
anxious to observe the girls in ecstasy

We arrived at Cosío at dusk, but started the climb to Garabandal at once. Our little mountain road was full of people coming down. Hundreds of people! They had come from other towns to see the ecstasies. We didn't stop to talk. All this was in July, and the apparitions had begun the 18th of June. Well, we arrived at the house and found Paquita, Conchita, and my mother. But I was anxious to see for myself what was up. I didn't have long to wait, for the next day came an ecstasy.

I didn't have to ask Serafín for his initial impression. The likeable, sun-browned farmer spoke in his normal expressive, almost musical manner, choosing his words carefully. "When I saw the girls for the first time, they were gazing up into the sky. Later, they said they had seen the Virgin, and I knew it must be a work of God because I knew my sister and what she was and what we are here in the village."

I had felt the same way the first time I met Conchita in July 1970. Nine years after the first apparition and almost five after the last, I had concluded the same—Serafín's sister could not deceive us. In America one gets around. You learn to know who's telling the truth and who the "used car dealers" are. I met no car dealers in Garabandal. There weren't even any cars except for Gabino's old taxi.

The reaction of their teacher had been the same when she saw them headed for the church, crying. "Is it true that you've seen an angel?" she had asked the four little girls that fateful June night of 1961.

"*Sí, Señora.*"

And knowing them to be sincere, she believed them immediately.[33] How valuable the reputation of trustworthiness. Even before I set foot in Garabandal, the characteristic that attracted me most to northern Spaniards was their honesty and mutual trust. In the bars, for example, the bartenders don't write down the bill. They ask what you ate and drank; you respond; they add up the charges and you pay. In such an atmosphere, although the villagers wanted to see for themselves, they took what the four girls reported seriously.

Serafín explained his initial deduction:

> When we were small, whenever we would see a stranger, someone from outside the village, we would stand and gawk because we
>
> weren't used to seeing people. But now, although the whole place was crammed with visitors from all over, my sister, with her head tilted back, and the others girls gazing motionless into the sky, were unaware anyone else existed. When I saw this, I thought, well there is something here. This is strange. This is an impossible phenomenon! It must be an act of God, or as the girls said, the Virgin was there.

From the beginning, and even more as time went on, I could see that it was of God. All that they have said between 1961 and 1965 until 1971, where we are now, has been fulfilled to the letter. "Priests are on the way to hell and with them they are taking many souls. Less respect is given to the Eucharist," they said. They also sang songs in ecstasy: "Styles are dragging people to hell; dress decently if you want to be saved."

Today in the world, it is said that many are dressing indecently. Many priests are going the wrong way. They didn't know then what would occur in 1971. Yet they said these things back in 1961

---

33 Francisco Sanchez-Ventura y Pascal, *The Apparitions of Garabandal*. (Detroit: San Miguel Publishing Co., 1971), p. 35.

and 1962. Where could they obtain such knowledge? Nobody had taught them or had prepared them. I know the education that my sister had in those times—little, more or less what I had myself. We had the same education, the same studies. Today she is smarter than I. Yes, without doubt she is more intelligent.

Conchita at the Pines

Serafín thus explained the impossibility of his sister and her friends foretelling through natural means what evils would occur in the future or, if this were not foreknowledge, how the girls, because of their isolation, had no way of knowing what was happening at that time outside their village.

I spent a month in Serafín's house during the summer of 1971. He had no television. I saw no newspaper or books, and he was describing the situation ten years previous (1961) before significant advances in communication had come to his village.

Although he has had much contact with visitors these past ten years, he still reacted in awe discussing the United States. "We hear some strange things about America. Do many people really get divorced there?"

"Oh, about one out of three. More in California."

"Really? What happens to the children?"

"They run away to San Francisco or Amsterdam or to your own Mallorca. Many suffer. I meet them every day in my classroom."

"America must be very bad. No?"

"Oh. I don't know if we are worse than anybody else. We might have more bad, but more good also. In America we are quite free to do what we want. Here in Spain, for example, by law and by circumstance your freedom is limited. In the United States, our laws, our money, our leisure time, and our education enable us to do much good but also permit much evil."

Serafín listens, and I enjoyed sharing my opinion on the strengths and weaknesses of American life; but fearing he might not talk again about the apparitions, I asked, "Did the Santander Commission ever ask you for your opinion?"

"No. That Commission is for me as if it didn't exist!"

"And did you ever see anything abnormal in the girls after the ecstasies?"

> Never! And I saw many ecstatic trances and marches. In two ecstasies they descended from the Pines backwards on their knees. Once I came down with Conchita from the Pines. And I suffering, thinking my sister was going to destroy her knees, felt like I myself was walking over the rocks on my knees. But I couldn't do anything until the trance ended. When we got to the house I said to her, "Let me see your knees!" Clean!

> With me that day, there were other villagers and witnesses from other parts of Spain, including a duke and a captain of the army and their wives. I saw many phenomena like this that were impossible to explain. Never can the Bishop of Santander say to me that this was natural.[34] You can't make me see as black something that is white.

Bisihop Puchol Montis

"What do you think about those who say the girls deceived the people, Serafín, or that you and other witnesses lied?"

He explained how this was completely implausible. Who could imagine how his sister and the others, although chronologically twelve,

---

34   On March 17, 1967 Santander Bishop, Puchol Montis stated in an Official Note, "that based upon the declarations of the involved [girls] all of the happenings that occurred in that locality have a natural explanation."

having a seven or eight-year-old's knowledge of the world, could deceive the numerous doctors and other learned people who saw them in ecstasy day after day? To attribute to them such a power would be unthinkable and unsupportable.

> I can say to the whole world that for me it is a thing of God. I believe and expect that which is announced. If the Bishop comes to me and tells me that it isn't from God, well I will tell him, "OK, but it's not natural either." And I, believing that it is not natural and believing that God exists and the Virgin also, well, I'll continue to say that this is a thing of God. For me there is no doubt!

Serafín didn't address the second question—that of him and others fabricating the whole story. In his book, *Garabandal el pueblo habla*, Ramón Perez' comment on this is revealing: "We would like to hear anyone, [be he] bishop or cardinal, say directly to [villagers] Benjamín [Gómez], Pepe [Diaz] or Simón [Gonzalez], 'You're a liar.' The spectacle would be amusing!"[35]

Later, Serafín and I headed for his closest field to stack the dried grass. On the way we looked into the American's new house.

"It's elegant. Look at that tile work. It cost him a fortune."

"How much would that cost to build up here?" I inquired.

"Well, I don't know exactly. For the rocks alone it would cost him a quarter of a million pesetas plus the cost of getting them up here which is no small sum. And that furniture is expensive. I would say, roughly, two million pesetas."[36]

Foreigners were moving in—most by acquiring old houses from the villagers. This was the most impressive of the new establishments, not counting the Sevillian's Castle.

"How does one acquire a field, Serafín?" We stopped on the bluff in back of St. Michael's shrine.

---

35 Ramon Pérez, *GARABANDAL el pueblo Habla. (Ediciones Resiac, Montsurs,1977).* *Edición en lengua española ampliada y actualizada sobre la 3.° edición francesa. P.393.*

36 $34,000, 1973 exchange rate.

By inheritance. Now you can't buy a field around here. The price has gone up since the apparitions. This one isn't mine. It belongs to Mercedes Salisachs. Or rather she gave it to some nuns, and they allow me to use it. It was the first piece of property that was sold after the apparitions. She paid thirty thousand pesetas (five hundred dollars). Now it would be worth about ten times that much—some 300,000 *pesetas*. The land over there on which the chapel stands belongs to this same plot. It's a good parcel, big.

The farmers who work the land close to home certainly have the advantage over those who walk two or three kilometers or more to reach their fields. It seems unfair.

Serafín continued, "A Filipino lady bought the field in front of my mother's house for 250,000 pesetas ($3,500) three years ago. She gave it to Father (Ramón) Andreu."

Serafín raked the grass into small piles. I stood and watched him draw all the grass within reach toward him, and then end with a curling motion. While watching him work I recalled the part the Andreu family has played in the Garabandal drama.

Fr. Luis Andreu, S.J.

Fathers Ramón and Luís, two of four Jesuit priests in a family of five boys, came to Garabandal shortly after the apparitions started. Ramón has left a detailed testimony of his experiences in the village.

Luís and Ramón

One day Luis, the youngest, was heard to cry out at the Pines, "miracle, miracle"! While riding home together that night to Reynosa, Mr. Fontaneda, the owner of the cookie company bearing his name, heard Fr. Luis say, "This is the happiest day of my life." Apparently asleep at their destination, the young priest could not be awakened and was pronounced dead. I recalled that the visionaries said that on the day after the great

Fr. Andreu in casket

112

Miracle, his body will be found incorrupt.

Serafín continued raking the dried grass. I tried to help saying, "You'll have to show me how. I'm not much of a farmer."

"It's easy. Look."

I tried not to mess up. I don't know how many *prados* (fields) Serafín owns or works: the one along the road, two more quite a distance from their house, one that he doesn't cut because the cows graze on it, this one which the nuns allow him to cut, and possibly others.

We gathered the grass for forty-five minutes without rest. Stacked in small mounds, it will dry further until Serafín piles it into one large stack. Thus arranged, the rain or night dew wets only the surface while the rest remains dry. Finally, he will store the hay from this field into the barn close to his mother's house. The hay away from the village is stored in winter barns called *invernales*.

"Do the cows like this dry grass as well as the fresh?" I would learn to be a farmer yet.

"No. They won't touch it when green is available. But in winter there is nothing else. Let's get a drink of water," he suggested. "The best water in the village comes out of this small spring. I keep a jar right here. Some people "baptize" the wine here in the mountains to make it less potent but they can't dilute the water."

We drank freely and then sat down to rest.

"Haven't you ever thought about getting married, Eduardo?"

"Yes, but not much recently."

"A man's got to have a purpose in life—somebody to work for."

Serafín sure worked for two gems in Paquita and María Conchita, I thought.

He continued, "One needs some responsibility. There goes Alejandro for example, the poor fellow. He's sick and can't work at times. He's alone and has no one to take care of him."

Yes! The single life did look sad—for Alejandro.

Paquita with María Conchita

CHAPTER NINE
CIRIACO

he mist rolled in, hid the mountains, and flowed down the canyon toward Cosío as it often does around one o'clock after the morning sun heats the moist ground.

From my observation post near the Pines, I could see over Garabandal's red tiled roofs to the road below. Fog engulfed the world beyond.

The bread was arriving early with either Josefa or her daughter, Natividad, coaxing the burro the final steps of the nine-mile round trip to Puentenansa. The arrival of the fresh bread meant dinner would be served soon, so I left my spot.

Approaching the village, I saw sharp-eyed Ciriaco Cosío sitting on a wooden stool in front of his house watching my descent. Sixty-one years old, but too sore to work the fields, he often stood around leaning on his cane or shuffled through the village in his albarcas, those awkward-looking three pegged wooden shoes. Profound and humorous, he was the type of character about whom you'd write a story.

"*Hola, Eduardo*," he greeted me in his guttural, raspy voice.

"*Hola, Ciriaco*. How are you today?"

"*¡Mal! ¡Muy mal!* My legs hurt horribly. Walter said he'd send me some balm for the rheumatism, but it hasn't arrived. I miss Walter. He visited every day. I'd like to write him a letter. Can you help?"

"Sure, whenever you say."

Ciriaco wobbled to his feet and leaned both hands on the cane to lessen the weight on his legs:

Ah, my legs hurt even when I sit. This is my favorite spot, here next to the lane. I used to sit here during the ecstasies.

115

Everybody else went running through the village after the girls but not me. I was interested, but not to chase all over. I watched mostly from a distance. I would follow behind or just sit here and wait. Many of the first ecstasies happened close to our door, so I got a good view. The girls often ran up here from the village, then fell on their knees right in front of me. I didn't believe it at the beginning. Oh, I believed I guess, but not like some of the others. *Ay, de mi.*[37] It hurts even to sit down.

People were always fascinated by girls in ecstasy

He adjusted himself again on the rough, homemade three-legged stool. "It's almost time for dinner, Ciriaco. One sure gets an appetite here in the mountains. I'll see you this afternoon."

"Yes, about the letter."

Why did he need me to write the letter? Was Ciriaco older than the village school?

Back up at the guesthouse, Paquita served vegetable soup, lamb stew, and, of course, red wine and crusty fresh bread. We would call it french bread but to the Spaniards it is just *pan*.

A short English lesson for Paquita followed. "Good morning. How are you? Fine, thank you. And you? Do you want breakfast now?"

Paquita worked hard to get it right. Serafín looked on with little interest in learning to speak English. Later, I headed for Ciriaco's.

"Anybody home?"

"Come in. Sit down." Ciriaco sat with a blanket over his legs. "I sit here by the stove in order to keep warm." It was the end of July but the afternoon fog chilled the air outside. In the tiny kitchen it was almost too hot for comfort.

"Would you like a glass of cognac, Eduardo?"

"No thanks, too strong for me." But I did like a shot in their thick, syrupy espresso coffee with sugar. In Barcelona, order a *carajillo*.

"Well how about a *blanco*?"

"Sounds good." He poured the white wine and set it before me on the table.

"Here's some paper and I've got an envelope somewhere. I'll buy some stamps."

"Do we write in Spanish or English?" I asked.

"Well, Walter understands Spanish. We'd sit here and talk all the time. Better in Spanish."

"*Estimado Walter,*

We miss you here in Garabandal."

"Do I write for you or from both of us, Ciriaco?"

"You know, Walter too."

"Fine, keep talking. Later I'll add my comments."

The old man dictated, "It has rained so much that we've been able to catch trout in your river."

I looked up perplexed, "Walter's river?"

"Oh, he'll understand. That's the drainage ditch he dug for the spring in front of Conchita's house."

Hmm, the old duffer was still sharp. He continued, "Clemente came to the Pines again last week. We in the village don't pay any attention to him."

"Ciriaco, that was you who happened upon the Clemente scene at the Pines last year! What did you think?"

"With Clemente it's not the same as with the girls. They were babies, incapable of pretending anything. They had never left the village. No, that [the ecstatic trances of the four girls] was the truth."

Still reluctant to initiate discussion about the Garabandal happenings, I jumped in at this opening offered by an eyewitness. The letter could wait. "Tell me about the ecstasies, Ciriaco. What happened and what did you think?" The old mountaineer shifted around on the chair:

My wife, Aurelia, preparing supper one night here in the kitchen, said to me, "Do you know what's happening in the village?" I couldn't know because I had been working cutting wood in the mountains. "Don't you know that the Virgin appeared to four girls?" And I said to her, "Look, you go gabbing about town so don't come to me with stories, because for me they are stories. You women are always speaking about saints, and you're the biggest gossips around. Don't talk to me about those things." So she didn't bother me again, and I didn't think more about it.

The author with Ciriaco's wife, Aurelia, in her kitchen (2015)

Some days went by, and a few of us in the mountains agreed to cut short the work and go see the girls. This was about eight or ten days after the first apparition. My companions and I walked home. I washed up, and as hoards of people crowded around, instead of going up the lane I went through the fields to stand where I could see the girls. I was a little ways away, but I could see perfectly.

Ciriaco seemed as intrigued by his story as I. He rubbed his legs but didn't stop talking. I put away the pen so the letter writing wouldn't sidetrack him:

When the girls fell onto the rocks, it made me cry. I returned home and said to my wife, "Well, this isn't for me—to see them suffer like that." I really noticed how they crashed hard to the jagged rocks onto their knees. It was something I had never seen in my life. Then one day Conchita came to my house and told me, "Don't worry, uncle, because for me it's the greatest satisfaction I can have when I am seeing the Virgin."

Loli and Jacinta in statue-like position.

"Oh good," I told her. "If it's ok for you, then for me also." Well, after that I followed the apparitions anytime I could. Not because I was a meddling sort of fellow, because I wasn't, but I always tried to be in a place where I could see them pass or in a place where they would remain quiet in ecstasy. When the girls came out of ecstasy, they were as normal, or more so, than I. Nothing of paralysis. Everyone commented on this. I saw things that I can state, as sure as my name is Ciriaco, that neither I nor anyone would be capable of doing—not little children as they were, nor an older person educated or not.

This was just what I was looking for, someone to pour out his impressions, to relive for me the historic months of June, July, and August 1961. Crippled old Ciriaco, still sharp of memory and wit looking for company, and I, a lone foreigner with leisure to listen and learn, made a good combination.[38]

---

38 The Santander Bishop's Commission, formed to investigate the happenings in the village, showed no interest in hearing Ciriaco, other villagers, visiting doctors or any of the thousands of eye-witnesses.

"Do the rest of the villagers agree with you? Do they all believe firmly in the supernatural origin of what they saw?"

Mari Cruz, Conchta, Loli

"I didn't believe much at the beginning, but I've thought it over well. Those girls—Conchita, Jacinta, Loli, and Mari Cruz—couldn't deceive us. They have to be telling the truth. Others have forgotten. It's hardly talked about."

Ciriaco used "believe" to mean knowing that God was the direct cause of the occurrences in Garabandal—that they were supernatural. The attendant phenomena (the ecstatic marches and falls, etc.) are acknowledged as facts. In my time in Garabandal and in the rest of Spain, I found no one who denies that these happenings (naturally unexplainable according to investigating doctors) took place. It is only their cause and importance about which a difference of opinion exists.

This general certainty of knowing what they had witnessed, but uncertainty of the cause, reminded me of the gospel account of Nicodemus, who saw Christ work miracles. He acknowledged that Christ was a wonder worker. But the certainty that he was the Messiah, the Son of God, is a supernatural gift which would be given later. "The wind blows where the Spirit wills."

"Then what do the villagers think of us coming in here? Do we bother you? Do the villagers think we are crazy?"

"On the contrary, what do you people think of us? Here we are ninety percent Catholics and very bad. Before, everybody in the village attended Mass and the rosary. Nobody stayed outside. Now, only a few attend."

That seemed odd. The people have become worse since God and his mother came to town? "What do you mean previously? When did some stop attending Mass?"

"Since the war (The Spanish Civil War of 1936–1939) the faith has decreased. Before that, Sunday was kept holy. Hardly anybody drank wine."

"Not even in the homes?"

"No." He must mean on Sunday. Without wine Spaniards would die of thirst.

"Only ten percent of you are Catholics, but you are good people. You believe in this. And you didn't see anything. You have only read and heard people talk." I savored every word. Ciriaco massaged his legs. "Everyone here, with the exception of one or two who might have been confined to bed, saw the ecstasies. At times, eight to ten thousand visitors came into the village."

It was becoming more and more evident to me that the strength of one's belief in the supernatural authorship of the Garabandal phenomena was not proportionate to the number of ecstasies witnessed. Faith is a gift. We returned to the letter writing, and Ciriaco's wife, Aurelia entered the kitchen to peel and slice potatoes.

"Would you like a snack, Eduardo?" she asked. "Here. Try this piece of ham. It's delicious."

Would it never fail? For me, the guest, the best snack in the house, the prized *serrano* ham. And for their own young daughter, María Eugenia? No, she didn't want a fried egg, only french fries. I continued the letter:

> You remember me, Walter, Ed Kelly. We met here last summer. Ciriaco misses you. He talks about you all the time and is anxious for the rheumatism medicine. Loli seems happier than last year. Conchita will visit for only ten days. A group of forty-five from the United States is due in soon.
>
> God bless you,
>
> Ciriaco (Cosío) and Ed (Kelly)

American Walter Kushion beside
his car on the improved Cosío road.

I did so well on that letter that Ciriaco dictated another: Yes there would be a room available in his house the nights of August 7 and 8 for an acquaintance from Reinosa.

"*Caramba*," I jumped up. "I'm late. I'll see you tomorrow."

"You don't visit very often. Walter used to come every day."

I sang down the rocky lane to the church, happy that Ciriaco had enjoyed my company as much as I, his. "But I've thought it over well," he had said. No doubt he realizes that his crippled body won't support his indomitable spirit much longer, and that he will soon be judged for the part he played in disseminating God's recent warning to the world. "Those children couldn't deceive us. It's got to be true."

I snuck into the back of the crowded little church, late for the evening rosary. "Ciriaco has a sore leg, God."[39]

---

39   A year later, in September 1972, Ciriaco, in bed dying from cancer, told me, "I have many pains. Perhaps I deserve them but I don't know why God gives them to me. I promised the Virgin half of my herd in alms if she would permit me to live to see the Miracle. If I had two cows for example, I would give away one. But little life is left in me." He died on October 2 and we carried him two days later in a plain box to the cemetery, where most of the grave inscriptions read: Mazón, Cuenca, Gonzalez or Cosío.

 AFTER THE VISIONS

aturday morning I started through the village on the run.

"Where are you going?" Gabino the cab driver and expert fisherman asked.

"To Mass." And he nodded to his jeep. That meant a free ride the three miles down the mountain to Cosío. Under forty, but turning gray fast, Gabino often offered me rides. It seemed a delicate situation to charge some and to carry the rest of us for nothing if he was going our way.[40]

Rakes and pitchforks stuck out the rear of the jeep-taxi. Inside were a butane canister, a cardboard box, and a burlap gunnysack. Grey-haired old Doña Vitoria, tears in her eyes, hung onto the doorknob of her narrow house.

"Don't forget the key," Gabino yelled.

"I gave it to María next door." Her shrill voice cracked with emotion.

"*Hola.*"

"*Hola, Doña Vitoria,*" I replied.

"I've got to leave. I've got nobody here. My son, Angel, is working in Asturias."

"I didn't know you would leave so soon."

"I don't want to move. This place is all I know. I have never left the village. All my friends are here."

---

40 Some visitors consider Gabino the "scalper" of Garabandal, but he won't admit it and asserts, "I haven't made a penny. Look, I pay five hundred pesetas to fill this thing up every four days and have worn out six cars in ten years transporting pilgrims up this road. I don't make anything." Although much improved from the 1961 steep, rocky path for burros and donkey carts, the "road" was still tough on cars at this time (1971).

How little have the poor. Were the few things in the jeep all she owned, and the two women around to see her off, her only friends? She said tearful good-byes to a couple more that happened along the road. Even the circle of friendship of the poor is limited by their lack of mobility.

With little income, and prevented by old age from working the land, she would move to Asturias, the province to the west of Santander, where a son worked. The demand for property in the village would have pushed up the value of her little place to enable her to sell and set up elsewhere.

"Come on, Doña Vitoria." Gabino winked at me. "You're not moving to the United States. You'll be back."

"No, I won't. I'll never get back."

I held the door, offering the inside seat, but she protested. "No. I have to sit by the window. I'll get sick."

"She's afraid she'll get car sick," Gabino chuckled. She carried a coffee can on her lap, and I soon found out why. "These people have never ridden in a car. They tell each other that it's horrible, that the ride will make them sick and it does." Darn Gabino took the sad situation so lightly. How could he laugh?

"Here, take this," he said. You'll get your dress dirty." He handed her a handkerchief. Gabino was thoughtful after all—and well prepared.

"They say that if you just relax and let the scenery go by without trying to stop it, you don't get carsick," I offered. But that advice didn't stop anything. Poor old woman.

And she had more than stomach problems. "Gabino, you take me to Asturias. You know me better."

"No. My brother is waiting below. He knows that road as well as I. I've got to go to Cabezón. You'll be all right."

"No. I'd rather go with you. Please, Gabino."

But down in Cosío they switched her, bag and baggage, to the black sedan already loaded with more possessions. A stove and some boxes stuck out of the trunk. Other household items and clothes filled the back seat. The gunnysack contained some *chorizo* and a large part of a *serrano* ham, most likely the same from which she had cut slices for me the year before. We struggled with the long rake trying to fit it into the car. Finally Vitoria knocked out the wooden nails and it came apart. Gabino gave directions and gas money to his brother, and the distraught old woman reluctantly changed cars with the coffee can still in her hand.

"*Adios, Doña Vitoria.*" I don't know how many people will pass your little house squeezed in between two bigger ones. Will we count them by the thousands or millions?

Someday, tour guides will point out the two houses a half block on either side of yours. "Mari Loli lived here, and Mari Cruz grew up here," they will say. I'm not sure what miracle the future pilgrims will experience, but none of them will be treated to fresh bread, homemade sausage, and good red wine like I was, while your own son ate a leftover fried egg and stale fried potatoes. None will be greeted by your warm, welcoming smile and high-pitched "*Buenos días,*" so comforting to a lone traveler. No, I know not what miracle latecomers will witness, but it will have to go some to outclass your kindness to me. *Que se vaya con Diós, doña Victoria, y que Él y su Virgen Madre le paguen.*[41]

"*Hola.*" Smiling as always, Danny, the crippled boy, at twenty-one or two, the same age as the visionaries, hobbled over toward me on his polio type crutches to say hello. He is one of three whom the girls mentioned by name to be cured on the day of the promised Miracle. The blind American, Joey Lomangino, and Javier, the son of author María Josefa Villa de Gallego, are the others.

"What happened last night at the Pines?" I asked. He shrugged his muscular overdeveloped shoulders. "It surprised me that so many of you followed that 'visionary' up to the Pines. Why?"

"Some out of curiosity, others to find fault with him later. Some people believe too much in apparitions; others, not enough."

Again it was the locals who detected the sham. Last night, a dozen or so people came in pilgrimage from Santander following a young waiter from that city. The word had spread that the Blessed Virgin would come and talk to him after an all night vigil at the Pines. When the group climbed the mountain bearing candles and chanting hymns, some of the Garabandal youth followed, laughing and scoffing softly.

---

41 May God be with you, Doña Victoria, and may he and his Virgin Mother repay you.

These young people did not often, at least with me, discuss the apparitions of the Garabandal visionaries, but never did I hear them disparage the girls or hint that visitors were wasting their time in the village. Yet, they laughed out loud at this new "visionary." Someone even hung a plaque high on the corner house at the village entrance. "*Chiflados* (quacks or fakers), we see through your deceit. You are not welcome here."

At 8:30 Cosío was just awakening. Mass wouldn't start for another half-hour. A woman swept out the café on the corner. One early riser drove in a load of freshly cut grass piled high on his donkey drawn cart filling the area with a pleasant aroma.

Then bells and horns, much more piercing than the familiar call to Mass, and not much less shrill than fire engine sirens, interrupted the peacefulness. A three-quarter ton truck pulled into the dirt square. The sleeping villagers will curse and stone this guy, I thought. The driver jumped to the ground and dropped the tailgate. "*Pescado. Pescado fresco,*" he yelled.

He didn't need to yell. The unmistakable odor of fish chased the pleasant smell of the newly cut grass from the plaza.

"*Sardinas, merluza, bonito. Sardinas, quince* [fifteen] *pesetas el kilo. Bonito fresco directamente del mar,*" he called while he set up the weights on his old-fashioned balance scale.

Women and girls in housecoats and *albarcas* (cumbersome looking pegged wooden shoes that last forever because they screw on new pegs when the old ones wear out) emerged from everywhere holding plates or dishes and lined up behind the truck. The proprietor counted out sardines, cut off and weighed slices from a tuna, and threw fish scale covered coins into a cigar box.

He worked fast, and then unhooked the scale, closed the tail gate and headed back out to the road to continue his route up the valley from the sea. Those fish wouldn't be fresh tomorrow, and he would want to reach all the villages in the Nansa River Valley before mid-day dinnertime.

After Mass in the damp little Cosío church, while crossing the bridge (over the Vendul River) which leads to the town proper, I spotted Mercedes waiting at her door.

"*Buenos días, Eduardo.* Come in for a *merienda.*" (Children often eat a piece of chocolate inside two slices of bread for this mid-morning snack).

Everyone in the area knows Mercedes or about her. "Be careful. She's a communist. Her husband fought with the *republicanos* during the war."

Be careful of what? Her husband, Vicente, sat at the kitchen table with a glass of wine and a wedge of *tortilla española* (potato omelet) in

Bridge over the Vendul. Mercedes' house is across from the white house.

front of him. Mercedes set the same in front of me, but needed no further winding up before starting in.

"*Y ésto, que?*" Meaning, and the Garabandal drama, what's new? What do you think?

She had asked me that before. And this time it was her husband, who didn't give me a chance to answer.

"*Un indiano*[42] brought this [the unexplainable Garabandal happenings] here." "*Un indiano?*" I asked. "Who?"

"Taquio. He and I went to Mexico together twenty-three years ago. He was one who always wanted to do something for his village [make his little hamlet seem important]. He came back and started this."

"How?"

"With drugs. He planned it all with that priest who died, Padre Andreu. He trained the girls. All that, the miracle of the host, that priest trained the girls to hold it in the roof of their mouths without breathing, but only Conchita

Conchtia after receiving invisible communion from the angel

---

42 People in the region call those who leave the area to work in Mexico, *indianos* (Indians).

and Mary Cruz could learn to hold it there for the length of time needed. And Mary Cruz wouldn't go through with the hoax."

He had certainly given his story some thought. It was difficult to hold back the laughter. I didn't. "But everybody says that priest was a very good man. Why would he do something like that?" I asked.

His wife jumped in. "He planned it all and took the girls up to the fields to train them. But Conchita was the only one who went through with it." Mercedes described how Conchita deceived most of the people, and named a witness who saw it clearly, and that he was close to Conchita.

"Yes," she said. "He saw clearly how she had the host stuck to the roof of her mouth trying to hide It."

"Wait a minute, Mercedes. In the dark of night he could see the small host stuck to the roof of her mouth"?

"No. no, plain daylight." (It happened at about 1:00 A.M.)

I continued, saying that Father Luis Andreu was well known to be a good, even saintly man. Vicente backed off, but Mercedes, with a big meat cleaver hacking slabs of beef from a part of a cow, steamed on saying, "No, this was the proof of what the man was like, that he did all this. He prepared the girls to fool the people. That's the proof."

Fr. Luis Andreu died mysteriously on August 9, 1961 almost a year before the miracle of the host but that didn't bother Mercedes.

"The parents kept it going," she said.

Doctor taking Conchita's pulse.

"How?" I asked.

"With drugs. The parents gave them drugs."

"Mercedes," I said, holding back the laughter and feigning seriousness, "I don't like to pass on information about Garabandal unless I can document it. Who told you?"

"*La madre.* Mari Cruz' mother. Yes, she wouldn't go along with it like Ceferino [Loli's father] did. You can see how he has gained from this. And Aniceta [Conchita's mother] also, coming down here every day to Mass. The hypocrite. It's not the daughter's fault. She is okay, honorable. It's the mother that kept this thing going."

"But Mercedes, how do you know this?" I hadn't heard a whisper of it from anyone else.

She explained, but not very clearly, that someone (she couldn't recall who) told the girls that if they took the drugs they would all get sick and you could see that it happened. They all got sick except Mari Cruz because she stopped taking them sooner than the others.

"They all got sick?" (Doctors tested the girls and observed them for lengthy periods of time and were amazed that, despite their going without sleep for many hours during the night and being constantly in the public eye, they were healthier than ever.)

Mari Cruz and Conchita enraptured

"Yes, all."

"What kind of drugs did they take?" When I went along, content to hear their unique explanation of the Garabandal happenings, Vicente got quieter and quieter. But his wife, the opposite. The more unreasonable her argument, the louder and faster she talked and the closer she got to me with the big, wide meat cleaver raised above her head. I couldn't hold back the laughter.

"Mercedes, I should have this on tape. You're quite an actress." She laughed until she cried. I hadn't noticed her drink a drop of wine, but maybe so before I arrived.

"Do you know anything about drugs, *señor*? What kind were they? They must have been a type I've never heard of in order to empower the girls to do what they did—reactions that the investigating doctors termed 'naturally unexplainable.' "

"I don't know anything. My friend Taquio . . ." Vicente didn't finish.

He sputtered to a halt like a car running out of gas. He hung his head in silence and soon afterward stood up and left the kitchen. I thought about those powerful wonder drugs. They would have been worth a fortune. Poor Taquio died too soon. The formula for his miracle drug is buried with him and lost forever. I turned to the cook who had finished carving up the cow.

"Mercedes, the people who went up from here, they all saw things they couldn't explain, no? The girls fell to their knees onto the sharp rocks. They walked forward and backward, at times moving three times as fast as normal. They revealed secrets about people's lives."

"They were carried away by . . . I don't know. They were affected by the situation. People thought they saw things. One woman here even claimed she saw the Virgin. And yes, Moisés Cosío told me about how the girls fell down hard onto the rocks and how rigid they were and how

Someone trying to move Mari Cruz's face

he tried to move them but couldn't" and she got excited, as all do, in describing how the ecstasies had impressed millionaire Moisés.

"Did you ever go up, Mercedes?"

"I'll go up when they show me miracles. I don't even go to church. I prayed for five years while my husband rotted in prison that God would deliver him." Now she moved into high gear railing against the (abusive) church and imprisonment without trial and what a horrible country Spain is and that you can't find out the truth, you slave away for enough to eat and the ministers abscond with millions, and they're making a movie of one of them—the one murderer out of many, that they found out. "Just go to the office of the housing ministry in Santander. You will see a thousand people in there doing nothing and living off us, but they never get fired because they are the one's doing the firing."

My ears hurt, and realizing why they had warned me to be careful, I bid my hosts *adios*, and quickly leveled the initial and steepest part of the climb back up the hill putting distance between us.

Not much traffic today. It was a good road for reflecting on my time on the mountain. Only Gabino's taxi, transporting the Florida women out, passed me. I put on my T-shirt, and puffing and panting, rounded the last bend. How quiet the village seemed from a hundred yards out. Yes, with the Floridians gone and the three road construction workers leaving for the weekend, I would be alone for the first time in the "hotel."

Not for long. Sunday at one o'clock, four Spanish women arrived from Santander and just behind them, a young Dutch-American couple and their eight children from San Diego, California, where the father is a construction foreman. I liked the man immediately.

At dinner they took up two tables. They were: María Goretti, about thirteen, the oldest child and only girl, Paul, Joseph, Dominic, John the Baptist, Vincent, Francesco and Daniel. I pictured the "boss" directing his construction gang like he handled his own brood—firm but fair.

"One of them is deaf. I bet you can't guess which one," the father challenged.

I watched the kids talking for quite a while. "Dominic?"

"No. Vincent. His mother works with him a couple hours every day. He reads lips well. The kids on the street don't know he can't hear. He went to a special school for the deaf, but now he's in regular school and keeps up."

"You've traveled a long way with so many."

"We left our nine week old daughter in Holland with relatives. We spent most of the time there with our families, so it hasn't cost much for food or lodging.

"Religion is weak in Holland. It shocked me," he said with a noticeable accent. "Even my own brothers and their families don't go to church. Fifteen years ago Holland was one of the most Catholic countries."

We talked much of the afternoon in Serafín's plain but comfortable dining room. After dinner I went out and helped stooped-over Doña Cándida repair her wooden shoe. Cándida is a little old lady of eighty who, always wearing widow's black, lives in the next house down the lane from Serafín. I liked to visit her. Although toothless, her Spanish came through crisp and clear. She seemed delighted to have visitors, and often called on me to translate when she had non-Spanish-speaking lodgers. Perhaps not being able to tell one foreign language from another, she called me in once to tell a German couple that she didn't serve meals. Whenever the communication faltered, she would shrug her hunched over, rounded shoulders and smile so broadly her eyes squinted.

Joaquín from Reinosa, forty miles to the south, stays there every weekend, and Chuck from California lived at her place last year.

"Where is Chuck, Doña Cándida? Have you heard from him?"

"He's in Ledeira, Portugal. Go visit him. Fantastic things are happening there. Hosts fall from heaven. Those who stay in my house saw it themselves. Look. They brought me some dried blood from a bleeding crucifix." Friendly and personable, she bubbled with excitement. Looking down at her small, squinty, but expressive eyes and her wrinkled old face, silly thoughts of witches crossed my mind. But she was friendly and personable.

"Doña Cándida, I'm not interested in Ledeira." Since the opportunity presented itself, I asked, "What happened here?"

"Here? Nothing happened here."

"Nothing?" I challenged.

"Well, that walking backwards impressed me, I guess. But even I could do that."

"Bah. What do you mean you could do that?"

"Well. I don't know," she answered with her winning, toothless smile.

"And all the other unexplainable happenings?" I pursued:

What about: the girls crashing hard to their knees onto the rocks so you could hear their bones crack, their returning the kissed articles without ever making a mistake, their being poked with pins and touched with hot items with no apparent discomfort, and Conchita holding her head craned way back for the duration of the ecstasy—sometimes for hours?"

Loli returning medal to correct owner

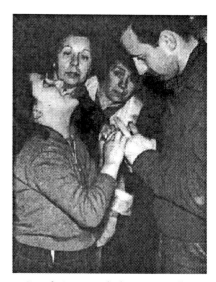
People intrigued observing Loli returning a wedding ring

"Well, yes. I guess those things impressed people, but not me. Others weren't impressed by the walking backwards. That's the way it was. Some things impressed some and other things impressed others. But now in Ledeira there are hosts falling from heaven, and when people pick them up they smell perfume. Now that's something. Nothing like that happened here."

Careful about chasing after miracles, Cándida, I thought. "I'm going to the dance."

The local youth gathered in the community center and, since I considered myself young, joined in. I danced with Paquita's cute younger sister, Virginia, and with Alicia who danced the Tango well. A girl coaxed me onto the floor to dance the *picayos*. Their regional folk dance isn't as simple as it looks.

It was the young Americans who stole the show. María Goretti danced with her oldest brother, and the younger boys joined in for the rock and roll numbers.

"Where did you learn to dance so well, María?" I asked.

"My father taught us, and my brother and I go to the school dances."

Even the littlest guy performed, and the Spaniards loved it.

I didn't last long. If I arrived before 10:00, Paquita would still be

133

serving supper, even though I had told her not to expect me. Her other guests would be easier to count on for meals. They went to Mass in the morning, walked to the Pines to say the rosary and talk, and then most of them just hung around in the guesthouse. I tried not to be a burden with my, "if-nothing-better-comes-up schedule," but I hated to miss any opportunity to listen to the villagers if they talked about the apparitions.

I did make it in time for supper, a favorite—*hake* in egg batter, fried in olive oil. Afterwards, two Catalans and I climbed to the Pines where we said the rosary, chanting the Our Father and Glory Be in Latin. "*Sicut erat in principio et nunc et semper et in sécula seculorum, Amen.*" The Hail Holy Queen followed and "*Salve Regina, Mater misericordie, vita dulchedo. . . .*" carried out over Garabandal and beyond.

People observing Mari Cruz speaking with her visitor.

Conchita, in an awkward position, and Jacinta,
both looking frightened.

CHAPTER ELEVEN

THE DIFFERENCE

onday morning, Father, or "Don Bernardo"[43] as they call him, tore into town on his motorcycle and celebrated Mass.

Afterwards, twenty-two year old Conchita, fashionably dressed in a knee length white coat and visiting from Barcelona, stood outside. Visitors crowded around to look at her, take pictures, and to say "*Hola*" if they could, or "Hello," "*Bonjour*," or "*Guten Morgen*." Mostly they just stared and sighed, "Oh isn't she beautiful? What a lovely girl."

How could she smile through it all? Not wanting her to see me as another foreign gawker, I walked away.

"*Hola, Cecilio*." Two doors from the church, Josefa's son-in-law stood in front of the house in which I had spent two weeks the previous summer. "How's the fishing these days?"

"Good. Caught ten yesterday morning. Mingo's the fisherman, though. He's upstairs. Go on up."

I climbed the stairs to the living quarters, taking care not to bang my head that still hurt from the previous year's encounters in the same house. "Anybody home?"

Domingo, about twenty-five years old, married Josefa's youngest daughter, Nati, last spring. He and Cecilio spend part of the summer in Garabandal to cut, gather, and store the hay—and to take the most delicious ten inch trout I've ever tasted out of the two streams that flow down the ravines that flank the bluff on which Garabandal sits.

---

43 The villagers don't use last names. Is it because so many are the same? I lived in Josefa's house in 1970 and never heard Señora (Mrs.) Cosío. Loli's father is Ceferino and her mother is Julia. Jacinta's mother is María and her father, Simón, although he is seventy-five years old. Thus their priests are Bernardo (stationed at Puentenansa) and Valentín (in Cosío) with the "*Don*" prefix as a title of respect.

"*Hombre*. How's it going?" Domingo greeted in his deep, melodious voice. He continued to sip his oversized bowl of *café con leche*. "Have you been fishing yet?"

"A couple of times but haven't done too well. I caught three in the river down below and only one in the upper stream. I saw lots of fish, but they spooked away before I could get my line in."

"You've got to sneak up on them. There are more fish in the upper stream. Look in the sink."

Fat trout spilled over the sides of the big pan. "Wow. They're beautiful. Where did you get them?"

"Up above where they're working on the new road."

Humiliating! In that same stream I had fooled only one, about the size of his smallest. Cecilio and his wife, Ofelia, joined us and spared me further embarrassment on comparative fishing skills. They readied their belongings for leaving. The hay harvesting over, they would return home to Celis some five miles from Puentenansa towards the coast.

Conchita with a friend

On my way back to the guesthouse, Conchita, walking with a girlfriend, recognized and greeted me. "You're here again. When does your vacation end?"

"The first week of September."

They continued their stroll, and I, mine while reasoning that her apparent happiness at seeing me lent credence to the veracity of what she has told us concerning her visits with the *Santísima Virgen*. She knew why I had returned for a third visit. She knew the distance from the U.S. and the expense of travel. Could she express happiness at seeing me if she had been playing games?

No one can pretend to be something he is not, for any length of time without it affecting his sanity. Were it all a hoax, impossible that Conchita could look me in the eye, smile, and welcome me back. She knows the importance of Garabandal.

Conchita has announced that: (1) soon everyone will experience a horrifying Warning; (2) within one year after the Warning, the greatest Miracle in history will occur at Garabandal, during which the sick who are present will be cured, unbelievers will believe, and sinners present will be converted; (3) after the Miracle, a sign will remain at Garabandal until the end of time; and (4) if we don't amend our lives after the Warning and Miracle, a terrible Chastisement will befall us, after which those of us who remain will live in peace with God forever.

The visionaries prophesied these events unafraid of being proven wrong. When they were little, they expressed their confidence this way, "The Virgin said so and she doesn't tell fibs."

I stopped off at the corner bar. "*Hola, Eduardo*," Loli greeted.

"That's pretty music you're playing."

She held out a record jacket. "One of the singers gave me this. She visited here last year."

The Sound of Music. "A former professor of mine is married to one of the Trapp Family singers."

Later, from Loli's small record player in the kitchen, I heard one of my favorite songs, "*Que lejos estoy del suelo donde he nacido. Inmensa nostalgia invade mi pensamiento.*"[44]

"Do you know that's the state song of Oaxaca, Mexico, Loli?"

"No, but Mexican music is my favorite," and she replayed it. How friendly she was.

"How's your English coming along?"

"*No puedo decir nada.*" (I can't say anything).

"Come on," I kidded. "With all the foreigners who visit this house, you should speak four or five languages by now."

How popular is Loli? Her nine-year-old sister Lupita gives us a hint.

Lupita Mazón

A few days previous, two or three little girls, Lupita among them, had approached me. "We're collecting stamps. Do you

---

44 "How far away I am from the land of my birth. Immense nostalgia invades my thoughts."

have any?"

"I have a lot back home in California. I could send them to you."

Lupita's chin dropped as she said in resignation, "They don't know me." (The "they" meaning those who move the mail from the United States to her house.) And then, after a minute's reflection on how she would ever get her mail if the postman didn't know her, she jumped in expectation, "Just put Lupita, Loli's sister."

Loli remembered me from 1970. I recall the evidence all too well. One afternoon when I had said, "*Buenas tardes*," she corrected, "Here we still say '*Buenos días*' until after dinner." The day's main meal, at times eaten as late as 3:00 P.M. in the summer, rather than the clock, divides the day.

Well, again the teacher was a slow learner, for on greeting her this year with a "*Buenas tardes, Loli*," she smiled and chided, "It's '*Buenos días,' Eduardo*. I taught you that last year."

The girls don't run a popularity contest. They don't encourage people to visit Garabandal, and in the village do nothing to call attention to themselves. Loli serves in the family restaurant-store-bar or stays in the kitchen working. Conchita lives in Barcelona and spends little time in the village. Her sister-in-law, Paquita, told me that Conchita had confided to her recently that she longed to escape from being "someone who saw the Virgin" to being just another girl.

The visionaries don't want to be the center of attraction and even, it seems, want to fade out of the picture. There was a lot to think about over one small glass of wine—about Loli and Conchita and their companions and about all that happened here starting ten years previous. The girls know that the messages given by God, warning of pending dire consequences for offending him, must be the focus of our attention in Garabandal and everywhere. The girls will leave the scene of their heavenly encounters in order to help "purify Garabandal of all that savors of the human, even of enthusiasm, until only the mark of God remains."[45]

"*Hasta luego, Loli*."

⊃•◆•⊂

45 *Garabandal 10 Años*, p.1.

Outside, her fourteen-year-old brother, Ferenín, greeted me so we sat down for a chat. Fishing interested both of us. Yes, with his parents' permission he could accompany me down to the stream. We would fish soon after a heavy rain when the Vendul colors up and we wouldn't spook the trout before getting our worm in front of them.

On Sunday I had noticed a late model, black BMW with German license plates park at the entrance to the village. A middle-aged balding man, impeccably dressed in a dark suit with white shirt and tie, had lifted a small bag out of the trunk and walked in the direction of the church. He stood out in contrast to some of the haggard-looking pilgrims worn out from busing to and from five shrines in a week. What was he doing here? Although people now referred to the widened path from Cosío as a road, it wouldn't remind this driver of the Autobahn.

Ferenín outside his home

I later found out that Hans worked for his government's intelligence department, that this was his second visit and that a Dutch couple allowed him to stay at their place in the village. He had agreed to take a walk this afternoon to get a closer look at the surrounding hills, so I took leave of Ferenín, went home for a quick meal and then hurried to the village entrance to meet Hans.

We walked a kilometer down to where the Cosío road divides and turned left to parallel the Sebrando River in the direction of the Peña Sagra Ridge. Hans said he wasn't allowed to say more about his work, so we enjoyed the sun and the sight of young calves in the green fields on the other side of the river before stopping to drink the

Dirt road paralleling the Sebrando River to the north of the village.

cold water flowing out of the side of the hill. Old Pedro, who often asked me to join him for a walk, invited us to sit down and rest.

Soon a young man jogged up the dirt road and stopped when we greeted him. His audible, "*Dos locos más buscando a nuestra Virgen María?*" (Two more crazy people searching for our Virgin Mary?) to the other Spaniard was not a compliment. But, no, he wouldn't mind if the German and the American walked with him.

Forty-something Mateo often jogs up from Cosío. We hadn't gone

Village church at the time of the apparitions.

a hundred feet when he started in. "I came up every day during the apparitions [five kilometers each way.] I haven't thought about this for years but I saw things you would never believe. Once, the four little girls walked across the narrow bridge over the stream in front of the church. I mean two of them walked; the other two floated across—one on each side. One day my friend, who easily lifts a hundred kilos, tried to lift Jacinta in ecstasy and couldn't budge her. Another time late at night . . ."

He wouldn't stop. Neither his two new foreign companions nor the panorama of the majestic 6000 foot Peña Sagra Ridge inching slowly towards us distracted him in the least.

Would it never fail? Like others in the area, after ridiculing our interest in the apparitions, once he thought back to the Garabandal of the early 50's, he relived for us what he had seen, heard and felt, as if everything had happened the night before.

When we came to the path on the left leading back to our village, Hans and I parted company with our new friend who then resumed his jogging. Back in the village within a half hour, I said good-bye to Hans and headed to the tackle shop to prepare for my date with Ferenín.

In the village's best supplied general store I greeted the tall, blond, hard-working owner, Adriano. "How are you doing?"

"OK. What can I get you?"

"Some fishing equipment. Let's see. Give me three hooks, some split shot, and some leader."

"Here they use three meters of leader tied to the end of the pole," and he marked off three arm-lengths of monofilament. "Will that do it?"

"Yes. I guess that's all. I'll catch them with this or come back and complain."

While the friendly proprietor added the bill, I spotted a newspaper on the end of the counter.

"Oh, and give me a *blanco* (glass of white wine), *por favor.*"

He filled the small glass with wine from the barrel, set the drink in front of me, then added, "Hooks, three *pesetas*; split shot, one; and line, three; with the wine, nine *pesetas* (about fourteen cents)." He wouldn't get rich in the fishing tackle business.

I gave him ten and left the one change on the counter.

"May I read your paper?"

"That's what it's for. Anytime."

"Not much business for you today."

"It's a nice day and everybody is out in the fields."

The men of Garabandal, and in similar mountain villages in the area, work long hard hours during haying season when the weather is fair. When it rains, many of them sit in one of the bars and play *tuti* or *la brisca*, games with that card deck of swords, clubs, gold and goblets. I have never seen money change hands, but they must play for stakes because they are deadly serious, keep score with beans, and often shout. Although wine and stronger are handy, many of them play without a drink in front of them. Is it because the two *pesetas* (three cents) a shot for wine and about three times that for cognac is stiff for many of them?

With our favorable exchange rate, at three cents for wine and a dime for a generous shot of Benedictine or Drambuie, one could have a good time in Garabandal even if he weren't interested in apparitions.

I perused the *Gaceta del Norte* and sipped the wine that I didn't like but felt I should spend something and that's what the village men drink before dinner. I hadn't read a newspaper in weeks. The astronauts were moving again. "Most important moon shot ever," it stated, "with more advanced and intricate tests than all of the other flights combined. Worden and Irwin will be on the moon for thirty-six hours."

Who cares? That's nothing compared to what visitors from further away than the moon did here. They could roam that rock until they found Swiss cheese yet wouldn't come up with anything like Garabandal. Did God's mother walk on every moon street like she did here? Did she visit all the houses on the moon? What language did she speak there?

I recalled the first moon walk in July of 1969. I was staying at a second class hotel just off the *Puerta del Sol* in Madrid. It was sweltering hot. I kept the radio on all night, and around 4:00 A.M. it awakened me. An astronaut was stepping out of the moon landing craft. I pulled on a pair of pants and tiptoed down to the television lounge on the second floor. Alone, proud of my countrymen, I sat in front of the black and white television and watched Armstrong step onto the moon.

The next day out on the street, a couple old *madrileños* gazed up at the day-faded moon. I eavesdropped. "*No. Es imposible.* I can't see anything. They can't be up there. It's a trick of the television. Not even the Americans could do that."

For a long while they seemed to ponder the evidence or lack of it— the great distance, no visible movement. They shook their heads and repeated with an air of finality, "*No. Es imposible,*" and walked away.

Old men from Madrid, New York or Singapore will doubt that the Blessed Virgin walked recently in San Sebastián de Garabandal. "No," they will say, "too far," or "Why would she want to visit a place like that? Those films of the four little children in ecstasy, those photos are a trick. The recordings of the girls praying in ecstasy and talking about *el Chiquitín* (the infant) are all a trick. Not even God could do that."

CHAPTER TWELVE

REPORTERS

 oming out of church the next morning, I spotted Manolín hauling cement. Pepe Díaz and two of his handsome sons were building a rock wall in front of their house. Manolín mixed and hauled the cement. The younger brother selected the rocks for Pepe, the stonemason.

The author with Pepe Díaz

"*Hola, Eduardo*," curly-haired Manolín greeted me.

"Everybody is working hard," I replied.

"A little." Pepe looked up, but didn't break his stride fitting and cementing the rocks. The wall grew in front of me. I saw why people called this oft-quoted eyewitness the hardest working man in town. I wondered if he ever stopped long enough to talk about the marvelous events he had witnessed between 1961 and 1965, particularly the miraculous appearance of the host on Conchita's tongue. Pepe's wife, Clementina, brought him a glass of wine.

"*¿Un tinto, Eduardo?*" she asked. It's good." She insisted and handed me a glass of red wine. I felt like a bum just standing around with everyone else working. I drank the wine, and then strolled off wondering about Pepe. He didn't seem much concerned about apparitions, only about completing the stone structure for his home.

In the afternoon I climbed towards the Pines and sat down in a secluded spot in the sun to jot down some notes. I hadn't written long when I spotted two girls walking along the path fifty yards below. It looked like Conchita. I watched them wind their way up towards me and hoped they would pass close by.

Sure enough, Conchita carrying her niece, and a girlfriend appeared just below. I walked over and greeted them.

"*Hola, Eduardo.* Are you sunbathing?"

"I haven't been to the beach all summer. I need it."

"No. You're tan. This is my friend, Ana, from Brazil. We want to take a picture."

"Let me take it of the three of you." I clicked once, then handed the camera back. They continued to the Pines where Conchita, with the baby still in her arms, knelt to pray. She knelt for some time before rising to talk to a priest dressed in a cassock and wearing a biretta.

I stretched out beneath the noon sun and reread my notes on what the reporters had written about her in the Spanish newspapers some six years previous:

> *Conchita es muy bonita.* She has a Spanish countenance. Conchita is an angel of God, a beautiful angel of God. . . . She is alert, alive but at the same time she blushes. In all of them I've observed a special smile. Here in Madrid I don't find that easily. Perhaps in my children. . . . The cause is obvious—goodness.[46]

And another wrote in the April 27, 1966 edition of *¿Por Que?* :

Conchita and Abrecht Webber

One reporter tried a number of times without success to enter her house but resigned himself in a Christian manner [to wait]. It was just the opposite of what occurs when the person to be interviewed is someone famous or important. . . . Conchita instilled a profound respect in all of us. Colleagues from Paris, Portugal, Madrid and operators of NODO [a Franco era news agency] waited impatiently, but without getting angry, the opportunity to speak with

---

46 Tico Medina and Enrique Verdugo, *Las Apariciones de Garabandal*, Pueblo, Madrid, April 15, 1966.

Conchita. I confess this was the most moving, thrilling moment in my life as a reporter. Never had anyone instilled in me such confidence and respect at the same time. She is no longer the child of 1961 when she had the first apparition. Today she is a woman. She is sixteen, very brown, exceedingly attractive with large expressive eyes, a sweet expression and a perennial smile on her lips. Her charm is extraordinary. Candor and charm combine in this young woman who stands before me and for whom thousands are waiting in the street.[47]

Many reporters, even one who wrote negative accounts of the happenings in general,[48] commented on the uniqueness of Conchita.

Teenager Conchita with village children

Her thirteen years older sister-in-law, Paquita, told me, "Everyone thinks she is attractive now. You should have seen her when she was fifteen or sixteen. With all the other girls her age so giddy and silly and trying to fix themselves up, she stood out even more. Conchita was so natural, so simple and frank. The people noticed this and clamored around her. I never tired of talking with her."

All three girls, Conchita, Loli, and Jacinta exhibit an outward, disengaged manner. Could it be that they are reliving the times they spent with the lady whom they called "my mother and my best friend," and would be bored listening to you and me after talking with the mother of God? When speaking, nevertheless, they break into captivating smiles that reveal their happiness and hope.

Conchita explained, "When I finished seeing the Virgin, it was like leaving Heaven [without seeing it] with a great desire to love the hearts of Jesus and Mary, and to tell people of them since that is the only thing that can make us happy—to speak and hear of the Virgin."[49]

---

47 Poch Soler, *¿Por Que?*, Barcelona, April 27, 1966. p. 7.
48 Margarita Landi, *No Hubo Milagros en Garabandal*, *El Caso*, Madrid, March 25, 1967.
49 A.M. de Santiago, *Garabandal 67*, (Zaragoza: Editorial Círculo, 1967). p. 37.

Later in the day, Mr. Courteville, a French biblical historian, came to our place with thirty or thirty-five friends and showed 1962 movies of the ecstasies, ecstatic marches, and mystical communions. The girls fall onto their knees so fast you can't see the fall! They are standing and in the next frame are on their knees. Courteville had visited the Bishop of Santander, José María Cirarda, and suggested that an impartial commission be formed with the right to review the original commission's findings. No luck!

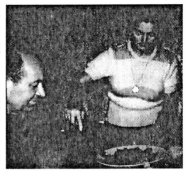

Jacinta serving Mr. Courteville in her home.

I liked Courteville and his business-like manner. He and his wife own a small house at the entrance to the village. "Visit Padre Lucio Rodrigo, the old Jesuit priest at Comillas," he told me. "He's a good one to talk with. He's eighty-six and been in the infirmary for some time. He's been very close to the visionaries. Conchita told him to take care of himself so he'd be around for the Miracle."

Wednesday morning I awoke after eight. Could I run three miles to Cosío on time for 9:00 Mass? I dodged rocks down the lane, and then jogged through the village. I hadn't gone far when the young French fellows from our *pensión* stopped and offered me a lift.

Although much improved since the previous year (1970), the road between Cosío and Garabandal still proved a formidable foe for their little car. When three or more passengers rode in a small car, at times some of us walked the difficult stretches.

There were two distinct worlds in Garabandal, that of the villagers and that of visitors. For example, here I was riding in a car to attend Mass (It would have been an extravagance to take the time off on a weekday to walk). We passed Alfonso, the bachelor, cutting grass in a field not far below the village. A woman spread the cut grass out to dry. We rounded the next curve and came up behind Josefa sitting high in her burro-drawn green cart. She held a parasol to protect herself from the hot August morning sun. She looked almost elegant—if a gray-haired old lady with a front tooth missing could be elegant.

"*Buenos días, Josefa. Que elegante está esta mañana.*"

"Hola. A buscar el pan."[50]

Making a little better time than Josefa, a man and a boy urged their cow along with a stick. For the cow it might be a one way trip.

Descending the final steep grade, we saw the Cosío women at the basins washing clothes. Others, laden with baskets full of clean clothes, headed for the bushes to spread them in the sun to dry. Out of Cosío we picked up two other church goers, the two men from Barcelona, Cataluña and continued up the highway a mile further to Rozadío.

Loli, Mercedes (the author from Barcelona), Conchita and her Brazilian friend, a few people from Rozadío, and the five of us attended. Father announced the Mass intention—a village boy killed in the war,[51] the son of one of the women present.

On the road home the Catalans talked about the Miracle and speculated about its date. "When do the American Garabandal followers think the Miracle will take place?"

"There isn't much talk about that. I'm in no hurry."

One passenger knew. "Conchita has said a few things privately that indicate the Miracle will occur the 13th of April [1972]. The Bishop will give permission to priests to go to Garabandal by the end of this summer, and the Warning will come in October."

Here was another who knew the date of the prophesied Miracle. Conchita knows the date and will let the world know eight days before it is to happen.[52]

"*¿Ne comprenez-vous?*" I asked in an attempt to include the French driver and his friend in the conversation.

"No," our driver and his friend answered. But that was the extent of my French. What a shame not to be able to talk to those to whom we were indebted for the ride.

That didn't bother the Spaniards who rambled right on. "It won't be long and this place will be mobbed. I wonder how we will all fit into little Garabandal for the Miracle. It will be a sight."

We passed a couple of road construction workers. What do they think

50 "Good morning, Josefa, how nice you look this morning."
"Hi. I'm off to fetch the bread."
51 "The war" to the Spaniards is their Civil War 1936-39.
52 Perez, *El Pueblo Habla*, p. 92

about the Garabandal phenomena? There was so much to learn. I longed to hike up to the Peña Sagra mountain ridge that rises four thousand feet above the village to the west, or to try for some fish like the beauties Mingo had caught, but there was no time for fishing today. And one and two day visitors continued to ask in amazement, "You've been in this little place for two weeks? What do you do here?" Two days in Paris had been enough, yet Garabandal fascinated me more each day. Maybe I hadn't found the exciting parts of the French capital.

I wanted to visit the old Jesuit Father Rodrigo thirty miles away in Comillas, but without a ride out of the mountains it would take hours to travel to the Coast. Luckily, the next day the

The Peña Sagra towers above a winter barn

multilingual Dutch doctor offered me a lift. He was on his way to Burgos to warn the Spanish bishops about the plot of the Dutch clergy. The latter, he mentioned, would launch a propaganda attack in September (1971) during the Bishops' Synod in Rome in favor of a democratic clergy. "The Dutch church is lost. There isn't a priest who says the rosary any more."

While we loaded the plush blue Volvo, Josefa's son-in-law, Cecilio, approached looking for a ride also. The Dutchman refused.

"Why don't you run down the first steep, rocky section," I whispered to Cecilio. "Maybe he'll pick you up down below."

My driver said, "Some of these farmers don't understand what it costs to buy a car like this. This road is horrible on a car, and I have to make it back to Amsterdam."

He did pick up Cecilio, who jumped out at Puentenansa, from where he would walk to his home in Celis three miles away toward the Coast. We turned east over Carmona Pass to Cabezón where the Dutchman and I parted company.

I hiked out of town, then hitched a ride ("auto stop," they say in Europe) to San Vicente de la Barquera. "Fishing village par excellence," says the tourist brochure. I walked through the busy center to the

The Picos de Europa rising above San Vicente de la Barquera

estuary where the cool sea breeze extended its low tide welcome. The medieval castle across the river mouth begged a visit, but I had other plans.

I entered a noisy restaurant overlooking the port. Spaniards talk out loud while they eat. Nobody watched the brightly painted green, blue, and red fishing boats swaying at anchor in the harbor. The mid-day meal is the focus of the Spaniards' lives and nothing distracts them.

Bottles of house brand wine and soda water on the tables gave the crowded place away as a local favorite. Many tourists wouldn't know that you get as much wine as you want when ordering the *menu del día* and wouldn't be accustomed to diluting the wine with *gaseosa* (or be able to pronounce the word) that is also included in the set price. Neither would many bring their young children or (especially if from the United States) allow them to sip the diluted wine.

I might not ever be able to probe the depths of meaning of Heaven's visiting earth nearby in the Cantabrian hills, but I was learning to enjoy the Spanish way of life. In San Vicente I outdid the dining Spaniards around me. The Spanish me relished the good food and wine while the visitor me imbibed the awesome colorful scenery.

After enjoying succulent *pollo al ajillo* (chicken with garlic and parsley, fried in olive oil) and red wine (undiluted), I headed for the taxi stand.

"*¿Cuánto me cobra a Comillas?*"

"*Cien* (100) *pesetas.*"

I could tell there was no use haggling. A twelve kilometer drive across and along the estuary and then through rich farmland brought us to the popular resort town.

"*La Universidad, por favor.*"

What a place—a football-field-long red brick building housing a Jesuit-run pontifical university overlooking the Atlantic Ocean! At the reception desk of the gigantic building the switchboard operator informed me, "Father Rodrigo is resting." He was awfully tired. I could come back around five that afternoon.

While I feared this might be a wasted trip, a priest approached and introduced himself—a Dominican from Madrid attending a conference

Pontifical University.

here on the development of the liturgy. "The Marqués de Comillas donated money for the original building," he informed me. "The Marqués was quite a man. He initiated the first steamboat run to America. That's a statue of him overlooking the ocean. His mansion is over there across the highway."

The priest showed me the chapel before pointing the way to the classrooms and residence area. Photographs of many illustrious graduates of the university hung on the walls of one long passageway. There they were, all the bishops who were careless in their investigation of, and reporting on, the Garabandal events: Eugenio Beitia, Doroteo Fernandez, Puchol Montis and José María Cirarda. What type of religion did they teach here anyway?

Conchita with Fr. Rodrigo, cerca 1965

I walked through the quiet rectory section trying to look as if I belonged. I just had to see Father after coming this far and didn't intend to wait three hours to do it. An elevator took me to the top floor where I met the brother infirmarian.

"Yes, you may go in and see him. He is very weak though,

150

so just for a short while."

I knocked at the door marked Lucio Rodrigo, S.J., and heard, "*Entre*" ("Come in").

I pushed open the door and saw a gaunt old man seated at a desk with his breviary in his hands. He peered up over his bifocals. Books lined two sides of the small room.

"Hello, Father. They tell me you know about the apparitions at Garabandal."

"*Pués señor, un poco, sí, un poco.*" ("Well sir, a little, yes, a little"). Where do you come from?"

"The United States. California. Have you ever heard of that place?"

Fr. Rodrigo

"Oh. We Spanish have been there for quite awhile."

The frail old priest didn't seem anxious to talk about Garabandal. He leaned far over toward me and cupped his hand over his ear. Maybe he hadn't heard me. His sickroom on the top floor of the building faced out over the ocean. "You've got a beautiful place here, Father."

"The best room in the house," he quipped. Then without preface, he began, "The proof of the supernatural origin of the happenings doesn't now depend on what the girls do or say, but on what we saw, on the cumulative chain of events witnessed by thousands and denied by no one. I don't go up to Garabandal any more. No need to. I will go for the Miracle."

Interesting! He's eighty-six, lives in the sick ward, but will go to Garabandal for the prophesied Miracle. It had better hurry.

The four visionaries with younger children at the Pines

"The punishment will come. Sodom and Gomorrah had nothing on these times. Whole nations are corrupt. Men commit sins against nature such as the world has never seen. God is infinitely merciful but infinitely just. The wrath of

151

God cannot be restrained longer."

I stared at the man, revered by his colleagues as an eminent scholar and a saint. Padre Rodrigo didn't wait for any agreement, contradiction, or comment. No, in a pontifical university, you pontificate—even from the sick ward.

He thinks the other recent visionaries around Spain are false and advised, "Stick with Fatima." But right beside the favorite saints on his desk stands a photo of Loli, Mari Cruz, Jacinta, and Conchita, and over his bed hangs a large picture of the Virgin of Garabandal.

He continued:

> I told that guy what I thought of him—that young fellow who works in the restaurant in Santander and goes up to Garabandal "to see visions." I wrote him first of all that he was disobeying the order of his bishop by going up there like that. The girls always taught respect for church authority. I showed Conchita the letter. She liked it and asked for a copy.
>
> The Commission made up its mind after just a few visits. That's no way to do it. I taught most of the members of that commission. They come here and say they agree with me [that Garabandal is of supernatural origin] but then they go off and state differently in public. I taught most of the bishops too. They all came here to school.

I asked:

> What can we do, Father, about the misleading statements of the present Santander bishop? He wrote last April in a letter to all the bishops in the world that his three predecessors agreed that the Garabandal phenomena have a natural explanation. Not true. Only Bishop Puchol wrote that. The two before him stated that it wasn't certain whether Garabandal was of supernatural origin or not. Cirarda also says that the apparitions aren't of special interest in his diocese where all, except a very small socially insignificant group, have been obedient to their bishops. Since when does the Catholic Church require its members to agree with their bishops on optional matters like apparitions? Doesn't he know that belief is a gift? Where did he study his theology? I kidded.

Don't worry. God will do all.

But I did worry. I didn't like Church officials teaching things that weren't true, so I continued:

Bishop Cirarda doesn't mention in his letter that the Santander Chancery told the local papers not to write about the apparitions or about the spectacular cure of Santander resident, Menchu Mendiolea after she venerated a crucifix said to have been kissed by the Virgin at Garabandal. Neither does he let the world's bishops know that Father Odriozola warned Menchu's father not to say anything about the crucifix, that it wasn't right to connect apparitions which were false with a spectacular cure like that of his daughter. I had heard this on the Santander streets, and Mendiolea confirmed that it was true.

Father Francisco Odriozola, one of five men appointed by Bishop Fernandez in 1961 to investigate the Garabandal happenings.

Author and Sr. Mendiolea, 1988

Don't worry. This is God's way, the bishops, the four girls, or Father Rodrigo notwithstanding.

What can we do, Father?"

Don't worry. God will take care of it. You will see. After our present pope, only two more remain before the start of the end times. Conchita said that the Virgin told her this, and furthermore she said that one pope would have a very short reign. Don't worry. God will do all.

Talk about lack of concern regarding the obstinacy and shortsightedness of the Santander bishops. His calmness disturbed me. I had felt all fired up to spread the Message of Garabandal and to rebut the illogical and contradictory statements in the documents published by the Santander Chancery. Now this venerable old theologian, who knew so much about the investigation and taught the investigators, tells me to take it easy. It felt like being ready to compete in a sport's event and having it cancelled.

We don't always find what we expect. Is it because we hope for foolish things? I had come to Father Rodrigo for help correcting errors and he kept repeating, "Don't worry. God will take care of everything." Maybe old age wasn't so bad if it brought the certainty that God is still in command of his wayward world. Father knows that, like the water porters at Cana, he only supplies the water. God turns it into wine.

Father looked tired. The hour visit had taxed his strength. "Will you give me your blessing, Father?" I knelt beside his desk. He didn't rise in order to call God's blessing upon me.

"May the blessing of almighty God, the Father, Son and Holy Spirit be with you and remain with you forever."

Here sat one Garabandal follower "pruned of all that savors of the human, until only the mark of God remains."[53] Will I be as wise as he when I'm eighty-six? There's not much time.

I turned to leave. As I closed the door, I saw Fr. Rodrigo return to his breviary to sing God's praises through the psalms of old and beg his mercy on himself, the strange Santander bishops and, hopefully, me.

Painting (based on the description by the visionaries) of the Virgin with child.

---

53 *Garabandal 10 Años*, p. 1.

CHAPTER THIRTEEN

RAMON'S MICROPHONE

I spent the late afternoon and evening in Comillas, where I walked the wrong way against an on-foot funeral procession, bought a guitar string, and paid a quarter for a guided tour of the Marqués de Comillas' brother-in-law's mansion during which the young guide stuck her nose in the air and talked to the walls the whole time.

Palacio de Sobrellano

The bus came through an hour late and arrived back after dark in tourist-crowded San Vicente, where I feared having to sleep outside like I had in Algeciras two years previous. But luck prevailed.

My bed secured in a musty old room, I went out to see what was up in the festive town. Hungry customers huddled on the street around women roasting sardines on large charcoal grills. Even in the dark, one could tell he was in a fishing village. I snacked on delicious *gambas a la plancha* (grilled shrimp), bread and wine, and then turned in for the night.

The Picos de Europa Mountains. Garabandal sits in the foothills fifteen miles from Spain's north coast.

In the morning I climbed the hill for Mass in the thirteenth century Gothic church of Our Lady of the Angels in which lies the valuable alabaster statue of the Inquisitor, Corro. But the majestic Picos de Europa towering high above the surrounding

155

farmland foothills impressed me more. Thirteenth century also?

After my breakfast *café con leche*, I caught an early bus headed east for Santander, but got off after twenty minutes at the resort town of Santillana del Mar. But no resorts for me today. I would use the day away from Garabandal to play tennis after visiting the famous prehistoric caves at Altamira a couple miles out of town. There was talk about limiting visitors and even closing down the caves to preserve the invaluable wall paintings, but yes, I could buy a ticket. Horses and buffalo paintings lined the walls! Eighteen thousand years old? There was no guide this time, but just as well after the Comillas museum "puppet" performance. I wouldn't remember anyway if the artists had used blood for the red and charcoal for the black and grey. Fire had been discovered by the time they painted these, no?

Altamira Bison

I had majored in history, but they were always making more of it before I could learn the old stuff. I became a Spanish teacher. Anyway, in a few years, people would be talking more about "my village" than they would about these old painters. "See you later, Altamira. I'm going to play tennis."

If luck held in nearby Cabezón, I might find a partner at the Solvay company courts. With no public courts in Spain and their play-by-invitation-only policy on the private ones, my Jimmy Connors Wilson metal racquet needed use.

Luck held—but not enough of it. I hadn't hit a tennis ball in a month, and not on red clay courts in ten years. After the match, with the closest public water ten miles away in the Atlantic Ocean, there was no chance to wash off the clay. I thanked my new acquaintance for the tennis "lesson." Yes, he played here every Friday, and every other day of the week except Mondays when he gave group lessons in Torrelavega.

By this, my third visit to the area, I knew the public transportation schedules by heart. The train took me west past Treceño, Roiz and San Vicente to Pesués, and then the bus, twenty-three kilometers up along

Nansa River Road signs.

the Nansa River from the coast to Cosío. Since it would be dark anyway by the time I hiked the three miles up the hill to Garabandal, I would lengthen the day and enjoy the great *cocido montañés* that the restaurant on the corner at the town entrance was famous for.

You use a lot of energy and work up an appetite here in the mountains even when you don't walk miles to and inside caves before playing tennis much of the afternoon. I was much more ready for supper than I had been for the day's tennis match.

"Para mí, la sopa de pescado por favor, y de segundo, el cocido." In the rural restaurants (and some in the cities), for the *menú del día* they give you choices for the first plate (appetizer), the second plate (main course) and third plate (dessert).

The fish soup came steaming hot in a large family size bowl. The bowl stays on the table with the spoon in it, so you serve yourself all you like. This was my kind of restaurant, especially when needing to refuel for the long hour's walk home.

Cocido Montañés

Next the waiter, holding another big bowl, ladled out white beans with generous portions of stringy roast beef, Spanish *chorizo*, salt pork and *morcilla* (blood pudding) topped with fresh collard greens. He took away the soup bowl and left the bowl of stew on the table. He would bring more fresh bread if I wanted and another liter of red wine if one wasn't enough. I would fly the rest of the way home.

Not quite. The road in 1971 was still a work in progress. Walking in the dark moonless night, I kept an eye on the ravine to the left. When I was about half way home, lights far below moved, and soon made a noise that got louder and closer much faster than usual for cars on this "little wider-than-a-medium-width logging road" road. I moved over to give the crazy fool plenty of room.

The sports car screeched to a halt. That meant a ride. I got in, fastened the seat belt and held on for the two or three minute race to the town square. We stopped and the conversation flowed. Censio Cosío was returning from visiting his girlfriend in Puentenansa.

"I've been around the world," he said, "seen everything: the Eifel Tower, the New York Rockettes, the theater in Mexico City, Hong Kong and London, seen and done everything, but this place is all that counts. Here there is happiness."

Now in his late thirties, he had left the village years previous to seek his fortune in Mexico. His car, worth *muchos pesos*, hinted that he had found it.

"When the apparitions started, we young men and boys threw stones at the visionaries in ecstasy—to see if they were faking. But I got to love those little girls and hugged them after every ecstasy. One time I said, 'Loli, I'll give you a million pesetas if you will fall to your knees onto these rocks.' She looked at me smiling and said, 'I can't.'"

What a well-educated, classy man this new friend was. We could compare the little knowledge that had stuck from my many years of education with Censio's "knowledge never learned in school," but one lopsided loss to a Spaniard was enough for one day.

Rocky lane at the western end of the village on the way to the Pines. The first and many apparitions occurred in this area.

Men from this whole area leave the country, work hard, set up businesses and thrive. Don't try to put something over on them, or on the women either. Those who think it would be only backwards mountain people from a Catholic country who could be taken in by the shenanigans of four little girls, should have a talk with this eye-witness, successful young millionaire.

It was late. "*Hasta luego, Censio, y muchas gracias.*" I snuck quietly into sleepy Mesón Serafín, took off my shoes and tip-toed up the stairs and quietly down to my room at the end of the hall.

The next evening while drinking an after-dinner coffee at the guest house, I met Ramón Pérez and his son with their big Grundig tape recorder and camera. A Frenchman with Spanish parents, Ramón spoke good Spanish. The sixteen-year-old son, also Ramón, outdid his young, bilingual father by also speaking a little English.

"We interview the people of the village and will write a book on Garabandal," Ramón said. "We'll call it *El Pueblo Habla*" (The Village Speaks).

Wow! They had just arrived and already had the villagers talking.

"We just recorded a session with Father Ramón de la Riva. Would you like to hear it?"

"Sure. I talked with him a few days ago." Although the proprietors had emptied Mesón Serafín to make way for the expected Americans, noisy talk forced us to retreat to my second floor cell.

"The Archbishop of Oviedo wrote Fr. Ramón a

Ramón Pérez

letter that shows the Holy See has not pronounced against Garabandal. Listen!"

You couldn't mistake Father's soft-sell style. "And during a recess in the conferences he, the Archbishop, came to me asking for information on Garabandal." This was what the priest had told me when I visited him at his home in Barro.

Ramón helped me transcribe father's biographical sketch from the tape. "I am forty-four years old. During the apparitions, as is logical, I was thirty-four. I haven't had advanced studies. I spent ten years in a parish near Villaviciosa, Asturias. The tenth of August I took possession of this parish of Our Lady of Sorrows and the next day I found out about the apparitions. It was the day after the mysterious death of Fr. Luis Andreu."

Approaching footsteps sounded loud on our wood floor hallway so we stopped. "Listen. Someone is coming."

"May I?"

"Mr. Courteville! You have finally come to visit me," I kidded, and thought that he must want something.

"We need your help, Eduardo. Can you come down to my house?"

"I'm rather busy right now. We'll be finished here in fifteen minutes or so."

"That's fine." He left without further explanation and we finished our work.

"Tomorrow we have an appointment with Conchita's Aunt Maximina. Would you like to come?"

"Sure. She's a talkative one."

I wondered what Courteville wanted in such a hurry. He had never come to my room before. Ramón Jr. packed up the recorder, and the three of us headed down the narrow hallway. "Watch your heads on the low-sloped stairway ceiling," I warned.

They sat down in the dining area for a drink, but I left to see what excited Courteville.

It was close to 6:00 P.M. when I arrived at the Frenchman's new stone house at the entrance to the village. "Is anybody home?"

Courteville's friendly wife ushered me into the small front room where three strangers sat with Mr. Courteville around a table. To such a meeting I had never been called before in Garabandal. Would we plan an attack on the Bishop?

"Oh, here you are," Courteville greeted. "We've been waiting for you. These are two of your countrymen, Ed and Steve Garber, and this is Jerry McDevit from Warpole, England. You already know my wife."

He got right to the business at hand. "Today Steve went to Conchita asking her to record some words of encouragement for the Garabandal promoters in the United States. Now we're trying to write out her talk and translate it into English for the rest of the Americans from Joey Lomangino's group when they arrive tomorrow from Lourdes. This is a rough draft my wife wrote. We want you to listen to the tape and make corrections."

Courteville handed me four pages of handwritten Spanish. His wife sat down beside me. Steve switched on the recorder. The group fell silent and we heard, "*Con mucho gusto hago ésto* (I do this with great pleasure) . . . because I believe and want it to be for the glory of the

Virgin, to save souls. I want to say to everybody that the most important part of Garabandal is the Message, the message of sacrifice, of prayer, of penance."

Conchita's voice was deep, mysterious—very different from the light-hearted, happy Conchita I met in her village.

We are now in the last warnings, in the final moments. God is giving us all that is necessary for us to change. If we continue [our sinful ways], he will send us the Punishment because it is necessary . . . Pray every moment. Prayer consists in being continuously praising God in our work, offering everything to God. We must make sacrifices. We must do penance. We must visit the Blessed Sacrament. This we must do for the love of God, but if that is not possible for us, let us do it in His name for our own good. I say for our own good because when a person behaves well and acts according to his right conscience, it makes him happy.

Mari Cruz and Conchita

I tried to hold back the tears and glanced at the three English speakers sitting patiently but passively in the dimly lit room. Conchita said:

[It was] the Virgin who asked God to come here to Garabandal. She asked it of him in order that in the final moment that remains to us, with the help of these words, these final warnings, the Warning that he is going to send us, [and] the Miracle, we might avoid the punishment. Although it won't be possible to prevent the punishment because we have now lost even the sense of sin.

Tears filled my eyes. I tried to hold them back. I didn't worry about my friend Courteville seeing me, but only about the fellows my own age. Conchita's disquieting warning flowed on. "But with the Punishment, those of us who remain will change a lot, and then we will live for God until the end of time."

Tears streamed down my cheeks—tears of awe at sensing the seriousness of the predicament of our world, but most of all, tears of relief knowing that God was still in charge. I looked up around me at the other young men who hadn't understood a word. I felt alone but happy. I recalled a line from an old Spanish song: "It's all right to cry. For when you cry, your burdens are lightened."

Conchita finished, "Let us pray a lot for priests. We ourselves are to blame for many of the priests who are on the way to hell because we do not pray enough."

How different was this from the self-righteous criticism one hears leveled against priests. Conchita spoke rapidly, never pausing to collect her thoughts. This was not the Conchita who smiled so readily, whose voice at times screeched in delight, but the solemn Conchita, the mystical Conchita in close contact with God the ten years since June 18, 1961.

Darkness! Although the power failed often in Garabandal, it still took us by surprise.[54] Mrs. Courteville lit candles and we continued.

"What do you think, Ed?" Courteville must not have seen the tears.

"It's powerful. This denotes a change from the two formal messages. Those state that if we don't amend our lives, God will send a horrible punishment. Now Conchita says that the Punishment will come.[55] That's frightening!"

Courteville shook his head. "I have never heard Conchita speak in such a solemn voice. Did you understand it all, Ed?"

"The meaning is clear. There are some difficult spots."

The imminence of the Garabandal prophecies hung over me. Previously, Conchita had advised us to tell the whole world about the Messages requiring prayer, penance, sacrifice, and visits to the Blessed Sacrament in order to restrain the wrath of God. Now it seemed she was advising us to save ourselves and our families, and if there was time, the

---

54 Just a few years previous, there were only low watt light bulbs in Garabandal. Now with new and reconstructed houses with their electrical appliances, the old generator couldn't bear the load. New power lines were strung up from Cosío in 1972 but the power still failed.

55 Later Conchita asked that we not pay attention to these, her words. The words of the Virgin, that stated that the Chastisement was conditional, were the important ones.

ones around us. How long do we have? Yesterday, sickly, eighty-six-year old Father Rodrigo had stated that he would come up to Garabandal for the Miracle. And Father de la Riva had said, "I don't believe that the Miracle and the Warning are far away from this date [August 1971]."

Courteville and the others broke for supper, but anxious to get at the transcribing and translation, I left with the recording.

Back in my room I started on a draft of the English translation, but, when the lights kept failing, went downstairs to join the Gonzalez family in the dining area. One young man stood at the bar. Milton, a big, handsome, silent type from Ontario, Canada, preferred gazing at, and nursing his glass of red wine to talking, or at least to talking Spanish.

Although it was late, Paquita seemed in no hurry to prepare supper but finally commented. "I couldn't cook because the lights kept going out. Are you hungry, Eduardo?"

"No hurry. Whenever it's ready."

The door opened and a pleasant surprise entered. Conchita brought a pitcher of milk for the extra guests and information on how many of the big American group would eat and sleep at our place the next seven days. How friendly and natural she was, talking about taking private English lessons in Barcelona.

"Well, let's speak English so you can practice," I kidded.

"No," she blushed. "I can't say anything."

So proper, and yet so personable, Conchita is a rare, fascinating combination. Was this the same girl, so solemn and serious that we had just heard on the tape? She glanced a couple of times at the young man at the bar and then said to me, *"A este señor le gusta beber, no?"* ("This guy likes to drink, no?")

She stepped closer, and for the first time I ever heard her speak English, asked him, "You believe in this, in Garabandal?"

Without looking up, and perhaps a bit irritated or at least surprised by the to-the-point question without any introduction, the Canadian muttered, "I don't know."

"Why you come?"

"I don't know, for the Holy Land." (The Holy Land was probably on the schedule for his tour group.)

Conchita was never so charming, and smiling continued, "What you think? You believe me see the Virgin?"

Milton looked up at her, and then down at his glass of red wine, "No."

Conchita didn't stay long. Her mother would be preparing supper, and with the lights back on, Paquita had started ours. I told her not to bother setting up in the dining room, that I would feel lonely. And eating in the tiny kitchen at the small table crammed in at the corner near the sink would provide a better opportunity to talk.

After Milton paid a few *pesetas* for his drinks and left, Paquita served Serafín and me a glass of wine and set to work peeling potatoes for a *tortilla española* (potato omelet). While we ate, she set apples on the table, and then cut up cheese to go with the apples (and wine) for dessert. She washed dishes by hand in between servings while the three of us talked.

"Where are your *compañeros*?" Serafín wondered. "We cleared out the pensión for them. They should have arrived much earlier."

"They might show up yet," I told him.

"No. It's too late."

"Where else would they stay? You don't know Americans."

Paquita worried about this first ever big onslaught of guests to "Mesón Serafín."

"I wonder if they will be comfortable here," she frowned. "Americans are accustomed to more conveniences than we can offer. Eduardo, you will have to talk to them."

"No," I kidded, "you have to get used to talking to foreigners. What will you do when I leave?"

"Tell the ones who sleep upstairs that they can shower with hot water in the basement."

"There's hot water in this house?" I exaggerated my surprise and hurt. Being treated like one of the family, at times brings disadvantages.

The big front door creaked, and soon Courteville stuck his head into the tiny kitchen. "They're here. The first group of Americans has arrived. The rest are still hiking up the road." It was eleven o'clock.

I slipped on my tennis shoes and headed for Ceferino's place to help. On the way, I noticed Milton standing alone and said hello. Light complexion, well built, in his late twenties (a few years younger than I), he didn't say much this time either, only, "Yeah, I believe she saw the Blessed Virgin. Conchita is beautiful. I could talk with her all day."

The boys of the village had already gathered at the edge of the town square. "Eduardo, are there any young girls in the group?"

"Present us to them," added another.

"*Sí. Una rubia bonita para mí*" (Yes. A pretty blond for me), Pepe Díaz' handsome son, Manolín, said, laughing.

Gabino lifted suitcases out of the jeep until they filled the bar entrance and overflowed out into the dirt square. The pilgrims arrived puffing in twos, threes, and fours. What a shock Garabandal was for some. The group leader assured them they would have a place to eat and sleep in the little mountain hamlet.

Courteville acted as coordinator with Margie, the group's secretary. He offered my services. "Ed, here, can help the people get settled in the houses."

By now, some thirty people fidgeted around hunting for their luggage. Others sat inside drinking beer or soda.

Ceferino surveyed the scene from behind the bar. The poor guy looked like a general helpless to prevent the invasion of his camp. "What a bother, coming in here in the middle of the night, no?" I offered.

He shrugged his shoulders. "This is nothing. During the apparitions visitors used to crowd in here at all hours of the day and night."

Fr. Joseph Pelletier, a serious looking, middle-aged priest, who has written two books on Garabandal, scurried around like an army chaplain assuring the troops that they could survive a week in this primitive outpost.

I helped some find the way to our *pensión* and the rest, guided by the village youths, headed for private houses. Mary and Ruth would share the big end room with bath next to my room; Mrs. Ferria

Fr. Joseph Pelletier

and her teenage daughter, the room on the other side of me; and the amiable little white-haired woman, the cubbyhole at the top of the stairs.

"No, there's been a change." A young couple entered and would stay here instead of at Conchita's mother's house. Secretary Margie kept cool. She took care of all the others and would sleep wherever was left. The married couple would take the double room with bath and Mary and Ruth would move to the basement.

These seven, plus ten or twelve more who slept next door at *doña* Cándida's or at nearby *doña* Clara's, would eat at our place. I carried suitcases upstairs and down. For a week's stay, some brought baggage for three months. What a night!

CHAPTER FOURTEEN

FOREIGN INVASION

unday morning broke clear, blue, and beautiful like many mornings on the mountain. But this one was special. After 8:00 A.M. Mass, the Americans in their clean, pressed clothes gathered outside the church. Such a show of United States finery would have embarrassed me five years previous in the poor Mexican village where I had lived as a community development volunteer, but San Sebastián villagers were accustomed to visitors and didn't seem to care, or even notice, how they dressed. The pilgrims meant some extra money for six or seven families with extra rooms to let, but they and the other villagers would keep harvesting hay.

Conchita, wearing a dark cardigan jacket and a white, pleated skirt, drew most of the attention as she had the year before. She and her blind American friend, Joey Lomangino, stood greeting those who waited to see them. Kodak should grant Conchita stock options. I would also take her picture if I could just sneak behind one of those women and snap a couple shots without her noticing me.

With Conchita home for a visit and forty-five Americans here, activity in the little village picked up. Fr. Ramón de la Riva drove into town in his clunky old Renault and entered Courteville's house with the American group's chaplain, Fr. Pelletier. Someone mentioned that they might be discussing the latest developments on Garabandal from the Bishop's office.

Wondering why I hadn't been invited, I retreated to Loli's bar to have a *tinto*. Inside, Margie was posting the suggested schedule for the group

167

of forty-five pilgrims.

"Good morning," she greeted. "Did you sleep last night with all the commotion? A Spanish priest, Fr. Ramón, will talk to us at 11:30 this morning up in Serafín's dining area."

"I visited him a week ago at his Barro-Llanes house. He will tell interesting stories." I glanced at the notice she had tacked up.

11:30 -- Meeting with Father Ramón

3:30 -- Movie of the ecstasies in the basement of the Sevillian's house

9:00 -- Rosary in the church

"N.B." at the bottom of the notice suggested that the pilgrims make use of their free time to visit the Pines and St. Michael's shrine.

Was this a tour, a retreat, or summer school? I preferred travelling alone, but that session with Fr. Ramón would be worthwhile.

Up in Serafín's guesthouse the people started gathering shortly after eleven. A dozen others joined the Americans. Courteville stood by the door speaking English with Father Pelletier. Father de la Riva stood alone to the side so I greeted him.

"*Hola Padre. Se acuerda de mí?*" ("Hello Father. Do you remember me?")

"*Claro.* You came to my house. From California."

The "*claro*" of the well-educated Spaniard contrasted with some of the mountain men's "*claru*" that I was starting to get used to. Fr. Pelletier turned to me. "I think we will use you to interpret for the group. Stand right here by Father, and you can use the same microphone."

It was a privilege to translate Father's words. It wouldn't be easy. In my Spanish classes I insist that the students never translate—that they memorize the new language code without bouncing it off any other code. Without daily classroom practice, their teacher hadn't learned to translate well.

Serafín again stood back as a bystander in his own home.

"It's quite a contrast to the quiet of last night, no, Serafín?"

"*Mucha gente*" (A lot of people). They crammed into every corner. Steve and Ed from the tape transcription session sat on the stairs, as did a few others. Paquita and her twenty-one year old sister, Virginia, peeked out from the kitchen.

"We're ready to start," Fr. Pelletier called out. "Father Ramón de la Riva will relate a couple of the events that he witnessed here. He is the pastor of Our Lady of Sorrows Church at Llanes on the coast. Ed here, whom some of you have met, will translate for us."

Talk slowly, Father, I thought. And he began:

> I had the privilege of witnessing some two hundred ecstasies. The bishop had prohibited priests from going to Garabandal without his permission, so I wrote asking to make a retreat in the place and in the manner that I considered most fitting to my needs. Of course, Garabandal was that place. After that, whenever I wanted to go up to Garabandal, I always wrote my bishop saying that if he wanted to forbid me, would he kindly reply by letter. He never replied. After Bishop Puchol published his Note stating that the happenings of Garabandal "could all be explained naturally," that it had been "something like a child's game," I began to go up without writing for permission. Since there was nothing of importance here, I reasoned, the prohibition was meaningless.

That introduction went well, but then came a challenge. Father had something that Conchita wanted but didn't know how to use.

"*Cilicio*," he kept repeating. What the heck was that? One can often catch the sense of a new foreign word by its context (so we advise students), but not this one. *Cilicio*?

I ad-libbed, hoping not to stray too far from Father's meaning, but soon stuttered to an embarrassing halt. Fr. Pelletier bailed me out. "No. It's a hair shirt worn for penance."

Cilicio, cilicio. That's a word I won't forget. Father Ramón was patient and understanding.

> Conchita saw the *cilicio* on my table and asked me what it was. When I told her that people wore it to mortify themselves, she asked if she could have it. I told her it was the only one I had. The next day we went up to the fields. I used to go up often

to the fields and *invernales* (huts in the hills, used for storing hay and for shelter during the winter) in order to spend as much time as possible observing the four visionaries. Well, when Conchita again asked for the *cilicio*, I relented. I soon obtained a new one but wanted to have my old one back now that Conchita had used it.

Conchita working under the hot summer sun

"Did you follow that after I tried to lead you astray?" I asked the group. A few nodded, but I doubted they all had understood that Father, realizing that some day Conchita might be declared a saint, wanted his original hair shirt as a relic after she had worn it.

The hair shirt story so intrigued me that I all but forgot I was the translator and feared I might not be so for long if Padre Ramón didn't keep his vocabulary below the "*cilicio*" level. Never raising his melodious voice he continued.

Although I was staying at Maximina's house as usual, one day Jacinta's mother invited me to eat dinner at their house. We were already eating when someone shouted, "Here comes Jacinta in ecstasy!" I didn't want them to see me eating, so I hid my plate under the table. They passed by the house and I finished dinner. Afterwards I felt guilty about having stayed to eat while the girls had an apparition, so I decided, as a penance, to get up in the middle of the night to follow Loli who had announced a vision for that night. Thus resolved, I set the alarm for 3:00 A.M. and went to bed.

Sometime in the night I heard a noise outside, then a knock on my door. I sat up and turned on the light to see a child fall through the doorway (a foot above the bedroom floor) and crash down to the floor onto her knees. Loli, in a trance, walked on her knees toward me. I prepared to kiss the crucifix she held in front of her, but she walked right past me to the wall where she prayed for a moment in front of the photograph of Maximina's deceased husband. She then returned to me, pressed the crucifix to my lips, turned and left.

Father told us that later he found out the apparition was specifically for him, and how afterwards he heard Loli converse with the Virgin about him. He concluded his talk by demonstrating how Loli took the Blessed Virgin's picture with a complicated camera the girl had never used before.

In the afternoon, the group went off to view Courteville's movies of the ecstasies. I had seen them before, but to spend time speaking English with my countrymen, accompanied them. Home movie specials, but intriguing. Cameramen have calculated the girls' falling time at 1/16 of a second.

I cringed at the thought of it, as had the eyewitnesses on hearing the little girl's bones crack on the jagged rocks. A children's game, Bishop? I again thought about Bishop Puchol Montis' 1967 Official Notice on Garabandal in which he stated that all this (the Garabandal apparitions) "had started as an innocent children's game."[56] Serafín had recently told me, "I know of some fifty thousand people who have come here who might not believe this (believe it's a work of God), but there wouldn't be one of those in his right mind that would call it a children's game. That it was not."

On Tuesday, the French Ramóns and I paid Maximina a visit. Widowed early with two young children, friendly Maximina smiles easily. She is one of three whom I know to be Conchita's aunts. (Ciriaco's wife, Aurelia, and Lucia's mother, Antonia, are the others.) When she leads the night rosary in church, she prays fast, like a freight train. I hope God understands her.

Maximina

The bespectacled, middle-aged woman stood at her gate as we approached. *"Buenos días,"* she greeted, and led

---

56 *Opispado de Santander, Declaraciones Oficiales de la Jerarquía Sobre Garabandal,* (Santander: Spain), 1970 P. 27.

us into her small kitchen where Ramón Jr. immediately set up the big tape recorder.

"May we take a picture before we start?" he asked. Maximina turned red.

"I look so horrible in pictures."

Young Ramón, audacious yet tactful, snapped shots of her sitting at the kitchen table before she could protest more.

Ramón senior got right to work. Maximina sat up straight. The interview seemed a big deal to her. Naturally lighthearted, she made an effort to be serious.

"Do you remember what you saw during the time of the apparitions, Maximina?"

"Oh, I remember everything, but when I see that (the microphone), I get all nervous and can't say a thing."

But at Ramón's directive, "Maximina, tell us about the night Loli came to your house in ecstasy," she picked up the mike and talked for two hours telling every detail of where her children slept and which pictures hung on the wall, of how at 3:00 A.M. Loli in ecstasy entered Fr. Ramón's room to present him the crucifix to kiss.

"Did you know all four visionaries before the apparitions?"

She laughed. "Of course! Here in little San Sebastián we all know each other whether we want to or not."

"And before the time of the ecstasies, how did the four girls deport themselves in comparison to the other children of the village?"

> The same. There wasn't any difference. You can't say God chose them because they were better than the others. We didn't believe them when they talked about the angel because at first they went alone to the lane. I thought that since Conchita was the oldest, it was something that she made the others see. We bawled out the girls and told them not to do those things, that people would laugh at them [and at their relatives, Maximina?]. They asked that four women accompany them. I can't remember who went, but as sure as anything, they saw the children fall down onto the rocks with their heads thrown back and how beautiful they became.

"Did the Santander Commission ever question you?" Ramón asked.

"No. They never came near my house, never asked for my opinion. Conchita went to Santander, and they questioned her, but they never talked to any of us in the village."

"Finally, Maximina, what can you tell us about the announced Miracle? Will it take place?"

I'll never forget her answer, "I will believe it when I see it. I'm like St. Thomas. When I see something I believe, otherwise, not."

I stared at smiling Maximina. She had witnessed so many ecstasies and other unexplainable phenomena. The most favored visionary, Conchita, is her own niece, yet she isn't certain that the prophecies will be fulfilled? But that's the way it is in Garabandal. All witnessed unexplainable happenings. Few seem certain that what they saw and heard was the work of God. I was learning what hadn't sunk in during theology courses—that certainty about the supernatural is a gift from God.

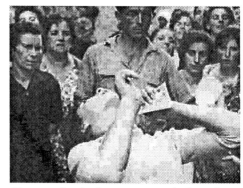

Engrossed onlookers never tired of watching the ecstatic girls. Maximina is on the left.

Conchita holding the crucifix up for the Virgin to kiss

I walked back to the "hotel" for comida at 1:30. Dinners were lively gatherings with all the Americans around. Paquita worked overtime. She watched over us, concerned. If she noticed someone not eating much, she would frown, "She doesn't like the chicken. Eduardo, ask her if she would like some eggs instead."

How could anyone complain, with delicious soup, chicken with rice, wine, abundant fresh bread and congenial company? They let me be waiter's helper. Some American visitors also asked, "What do you do for so long in this place?" Life got so hectic that second week of August that I didn't even take time to fish.

Margarita Huerta

After dinner, Margarita Huerta, the Catalán and I corrected my transcription of Conchita's August 7 recording. What a job! I had already worked hours on the ten-minute recording. Margarita, retired from Spanish government work, showed her expertise on the impossible punctuation. We argued. Don Pedro wanted to write it immediately in Catalán so he could publish it for the people in the Barcelona area.

"No," I countered. "We need to perfect it in Spanish first. We can't all be working on something different. Later you can have a copy to do with what you want."

The tape wasn't easy to follow. We argued over many words.

"She says '*ya*' there. And this is improper grammar."

"That doesn't matter. That's what she said, and we should write it that way, correct or not!"

"What does she mean here, '*Por eso es preparándonos cada uno que oiga estas palabras?*' That doesn't sound right."

"No. It's not. She should say, '*Por eso debemos prepararnos.*'" (Therefore we ought to prepare ourselves).

Margarita complained, "Oh, this is horrible!"

What a turn about! Earlier in the day I had told her that the work contained many errors, and that it would be almost impossible to translate. But now with a rough draft completed, I was confident it could be done. "The meaning is clear," I assured them.

Margarita worried on. "I talked to some priests this morning, and they agreed that Conchita should correct it. You take it to her, Eduardo."

Oh brother! I, a foreigner, tell Conchita that she has a dangling participle in her talk.

Later that afternoon I approached her house hoping she wouldn't be in. No such luck. There she was, talking with a small group gathered around her doorstep. My French had improved to the degree that I could identify the language. Furthermore the group looked French. I waited.

A couple with two little towheads moved up and greeted Conchita in an unfamiliar language. She smiled, signed holy cards, and then stood allowing the family to take pictures and to look at her, God's intercessor. No interpreter was needed. The family said good-bye and walked away delighted over their "talk" with Conchita.

Even though I hadn't noticed many visitors around except for the Americans, other strangers kept arriving. I stood back, not wanting to make them wait if Conchita decided to revise the paper. People came to me to translate the words Conchita had written on their holy cards.

"What does this say?"

"What did she write? Oh, that's strange. How did she know I was worried about my husband?"

I finally moved up to the door. "You are very popular today, Conchita."

"If this were the only day," she smiled.

I treasured that reply, daring to think she wouldn't confide to everybody that being in the public eye bothered her. She glanced at the manila folder I carried and didn't seem overjoyed to see it.

Author with the transcription of Conchita's taped message at her doorway

"What do you want?"

"This is a copy of the message you recorded the other day. There are a few points we don't understand and that will give us trouble in translating." She glanced at the paper, out at the group in front of her, and then at me.

"What don't you understand?"

"This part here where you say, 'consecrated by the Virgin.' Do you mean 'consecrated to the Virgin?'"

"Yes, that would be better."

"And here you start a sentence, 'She asked it of him [God] in order that in this final moment that remains to us, these words,' but you don't end the sentence. There is no verb."

"Well, you look for [supply] the verb."

Wow! She wanted me, with my non-native Spanish, to tamper with her work? I had hoped she would correct it at her leisure, but no, she just read while I held the papers. She wrote nothing; I would have to remember her corrections and comments.

"And here, Conchita, this seems like a contradiction. You advise us to pray, to make sacrifices, to visit the Blessed Sacrament in order to avoid the Punishment and then you say, 'although we won't be able to prevent the Punishment.' Isn't that a contradiction?"

"Yes." Then she pointed to the words starting with *aunque* (although) and said, "These are my own words." She did not want us to confuse her own opinion--that the Chastisement was inevitable--with the words of the Virgin in 1961 that God would send a chastisement if we didn't amend our lives.

"*Conchita, te molesta si publiquemos este mensage?*" ("Do you mind if we publish the message?")

She answered a clear, "No, I don't mind."

I left Conchita to her admirers, inserted some clarifications, and then went to look for Father Pelletier, the chaplain of the American group, in order to give him a copy. I found him beaming with happiness.

"Conchita just wrote me a note which I will use as the introduction to my book." He handed me the manuscript, a translation of Conchita's diary with notes. Preparing a book is an imposing task. "Thank you for this paper, Ed. I'll read it to the group on the bus tomorrow on our way to Ávila and Fatima."

It saddened me to see them go. The thoughtful group secretary, Margie, must have noticed. "You are welcome to come," she invited. "We have extra room on the bus, and since Frank and the doctor are remaining here, you might as well use their paid-for room in Fatima."

Tempting! Let someone else make all the travel plans. Fatima had been on my itinerary for two years, but I kept bogging down here. "Thanks, Margie, but I couldn't get packed on time."

Early Wednesday morning the big American group hiked down the mountain, and with the village once more at peace, we got back to polishing Conchita's words to Garabandal promoters. It still didn't satisfy the meticulous Madrileña, Margarita. "Aye, she's done much better than this! It will go around the world. Bring it back to her, Eduardo."

"Margarita, I don't want to bother Conchita again."

"Go ahead. She'll be grateful to you. You'll see. Here. I'll go with you."

Conchita wasn't in, but her mother, Aniceta, proved a worthy substitute:

> That's the way Conchita said it and we shouldn't change anything! She didn't prepare a speech. When that fellow came over with the recorder, she just took the mike and talked. It came straight from her. I understand it. That's the way we talk. Neither one of us is educated. It was the same when she was younger. No one told her what to write. What's the difference if she says 'evitar al pecador' or 'evitar que el hombre peque?[57] It's all the same. We should do what Conchita says. She's mad at an author for not following her directions. He went ahead and wrote about those reported recent apparitions down in Portugal after she told him not to mix anything with Garabandal.

I couldn't get in so much as a "sí" or a "no," with the two ladies, and just listened. Margarita talks even faster than Maximina reciting the village rosary. At Aniceta's remark, she tensed like a bantam rooster and the gossip flew. "Why, do you know that down there the so-called visionary is living with a man that isn't her husband?"

"I would never do that," the staunch, widowed Aniceta replied.

Margarita steamed on, "Why, if one of the visionaries here would scandalize us like that, for me it would be 'good-bye Garabandal.'"

------◆◆◆◆------

57 Avoid the sinner vs. prevent the sinner from again falling into sin.

"No, Margarita. Garabandal will last because it is of God, regardless of what the girls do, and I say that even though one of them is my own daughter."

Aniceta, quick and perceptive, held her own against the Madrid professional. Margarita stood corrected. "Yes, you are right."

I left the manila folder on the shelf in the kitchen. "Give this to Conchita, Aniceta, and ask her to correct it."

Back at the pensión, an Irish lady chatted with an American doctor. Earlier she had been with a group at Conchita's door. "All the time I was there with her I felt so happy, so special. Even though she looked around at others in the group, I felt present to her and important." Here was another who thinks Conchita is unique. Does anyone consider her ordinary?

Serafín sat relaxed in the kitchen, resting from his day's labor of cutting and stacking the hay. "Eduardo, when are you leaving? Conchita asked if you wanted to accompany her to Bilbao tomorrow and share the cab fare."

I looked at the guy. He wasn't one to joke.

" Sure." Bilbao, Siberia, the Sahara Desert!

Serafín said no more. I feared to ask if he meant it and left to check with Señor Pérez. After having accompanied him for the interview with Conchita's Aunt Maximina, I didn't want to miss the talk with Pepe Díez. Yes, the tape recorder was repaired, so tonight at 10:00 o'clock we would hear Pepe.

I went on to the church for the rosary, back home for fast ham and eggs with french fries, and then cut through a dark but short lane towards Pepe's house, wondering why Conchita would invite me to accompany her to Bilbao.

 PEPE'S THREE MIRACLES

orty-three-year-old Pepe works hard. People call him the most ambitious, hard-working man in the village. His wife told me that he never stops. The other day he didn't stop his masonry work to talk. Many consider him the most important eyewitness to the Garabandal happenings, especially for the 1962 Miracle of the Host.

When I entered their kitchen out of breath, Pepe's pretty wife, Clementina, sat talking next to Ramón holding the microphone. Black haired, mustached Pepe stood up, motioned to me to take his chair, and hopped up to sit on the counter. Lines creased his determined face. An able looking fellow one might take for a doctor, a foreman, a winner—someone you'd want on your team.

In order not to disturb the recording, I took the chair without protest. His wife was speaking:

> I saw the second apparition; the first, no. On seeing them in ecstasy I got excited and called out loudly, first to Loli, and when she didn't answer, to Mari-Cruz. Then I attempted to call Jacinta, but I don't know what happened; something took away my voice, so I poked Aurelia. "Get up, Jacinta," Aurelia yelled. "There's a herd of animals coming that will trample you."
>
> Angelita, another woman by the name of Serafina, and my oldest boy, Manolín, who was ten, joined us. I pulled myself together and cried out, "Conchita, call the Virgin of Carmel. Call the Sacred Heart. Tell them something. Ask Him what He wants of us."
>
> And the others, Aurelia and Concesa, laughed at me. "Tina," they said, "Don't. It's probably a work of the devil." I got very nervous and said I was going to get the priest and everyone, that if you

didn't believe in this, you didn't believe in God. And on saying this, we heard Conchita say, "*Virgen Santísima*, they don't believe us," and I shouted, "Yes, we all believe you." We were there until 10:00 P.M. watching them, how they had their hands up like this.

His black, bushy eyebrows partly covering his eyes, Pepe frowned, then smiled and pointed to himself. Did he want to speak that badly? He must have heard, and told the same story many times. He waited, attentive, alert, while his wife continued.

When they came out of ecstasy, they told us they had seen an angel but he hadn't spoken, that he had laughed and shook his head at the expression, "*Virgen Santísima*." The next day everyone asked us if we had been at the apparition. We told them we didn't see anybody. We could only see the girls and nothing more.

Pepe with the Gurardia Civil at village entrance

Around 11:00 P.M., when Clementina rose to send the youngest of their four sons, Antonín, to bed, Pepe jumped into the chair and started to talk.

While Ramón switched tapes, Pepe explained, "Yes, at times the girls feigned ecstasies, but it was easy for us to see the difference between the faked ecstasies and the real ones, and after telling the little girls that they couldn't fool anybody, they didn't do it anymore."[58]

Aye! Why were we wasting important testimony? But like good Spanish wine that tastes better and better, the story improved as he talked. When Ramón signaled, "ready," Pepe related his story.

---

58 Since all of the girls weren't equally favored, and at times some of them went for periods of time longing to see the Virgin, witnesses surmised that perhaps the children thought that by putting themselves in the line with the others they would have a visit. They didn't.

And what a story he told! For two and a half hours he held us spellbound with accounts of the girls' ecstatic walks, levitations, crashing falls, their mysterious returning of religious articles, the miracle of the visible communion, and more. He relived the scenes of nine and ten years previous, enthusiastically, and at times humorously, never faltering for a word or fact:

Loli handing up religious articles to be kissed by the Virgin

There was this big fellow from the village of Polaciones. Cirilio they call him. Young, twenty-five years old, but big and strong. We men in the village chided him, "You can't lift Jacinta off the ground. Let's see if you can lift her." And he went up to the statue-like child in front of the church, but he couldn't lift her. All embarrassed, he moved around to get a better hold, but the poor fellow still couldn't budge her.

Pepe laughed on recalling his story.

And the guy, all flustered from not being able to lift the little girl of, let's say, forty kilos, and we, accustomed to lifting one hundred kilos in the fields, stared at her with his mouth open, then looked

181

around stuttering, "I--I--I can't lift her. How is it possible? If I go to Santander and tell them this, they won't believe me."

Then Jacinta came out of ecstasy. So we returned to the big guy and asked him, "Let's see if you can do it now." And he turned scared like a baby. "No," he said, "I don't know. I'm afraid of that!" But we talked him into it, and in front of her father I asked, "Jacinta, how much do you weigh? Don't worry if this fellow tries to pick you up." And the boy got set like he was going to lift a tremendous weight, grabbed Jacinta, and lifted her into the air like a rag doll.

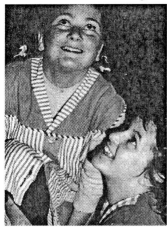

Loli effortlessly lifts up Jacinta
to kiss the Virgin good-bye.

Ecstatic girls were made heavy to others and light
to each other.

Pepe enjoyed our laughing at the plight of the poor, overgrown farm boy. It was after midnight. I hoped we didn't disturb his sleeping family. After a break he directed, "Don't turn that thing on yet. I don't want this recorded."

One night I decided not to follow the girls and stayed behind to talk in front of Ceferino's place, you know, where the men gather on the log? Well, thinking that I didn't want to miss anything, I jumped up and hurried to catch up with the group. Wanting to be near the front, I dashed around the corner and conked my head on a low hanging balcony. "*Aye. Me cargo en San Pedro!*"[59] I saw stars and cussed out all the saints in heaven. Even God himself suffered that night.

59 "Aye, I (vulgar expression deleted) on St. Peter."

Ramón and his son muffled laughter. "That's filthy, horrible. Did you get that, Eduardo?"

"More or less, but those exact words aren't in our Spanish textbooks."

They tried to explain the phrase and laughed again at turning Pepe's vulgar expression into a language lesson.

Pepe continued, "Well, there I was holding my aching head and uttering foul oaths, when the three girls in ecstasy rushed backward down the path toward me. In an impossible position, they jammed their crucifixes against my mouth."

Presenting the crucifix in awkward position

We stared at the guy. His rapid, mountain-style Castilian could strain a school-trained Spanish brain even at a decent hour, but now, far into the night, aided by his lively facial expressions and demonstrative gestures, I savored every word. Pepe dramatized history as if it were more his pleasure than ours. All students should have professors like him. He steamed on:

> At the beginning, I didn't know what an ecstasy was. It was something I didn't understand, and the first time that I had seen anything supernatural. Some days there were two or three ecstasies. They might happen at three or at six in the afternoon or at three in the morning. I couldn't sleep because I didn't want to miss anything. They, twelve-year-old girls, would move at such an enormous speed that young men of twenty-five and twenty-eight, accustomed as we were to hiking fast through the mountains, sometimes carrying heavy loads, couldn't keep up with them. They took normal steps but advanced three times as far as normal. To keep up with them was impossible.

Loli and Jacinta walking over the
rocks at night while gazing upwards

Three times he repeated the speed at which the girls moved. Considering himself fit and the best in any endeavor, their speed and his inability to keep up had surprised and confounded him.

> I always tried to be in front, but I couldn't catch up with them, even though nobody outdid me in those days. They still don't often beat me at forty-five, but even less so then. On following them you lost your tiredness. Even sick old people followed them all over. I never got tired. I don't know why—the desire I had to see them or to learn what would happen.

"And when they walked backwards, Pepe, did they move as fast?"

"No, but a normal person, let's say of middle-age, couldn't keep up even then. Doctors came with their apparatuses examining them."

Then, recalling another incident, Pepe digressed:

> One time this man in back of the girls pricked them with a needle, and at that moment the little girls with smiling faces—I'll never forget how they looked on seeing their apparition, let's say the Virgin—said, "He's pricking us? But it doesn't hurt." I heard this myself. I can't say what tests all the others performed but I made my own. I would. . .

Doctor taking Loli's pulse

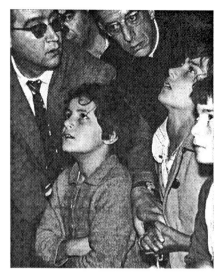

The pulse was always normal after the girls had moved faster than anyone could keep up with them.

Darn Ramón cut him off. "Pepe, what is your opinion of the girls now?" That was no way to interview. It was Pepe's digressions and anecdotes that brought the Garabandal history to life. We should allow him to ramble on at will. But Ramón stuck to his written list. Who cares what he thinks of the girls now, I thought, and didn't listen to the answer.

"Pepe," Ramón continued, "did the Commission[60] ever call you?"

"No. I would walk to Santander tomorrow if they would hear me."

This guy was great. He could convince the Bishop, the Pope, or the devil himself of the veracity of the apparitions. No, he shouldn't mess with that last-mentioned fellow. He knows they are true, and has been confusing people, especially the Santander bishops, ever since things began here.

"Pepe," I said, "I'm grateful. Last year when I returned here, it discouraged me to hear that the people of the village wouldn't talk about the events. It's great that you will tell us these things."

<hr>

60 The hastily formed Bishop's Commission consisted of: Doctors Piñal and Morales and Fathers Saiz, Odriozola and del Val Gallo. The evaluative *Notes* published by the various bishops who have occupied the Santander Diocese since 1961 were based upon the findings of this Commission.

"Well, I look at it like this. We all need each other. If I were to go to your country and were to ask for directions, for example, it would not be charitable for you not to help me. I know why you come here and I'll tell you anything I know."

> The most important event for me was the miracle of the *forma,* the miracle of Communion [Foretold by Conchita July 3, 1962, it occurred July 18.] I had seen many ecstasies, but when I heard, "miracle," I wanted to see something more. When Conchita announced it two weeks ahead of time, I knew thousands of people would come, and I worried how I would see it. The people had flocked in here all along, and many more would come for a miracle. Then the day before, Aniceta came to me and said, "Pepe, will you accompany my daughter and protect her from the crowd?"

Pepe threw his hands into the air.

> "Oh!" I said to myself, "that's a miracle right there," guaranteeing me a front row seat, so to speak. I stayed by her all day from seven in the morning. Late that night, or actually early the next morning, Conchita went into a trance in her kitchen, and then walked out to the lane behind her house. I held onto her arm, and the people grabbed me and tore the clothes from my back trying to take my place. I was naked to the waist but didn't care. It was a horrible brawl. Anxious to see, people knocked down old women and walked right over them. That was another miracle, that nobody got hurt.

> Well, in the lane with thousands pushing in to see, Conchita fell onto her knees and put out her tongue. It was easy to see that there was nothing on it. This disturbed me. I had expected to see the host when she put out her tongue, but it wasn't that way. We knew that the angel would give Conchita Holy Communion, but we didn't know just how. I was confident because everything Conchita predicted had always come true, but still I was anxious to see how it would be.

"How far away from her face were you, Pepe?" Ramon asked.

Close, maybe fifty centimeters. I can swear that I didn't glance away for a second. She held her tongue out that way for maybe a minute without moving or swallowing. All of a sudden the host was on her tongue! I didn't see it come.[61] There wasn't any movement of her face or her tongue. The child remained motionless from the moment of putting out her tongue. The host appeared perfectly formed, a normal host like the priests use. After some three minutes, it grew bigger like a living substance. I felt like I was next to a miracle. When it was over, I noticed I had no pants on. People had also ripped off my pants, so I ran home, embarrassed, in my shorts.

About 1:30 in the morning, Ramón asked, "Shall we quit now, Pepe, or continue?"

"It makes no difference to me. I'll just have another cigarette and we'll go on, or we can finish tomorrow."

Finish? Pepe was a bottomless well of information. There weren't enough days left in the summer to finish.

"During the apparitions," he said, "I averaged two hours of sleep a night for a year and a half but always woke up refreshed." And now, still in work clothes, he was willing to talk on through the night! He had no time for banal gossip, just for physical labor and this—telling us what he had lived through between 1961 and 1965. Would I wake up refreshed? Tomorrow could be quite a day. We decided to call it a night.

"*Buenas noches, Pepe, y muchas gracias.*"

"*Nada, hombre.*" (Don't mention it). And he extended the firm, strong hand of a man I knew I could trust to help in time of need, and to tell the truth.

---

61 Nor did anybody else see it arrive. People knew the angel would give Conchita communion and that they would see it, but nobody knew exactly what they would see. After the event, some thirty witnesses testified that they saw the same thing in the same sequence; all told it in different words but agreed on the essentials. None, for example, reported that he or she saw the angel, or saw the host falling onto her tongue, or that it moved out of a ciborium.

Outside, we strolled through the slumbering village. The night was fresh and bright. I paid Ramón for the tapes. Eight hundred pesetas seemed a lot.

"I'll duplicate the recordings and send them," he assured me.

I sure hoped so. "That will be great," I encouraged, "especially of Pepe and Maximina." I would stay and copy them myself, but if it was true that Conchita invited me to accompany her to Bilbao, I would leave the next day.

"Shall we climb to the Pines?" Ramón suggested. The large rocks, such obstacles even in the daytime, seemed helpful stepping stones in the middle of the night. In no time we reached the top and looked out over Garabandal. A dozen lights dotted the sleeping village. Would it be the same on my next visit? Not if the Miracle happens before that. Many are anxious for it. Not I. When the people flock here, Serafín won't have time to sit on the steps and talk. Paquita will be much too busy for English lessons or to chat, and the fishermen among the hordes of visitors will deplete the trout population in the streams.

Ramón interrupted my thoughts. "Shall we say a decade of the rosary? You lead and my son and I will answer."

"*Dios te salve María, llena eres de gracias, el Señor está contigo.*" I began. And from Ramón Pérez, father, on one side and Ramón Pérez, son, on the other, "*Sainte Mere, Mere de Dieu, preiz pour nous pecheurs, maintenant et l'heure de notre mort. Amen.*"

Later, down below, I tiptoed through the sleepy household so I wouldn't wake the other guests. Preparing for bed, I wondered about that invitation. Why would she ask me to accompany her? During her short visit home, we had hardly talked. Yes, I had mentioned leaving, but I had been doing that for a week, and I had never said anything about going east toward Bilbao. Just yesterday I had talked with an American visitor about travelling together in his old Volkswagen bus, west along the coast to Galicia, Portugal, and Fatima.

Just in case Conchita meant it, I threw most of my belongings into my one small suitcase, opened the door so I'd hear the American women rising for early Mass, turned off the light, and jumped into bed. It was 3:30 A.M.

CHAPTER SIXTEEN

INVITATION

ay arrived quickly. When the neighbors stirred, it was just 6:00 A.M., but I roused myself with the same anticipation as for boyhood fishing trips, and finished packing before heading for Conchita's house. The sun poked out from behind the mountains over Cosío. Aye! What if she had other plans? I'd better not go too near her house this early. Yet I'd hate to miss her. Someone is in the kitchen. No, I'd better not knock. I walked back through the village.

Not much action in Garabandal at 6:30 A.M. I headed back to Conchita's house thinking, *Que será, será* (What will be, will be).

"Hi. Is your daughter here, Aniceta?"

"She's in her room packing."

"She's leaving at seven isn't she?"

"Whenever the taxi comes."

Talking to myself, I returned to get ready just in case it was true. Would Jim be angry if I didn't travel with him through Galicia and Portugal? To ride in his van and stop and visit the small fishing villages would be a great trip. Moreover, I had suggested it. Traveling with Conchita, cab driver Gabino might monopolize the conversation, or Conchita might not talk in front of him.

Serafín burst into the house. "Eduardo, when are you leaving?"

"I'm not fussy, anytime."

"Well, Conchita wants to know if you want to ride as far as Bilbao. I'll tell Paquita to fix you breakfast."

I shaved, wrapped the cognac glasses in newspaper, tied the package with the frazzled blue ribbon saved from Father de la Riva's mother's lunch package gift, and then wrote a brief note to my hosts:

Queridos Serafín, Paquita y María Conchita,

A remembrance from one who remains grateful for your hospitality and friendship.

May God repay you,

Eduardo

A longer, more profound note would have been appropriate, but there would have been mistakes with the Spanish "*vuestro*" and "*os.*"[62]

Poor Paquita worked so hard. Out of breath now from running up the hill to make my coffee, she still smiled.

A few minutes later we walked together through the awakening

village to Conchita's house where Gabino already waited with the jeep. I said good-bye to the few women standing around and paid Serafín 3,200 *pesetas* (about $45) for three weeks board and room.

Hasta luego Aniceta, Serafín, Paquita, and María Conchita.

On the road we picked up a fellow who climbed into the back of the jeep next to me.

"*Buenos días,*" he greeted.

"Are you from Garabandal? I don't remember seeing you."

Serafín and his daughter with Conchita a few minutes before she leaves the village

"I spend a lot of time in the mountains with the cattle. I've seen you. Last year, also."

"How many cows do you have?"

"Oh, about thirty."

"You must be rich with that many."

"Rich? Nobody around here is rich."

---

62 Spanish pronoun forms which differ from the Latin American pronouns used by the author.

Gabino, from neighboring Cosío, disagreed countering, "But the banks [three or four of them in little Puentenansa] are full of Garabandal money."

Almost everyone in the village has cows. Our new passenger couldn't offer an average number. Many have one or two. Some have twenty or thirty, and one or two might have as many as fifty. The total number decreases as the people move out of the village. "Seventy families lived here when the apparitions started, now about fifty," Serafín had told me. In Cosío we let off our extra passenger before changing from the jeep to Gabino's black sedan. Minutes later we stopped in Puentenansa where I dashed up into the big pensión, said a fast "hello" to the friendly, fish-frying, free-talking *señora* standing at the rail at the top of the stairs, grabbed the knapsack that I had left there the week before, and ran back down the stairs.

"The bishop wrote that the girls have denied seeing the Blessed Virgin," she yelled down.

"I can't talk," I called back up to her. "I'm in a hurry. See you next year."

I chided Gabino and Conchita for telling people who wanted a ride to Cabezón or Torrelavega (to the east) that we were going to Reinosa (to the south). How friendly she was! It would be a good trip. But then a half hour later, when we stopped to say a good-bye, Conchita asked, "Will it bother you if my aunt and cousin come along for the ride?"

Conchita outside of her aunt's house

Gabino said "No," so what could I say? *Caramba* (Gosh), I thought.

191

I'm not paying for half of a four-hour taxi ride to listen to her old aunt. Oh well, maybe her cousin would be like Conchita.

Not quite, but Aunt Antonia was a riot.

"I wouldn't let my daughter go off by herself to the city. God only knows what could happen. Why, even here in our little Torrelavega, I see people kissing and embracing right on the street. Now I didn't let my husband kiss me until we went to the altar, and that's how it's going to be with my daughter."

Gabino nudged me and grinned, "I told you this was going to be a good trip."

About ten minutes along, Antonia's asking, "Is this Bilbao?" provided a good laugh.

We talked about the poor wages in Spain and the impossibility of living well and about "old" Gabino's late marriage and that there was still hope for me. They all preferred older men. Conchita remarked, "I, at twenty-two, would marry a man of forty."

"Younger men don't have much sense," Antonia added. For miles we tried to convince her to let her daughter, Lucia live with Conchita in Barcelona, but she laughed when issuing the maternal veto to all our reasons.

The author with Lucía in 2015

In Bilbao we checked our luggage at the station. Conchita's train wouldn't leave until 9:00 P.M. What a break! Would she agree to have lunch with me? I would have to ask her soon because the others would head right back home. It would be difficult for a Spanish girl to accept, and more so with an aunt looking on to report back to her mother. But somehow with Conchita it didn't seem such an awesome task. I knew she would be kind in refusing and not make me feel bad.

"Will you look for a place to stay now?" she asked.

"No. I'm in no hurry. I still want you to look at our transcription of your taped statement. May I invite you to lunch?"

"OK."

Did I hear that correctly? And my shoes hadn't been shined in weeks. We gave auntie a quick tour of the booming Basque port city, and then stopped and waited while the women jabbered lengthy "good byes." Come on, Gabino, I thought. Put that cab in gear before her aunt convinces Conchita that it is improper to have lunch alone with a foreigner. At last he pulled out of the driveway behind City Hall leaving us alone on the street.

 BEAUTIFUL BILBAO

 day later I sat in a Bilbao hotel dining room writing the wonders of the previous day. Oh for a recorder to preserve all that I had heard and felt! Highlights? The whole day! And I had worried about making the wrong decision—travel to Bilbao with Conchita rather than to Galicia and Portugal with Jim.

When I recalled the long-ago circumstances that preceded and made the day possible, tears dropped onto the notebook in front of me. Twice I had been relieved of basketball coaching positions, forcing me to concentrate on teaching (and learning) Spanish. I had cried out, Job-like, to God for allowing the principals' injustices to me. Without them I wouldn't be telling this story.

And do even the astronauts have a more thrilling story to tell? How barren the moon! Two nights ago as it shone over the Cantabrian Mountains after Apollo XV had left it, I had thought that any of those moon visitors would have changed places with me. And that was before yesterday! The waitress set the *arroz con leche* (rice pudding) in front of me. It would be difficult to return to teaching. Maybe teach half a year, and the other half tell people about Garabandal. Relating the recent, extraordinary history of the village would be easy, but how do you explain Conchita?

Was it that having spent much time with the Blessed Virgin, she has become like her heavenly visitor? Dom Hubert Van Zeller reasons that with friends (The visionaries called the Virgin their best friend), the virtues of the stronger are often acquired by the weaker.[63]

---

63 Dom Huber Van Zeller, *Ideas for Prayer* (Springfield: Templegate, 1966), p. 97.

He says:

> . . . that God asks us . . . to stand humbly in front of him and reflect him. Souls preoccupied with themselves cannot properly reflect God; their own image keeps getting in the way. . . .Shafts of light can come from it [a heliograph] only when its casing has been removed and there is no shadow lying across it. . . .[And] even when the obstacles have been removed . . . neither the light nor the message which it transmits is its own. The instrument cannot pride itself on the brightness of the sunshine or the wisdom of its communication.[64]

Mary didn't block out the son. Her soul proclaims the greatness of the Lord, not of herself. Conchita, like her best friend, and likely imitating her, doesn't get in God's way either. Although others attempt to put her on a pedestal, she knows that she wasn't then, and isn't now, anything special for having been in the group playing when the angel joined them. She reported, "At first there were just the five of us: the Angel, Loli, Mari Cruz, Jacinta and I." Father Pesquera comments, "The observation is delightful. . . .We see the powerful angel of the Lord on the same line with the poor daughters of Garabandal . . . a strange squadron in the skirmishes of the Lord God of Hosts"![65]

Conchita at time of first apparitions

Who, but a poor village daughter would put herself in the same line with the powerful archangel, without any fear of being accused of wanting to be considered important?

After Gabino had driven away, cars, taxis, and busses had whizzed by us at the start of the two and a half hour dinner break. It would be good to be able to lead Conchita to a proper restaurant. As we walked, she seemed to know where she was going. The tall, tan, twenty-two-year old looked sharp

64 Ibid. p. 107.
65 Eusebio Pesquera, *Se Fue Con Prisas a la Montaña Primera Parte*, Vol.1 (*Zaragoza: editorial Círculo*, 1972) p.48.

in a sleeveless V-necked white dress, with a navy blue sweater that she alternately wore and swung along beside her. Her dress fell in pleats to her knees. Classy!

Walking in bustling dinnertime Bilbao, I feared people would critically inspect the guy beside such an attractive young woman, so I smoothed out my well-traveled sports coat and wiped the tops of my shoes against my pants.

I noticed how she walked. Like a lady of course, but young and happy, very different from many young women who look like they are carrying the burden of the world. Paradoxically, she is the one who has been doing that. She knows the weight of our sins and how they offend God. She miraculously previewed the Chastisement for these sins, senses its imminence, and begs God's mercy. She carries the burden of having announced to the world that God will send all of us a terrifying warning and then perform the greatest miracle of all time.

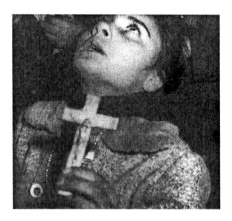

Everything about her seemed to testify to the fact that for ten years, since 1961, she has been striving to make herself pleasing to God, and thus was so irresistibly attractive to others.

What do you say for openers to such a person? *"Tienes hambre, Conchita?"* (Are you hungry, Conchita?) I had worried about a wrinkled coat and un-shined shoes. Nobody looked at me.

We passed a couple of restaurants before stopping. "I used to eat here when I lived in Bilbao," she told me. Restaurante Mesina. I hoped it would be a nice place for her. Are there people like Conchita in Heaven? I must go there. None of the tourist brochures recommend industrial, smoggy Bilbao. Is there a more fascinating place on earth?

Bilbao in early 1970's

It was quiet upstairs where people in business dress occupied three quarters of the twelve or fifteen tables. When I held out her chair, Conchita moved around to the next side where we repeated the performance. It looked like musical chairs. Hadn't anyone held out a chair for her before?

"Do you like *paella*, Eduardo? Do you prefer fish or meat? This fish, *mero*, is very good," she offered, trying to help.

I chose a favorite Spanish dish, roast lamb.

"For me, *ensaladilla rusa* and macaroni."

"There isn't any macaroni," the waitress advised.

So she ordered breaded veal, *ensaladilla*, and Coca-Cola.

Garabandal girls drinking Coca-Cola (1999)
Raquel, Mónica, Virginia, Alicia

"Don't you know that Coke is the worst thing you could drink?" I admonished in my Irish manner of joking about serious things.

"¿*De veras*?" (Really?)

"Yes. A nail corrodes in that horrible drink. Once when prospecting for uranium, a partner showed us how bad Coca-Cola . . ."

"What do you drink in the United States?"

"There's really no national drink: water, milk, beer, wine, lemonade, tea, coffee, Kool-Aid, Coca-Cola."

"What do you like best about Garabandal?"

Not expecting such a provocative question so soon, I asked, "May I wash my hands before answering?" On returning to the table, I started, "What do you do, Conchita, when people ask you difficult questions?"

"I don't answer."

"Two years ago I came to Spain to meet the people whose language I teach, and happened upon the Rionansa area. When I returned last year, I heard intriguing things in Garabandal and asked myself, "Where are you going? Here there is happiness and hope." This year I came back again to learn more, and thus be better prepared to help my countrymen when telling them the story."

She could probably see through that pious talk, but I meant it, mostly. I couldn't very well give speeches about the Blessed Virgin and her Messages of prayer and penance and not try to grow in virtue myself. In the Liturgy of the Hours for Doctors of the Church we read in the antiphon for the gospel canticle, "Those who instruct people in goodness will shine like the stars for all eternity." That sounded like a good deal.

"Do the villagers believe in the supernatural reality of Garabandal?" I asked.

"Basically, I think so, the majority. Some forget; but if you question them, they remember."

I recalled how the other day, "unbelieving" *doña* Cándida wouldn't part for anything with her rosary the Virgin had kissed, and how Gabino's mouth had fallen open and how he stared at Conchita's brother, Serafín, in disbelief and asked, "You mean that out of all the kissed medals and rosaries there isn't anyone in the whole village who would sell me one?"

Serafín had looked at his friend, and answered in his slow, well-thought-out manner, *"Lo dudo. Lo dudo mucho."* (I doubt it. I doubt it very much.)

"Does it bother you, Conchita that some people forget about the apparitions or don't believe?"

> No, I think it's natural. The pilgrims to Garabandal help a lot. Some make big sacrifices in order to come; it's not easy. Those in good faith, those who come for the Virgin, are very impressive. It is you who help the people of the village. It is we [the visionaries] who are to blame for the people not believing. They expect something of us, but we don't act the way we should. The people of Garabandal are very good. I love them a lot. The young people are respectful.

The waitress brought Conchita potato salad and me, lettuce and tomato. How could the young people not respect her? She knows who they are—princes and princesses, the sons and daughters of a king, the king of kings, and she treats them as such.

"Have you always been a practicing Catholic?" she asked. When I didn't answer at once, she specified, "Have you always said the rosary and attended Mass?"

"Yes, I've tried."

"More or less after Garabandal?"

I stared at her amazed; she didn't waste words. Unlike so many of us who babble insignificant trivia, everything Conchita said seemed important. I managed a weak, "the same," but when that didn't sound right added, "Certainly it's easier to pray and be good in Garabandal, but on returning to the world it's more difficult. How can we remember, Conchita?"

"Thinking about God and *venciéndonos.*"

"I don't understand. Mortification?"

"Yes." She twiddled a piece of paper napkin and explained about leaving it on the table when you feel like playing with it. "And all the better in small things."

And to make sure I understood, I asked, "Like not having a cup of coffee when you want one?"

"That's right. It's also good to think about death. I fear to arrive before God and have him ask me what good I have done."

Was she thinking about her request in 1965 to go with the Virgin back to heaven and the latter's answer? "You need to present yourself before God with your hands full of good works done in his name, and now your hands are empty." I looked at the beautiful girl whose most serious offense might have been taking a green apple from a neighbor's tree when she was twelve. Not worthy to go to heaven? Where did that leave me?

"I mentioned to my public school Spanish students this year how it helps to think of death. I'm a good one to advise others."

She laughed. "Me too. I don't think I've ever spent a perfect day in my whole life. In the morning, yes, giving myself to God, but then by evening I forget."

She talked about present life in the village. "I'm nervous in Garabandal. I can't enjoy my vacation there. I left early in order to spend more time in Barcelona."

Knowing that of her month's vacation she had only spent ten days in the village, I persisted, "Is it really that bad?"

Crowd that included many visitors outside the village church, 1970 or 71

"Yes."

"Can you be alone in Barcelona?"

"There, nobody knows me."

"Some famous people use fictitious names," I suggested.

"*Oh, en Barcelona, mi no Conchita, mi María.*" There it was again— no predicate. Leaving out verbs and using the objective or possessive case form, "*mi*" instead of "*yo*", the engaging young lady in front of me wouldn't receive a top grade in Spanish class.

"Even the woman I live with doesn't know that I'm Conchita." Sitting at the table with her, I looked forward to telling people that I knew her and had talked with her. How difficult it must be for her to hide the transcendental experience of her life.

"But at times don't you feel you just have to tell her?"

"Nooooh." Her concerned look evolved into a prankish grin and I glowed at her taking me into her confidence by her saying, "The other day in [the big department store] *El Corte Inglés*, a woman recognized me and said, 'Pardon me. Aren't you Conchita Gonzalez of Garabandal?' I stared at her and said I didn't understand, and that she must be mistaken."

I wondered how long she could remain incognito anywhere. Her mother had told me that when somebody recognized her at Lourdes, the people mobbed her. And while studying nursing in Spain's fifth largest urban area, Bilbao, she became so well known that she retreated to Spain's second largest city, Barcelona. With Conchita in a group of beauty queens, would anyone look at the others?

I took another bite of the roast lamb that wasn't as juicy as that at Casa Pepe in Burgos. I recalled aesthetician Doctor Jean Caux's revealing comments:

Having studied thousands of countenances, cut, sewed, and above all, tried to free them from their complexes, my specialty as an esthetician had disposed me to receive the 'shock' of Garabandal. The ecstasies of the four young girls came suddenly, to crown my studies of the mystery of human beauty. It was for me a veritable 'back to the drawing board,' focusing in front of me the primacy of the interior life, dominating and totally freeing the human body of its often unaesthetic expressions."[66]

Conchita with Dr. Caux.

"Eduardo, wouldn't you like to live in Spain and give English classes?"

"No. I'm happy teaching Spanish and living in **Santa Clara**. Santa

---

66 Pérez, *Garabandal el Pueblo*, p.187

Clara is where I'm supposed to live." I pecked at the food. It didn't look bad, but for once in my life, eating seemed unimportant.

Old thoughts competed with new. Why had I become a Spanish teacher? Now I knew, and laughed to myself at the irony of it all. Spanish had been a joke in college where we had to "take" two years of it in order to get a degree in history. Like many students, I didn't learn to speak the language; I just took it like one takes medicine.

One teacher had expounded the weaknesses of progressive education and the evils of eating meat. "But when you eat out, Señor Perotis," we had protested, "how do you avoid offending the hostess by refusing the meat served?"

He looked up over his thick bifocals and answered in all seriousness, "Why that's no problem. Just carry a small jar of honey in your pocket, the pure imported kind, and after each bite of meat you take a small spoonful of honey to counteract the bad effect of the meat in your stomach." He kept us laughing, but no Spanish.

During my first year teaching Spanish in Oroville, Washington, I had laughed at myself many times. You've got to be kidding, I had thought. Me, a Spanish teacher? And the teacher stayed up nights practicing "*buenos días*" and "*hola Isabel*," wondering how long it would take before they found me out.

Not soon, and the second year they appointed me varsity basketball and tennis coach. Now that was more like it. After one season, however, they hired a new coach but said they still appreciated my Spanish teaching. Yeah, they did. That spring the Federal Government accepted me and other bad teachers into a Foreign Language Institute paid for by money appropriated under the National Defense Education Act. The director had even called long distance from San Francisco to test if I spoke poorly enough to qualify. The acceptance letter arrived within days.

Now, sitting at the table, everything made sense. I stared at my half-full plate. Live in Spain and teach English? Maybe teach Conchita English? Not wanting to pass up any openings, I added, "Maybe next year," and explained sabbatical leave possibilities.

"You mean you get a year off with pay? My salary is twelve thousand *pesetas* a month, and that is a lot for Spain. I'm very lucky. Twice a year they give me twenty thousand *pesetas* extra. How much do you earn in the United States?"

Now she will really consider Americans filthy rich, I thought, and avoided the question. Together we calculated her salary in dollars— about one hundred seventy-five per month.

"How long do you work every day?" she asked.

"Five classes of forty minutes each."

"Forty minutes?"

"No. Five times forty minutes." We figured it out together.

"Aye," That's very little."

"No. It's a lot. It's too much, and more time correcting papers, planning, and counseling students."

"Here, eight hours every day. And at times I work at night in order to afford to buy things for my house."

"Ah, Conchita, you're getting like the Americans, thinking about more money and amassing material goods," I kidded.

"No, no. Look, I never buy clothes! Previously, yes."

"I noticed. You always dress elegantly. All Spanish girls do. Is it because they think mainly about attracting a man and getting married?"

"I don't know how to get along with boys."

You've got to be kidding, I thought, and stared at the tall, beautiful girl, bronzed by the Garabandal sun. What do you mean you don't know how to get along with boys? You enchant everyone who sees you. Then I recalled the chair difficulty. What a strange world! All girls should have your problem, Conchita.

"I went to a dance in Barcelona and I was very nervous. I wanted to leave. I like to dance in Garabandal. The city dances aren't healthy. If you dance with another girl they look at you as if . . ."

We were the only ones left at the tables,

but since Conchita seemed content, I didn't suggest leaving. She talked about life in the big cities.

> Last year I met two actors in Madrid . . . I also know an actress in Barcelona. She always invites me to meet the theater people, but I don't want to. I don't like that life. We went out together a number of times. Once at Mass she received Holy Communion without going to Confession. I felt very bad. That offends God a lot. I talked to her about it. She told me that she hadn't committed any sins, but she had, because I knew her life. I read her the Ten Commandments.
>
> People in America are less respectful in church, no? They enter without a *mantilla*. That's not very much trouble. What I like best about America are the Americans. They are very open. But some take too much for granted, take too much liberty, assume your friendship and meddle too much in your personal life . . . Eduardo, you have received many graces.

Hmm. She didn't say I was good, only that I had received graces.

"You have helped me a lot, Conchita—speaking with you."

"And you, me." I hoped she didn't say that just to sound proper. What a long lunch! It was almost six o'clock. Three and a half hours and the food wasn't anything special. She ordered flan with a pastry, and I, ice cream. I asked for coffee and she, hot milk, which she said she has every day. When it came cold she sent it back. She gave me one of her custards.

"Shall we see what time Mass is?" she suggested.

We left the restaurant and walked to St. Nicolas Church with me asking the way.

"I don't like to ask directions and have wandered for hours

San Nicolás Church, Bilbao

trying to find a place," Conchita admitted.

The church houses an eye-catching Pietá sculptured by Juan de Mena in the 16th century. We knelt in front of it. After a while she asked, "Since we can't hear Mass, shall we say the rosary?"

"Sure." If she had suggested a forty-day fast, I would have considered it a great idea.

"You can answer in English if you like. An act of Contrition." She started out in a whisper but got louder and louder. "*Padre nuestro que estás en el cielo ....*" When I faltered on parts of the Our Father she helped immediately.

"*Dios te salve, María . . . .*

"*Santa María, madre de Dios . . . .*

"The Litany of the Blessed Virgin Mary. *Señor, ten piedad.*"

"*Cristo, ten piedad.*"

"*Madre del Creador,*"

"*Ruega por nosotros.*"

"*Madre del Salvador,*"

"*Ruega por nosotros.*" I got lots of practice on the trilled Spanish "*r.*"

"For the Holy Souls in Purgatory, an *Ave María.*"

It was difficult to concentrate on talking to the Lord and his mother. I worried about perspiring too much in the hot church. How many people had Conchita taught to pray? Imagine! Helped with the prayers by a girl whom God's own mother had shown how to pray—someone who had been under the personal tutorship of the Blessed Virgin for four years. Can you believe that?

Back on the street thinking what a privilege to be with Conchita all day, I feared that now she might need to run some errands or just want to ditch me and be alone. To free her to do so, I asked, "Conchita, perhaps you have other things to do like shopping or something?"

"No, nothing."

Fantastic! I would be with her until her train left at 9:00 P.M. "Do you know, Conchita, that after your help, you will have to pray doubly hard for me that I comply with the graces received?"

She smiled. "And you for me also."

"Even last year I was afraid of becoming too proud over talking about Garabandal."

"That's good."

We jumped into a cab to go to the Jesuit Church. "I get turned around easily. Do you have a hard time in a strange city?" she asked.

Mass wasn't until 7:30. I knelt beside her in the ornate church that elicited reverence and piety. We knelt for a long time.

"I'll leave these things (her purse) here. I'm going to confession."

What would she have to confess, that she had wasted a whole day talking to me? People claim that the messages that she writes on holy cards are related to their personal lives. Would she tell me some secret about myself?

Nah! Signs from God, odor of perfume from medals kissed by the Blessed Virgin? Hogwash. She returned to the pew and whispered, "I asked for Communion before Mass." When she walked up to the front to receive Communion, I got up to look around the church and read that in Jesuit churches one can gain a plenary indulgence on the feast or vigil of certain Jesuit saints. Could it be just my luck? How much God gives us!

"Pardon me, Conchita. We can gain a plenary indulgence. Today is the vigil of the feast of a Jesuit saint."

"*Quién, San Ignacio?*"

"No."

"*San Francisco Javier?*"

"No, another."

"How [do we gain the indulgence]?"

"Well, in the ordinary way. Pray for the intentions of the Holy Father."

The Mass started. "*En nombre del Padre, del Hijo y del Espíritu Santo* . . . Today, the 11th of August, is the anniversary of the death of **Santa Clara**. Born in Asís in the year. . . ."

I couldn't help from smiling inside and out, a happy, grateful smile. The beautiful girl at my side turned to me and whispered, "Did you hear that?"

How generous God is with His gifts. I had certainly received more than my share for one day. But God doesn't portion them out stingily like I do. He, to me who has offended him so many times, showers his blessings as if I were his best friend. And I to him give reluctantly and little. Strange relationship! I sniffed the Garabandal relic just in case.

As Mass was ending, Conchita whispered, "Wait here. I'm going for my ticket." Benediction of the Blessed Sacrament followed Mass. It had been so long since I had attended Benediction that for a moment I didn't realize what the priest was doing. Ah, could that be the reason for my present good fortune? Did God remember that every Sunday afternoon when I was nine and ten and older, I had left playing football at Seattle's Lincoln Park to go to church for the rosary and to receive His sacramental blessing? I don't recall what favors I asked for, but it was probably for a new baseball mitt or to make the grade school baseball team, and certainly not that I meet a Spanish girl who had spent much of four years visiting with his mother. God has a good memory!

Conchita didn't return. Should I run to the depot? I still wanted her to check over the transcription of her recorded talk. There wouldn't be time if I waited. Hurrying down the street I wondered about being able to spot her in the train station. Minutes later in the crowded lobby she was the only one I noticed.

"When are you coming to Barcelona?" she asked.

"Oh, in about a week. I'll spend a few days here before going to Madrid. And the transcription of your recording?"

"*Mejor en Barcelona con más tiempo.*" Did I understand her correctly? Was she suggesting that we meet in Barcelona?

"Here. I'll give you my telephone number," she went on. "Write it down. My suitcases are upstairs. We had better go up."

Aye, did that poor girl carry those heavy bags up the stairs? Some help I've been.

"Here." She handed me a caramel. I tossed away the green wrapper and popped the candy into my mouth. Up at the gate, she extended her hand saying, "*Hasta luego,*" and I watched her fade into the flow of hurrying travelers. I descended the stairs, happy.

Down below, I checked all the candy wrappers on the floor looking for a green one. I bet Conchita González didn't buy a caramel for everyone. I went up again to the platform area to catch a last glimpse of her. Eating a piece of bread, she came running toward me, "I'm trying to get a place to sleep." Then she turned, ran after the conductor and jumped onto the train as it pulled out of the station.

I felt sorry for her going off on the train alone at night, arranging for a place to sleep. I stood and watched the train disappear into the night. That conductor would treat her right if he knew who she was. *Hasta luego, Conchita.*

I wandered around the station lobby in no hurry to leave. *"Hola, María. Cómo estás, María?"* It would take some practice not to call her Conchita in Barcelona.

CHAPTER EIGHTEEN

ARÍA

fter seeing Conchita off on the train, I locked myself in a hotel room and wrote for two days—about the eventful day before. I then took the train to Madrid, picked up the problem pants and enjoyed a couple days in Spain's bustling capital before taking the train to the country's second biggest city. In Barcelona, Conchita said she had been waiting for my call.

That evening the owner of the flat led me to the back room where I heard accordion music before seeing Conchita playing it. What a picture: orange pantsuit, yellow scarf, a single strand of pearls and the typical, attractive pierced-ear earrings. She stood up to greet me.

"*Hola María.* Continue playing."

"No, I can't. I just started taking lessons." She obliged and it didn't sound bad. "Do you know anything about cameras? This is new and the flash doesn't work."

"Not about those fancy ones." She handed it to me.

"The housekeeper here, Enrieta, is getting married next month. They don't have money to pay for a professional photographer so they asked me to take pictures. I will have to learn. Try it."

To the surprise of both of us it flashed. I would like to have that nice close up of the noticeably relaxed "María." Women in Spanish cities dress fashionably. The girl in front of me would have to work not to stand out among them.

Who would guess that until just ten years previous, she had spent only a few years in a one room elementary school house, had never seen a movie or television, and had spent her life hidden from the world in the foothills of the Cantabrian Mountains tending cows and sheep?

We decided that she hadn't been pressing the shutter far enough. Practicing, she took a photo of me, and when Enrieta entered, I took one of the two girls before the young housekeeper returned to her chores.

How could she keep from telling people who she was, and how long could she stay unknown when people all over the world were talking about her? "How long do you expect to stay incognito here?"

"I hope for a long time. At Mass the other day with the woman who owns this flat, I saw a Garabandal holy card in her missal. She still doesn't know that I am Conchita."

"At times don't you feel like you just have to tell her?"

"Nooooh. I hope she never finds out." Relaxed and out of sight of (most) admirers, she was even more attractive as "María." I recalled how her mother had described her as somewhat curt with people so they would not idolize her, but at home she was the perfect daughter. How different from many of us.

It seemed strange to hear the *señora* and her housekeeper, Enrieta, call Conchita "María." I pondered how hard it would be not to share the most profound experiences of your life with people close to you. In the days since Bilbao, I had practiced, "*Hola María. How are you, María?*" so I wouldn't give her away.

After an hour or so we got around to the August 7 transcription. She didn't want to correct it, but knew it had to be done.

> Ah! It's horrible! It doesn't make any sense. Should I write a whole new one? I didn't mean this for everyone. I just felt it, so I said it. Now after thinking it over, I'm sorry I did it. Everything is already in the Messages of the Virgen. I don't want people to think about me. I don't want it to be published.

Although she had said, "ok," back in the village, now she worried that readers would focus on her opinion that we can't avoid the Punishment, and would overlook, or minimize, the importance of the Virgin's words that the Punishment was conditioned on whether or not we amended our lives. She made a few corrections before a smiling, sun-tanned girl entered the room. Conchita introduced her, "Eduardo, this is Milagros, my best friend in Barcelona."

"*Hola Eduardo.* María and I were both new in the city and didn't know anybody so we became friends. I'm from Salamanca."

They made their plans for going to the beach the next morning. "Do you want to come with us?" Conchita asked.

I was speechless. I didn't want to spoil her day at the beach—but she invited me, didn't she? "If I decide to come I'll see you outside on the sidewalk at 8:00 A.M. But don't wait for me." I said good-bye and meandered along the promenade of Barcelona's main street, *Las Ramblas,* in the general direction of my hotel.

Las Ramblas

In the morning Conchita and Milagros were waiting when I arrived. We took the subway from *Paseo la Gloria* to *Correos* and then hurried to the train station where I bought three roundtrip tickets to Vilasar. On the train the two well-tanned Spanish girls sat across from me and turned on the music. In such delightful company, the half hour ride passed quickly. When we hopped off at the first Vilasar stop, the fresh salt air filled my lungs.

"Which beach do you prefer, Eduardo?"

"It doesn't matter to me. You choose." Just being there with them made my day. They decided on the nearer beach, a small cove with fishermen at the shore washing out a dozen or so green, blue and red boats. We picked a spot on the uncrowded beach and spread our towels. Although it was still early, Conchita and Milagros spread on suntan lotion.

"Do you want some?" Conchita asked. "Let me put some on your back. The sun will soon be hot." Milagros headed for the water.

"I thought you didn't like the beach, Conchita."

"I didn't. I came yesterday because Milagros didn't have anyone to go with. Yes, I enjoy it now. The sun feels good and I like to be tan. It's good for the body but not for the soul. When I start back to work in September I won't come here anymore."

"How can you like Barcelona with all the noise and people?"

"It's a big city and I can get lost. Although it's crowded, I can be alone. In Garabandal I am nervous and ill at ease all the time."

"Is it that bad?" I pursued.

"Yes." She joined Milagros in the water and called to me, "Are you coming in?"

Milagros and I tried to teach her to swim. "I can't. I can't. I don't know how. I went to the beach for eight days when I was twelve." Yes, during her much publicized stay in Santander, at the invitation, or rather instigation, of the Bishop's Investigating Commission. Its leaders arranged for her to be taken to the beach every day to wash away the apparitions. They also had her hair cut, thinking that perhaps she was casting a spell on her three younger companions with some magic potion hidden in her braids.

I demonstrated the easy dog paddle stroke and the breast stroke while Milagros held her up. She wasn't a good student. Milagros had more patience than I saying, "Just relax, María. It's easy."

Back on the sand we soaked up the Costa Brava portion of the Mediterranean sun. Milagros was a real fish and stayed in the water. I was happy to talk with Conchita again. "Do you remember your father?" I asked.

"Yes, very well. He was like me—tall and dark. He died sixteen years ago."

She tells people that she is from Santander. I wondered if Milagros suspected that her friend was special, someone chosen by God to announce to the world a "worse than the pains of death" divine Warning, and that we would soon be in the end

Conchita, her mother, grandfather, brother, aunt Maximina and Mary Carmen, Maximina's daughter.

214

times. It would be interesting to hear her opinion of María.[67]

Milagros finally gave up swimming and when she joined us, the Spanish guys spotted the extra girl and moved closer.

"Are you hungry, Eduardo?" Conchita asked.

"Sure." At a stand near the road we ordered a salad and *sangria* and then picked out a vacant table underneath a protective awning. Music from a loudspeaker over the food stand roof accompanied us. I never liked rock and roll, even when I was fifteen, but now it sounded just fine.

"Do you prefer *tortilla española* or *bonito*?" Milagros asked.

"I like them both." Potato omelet in "French" bread might seem like plain fare, but that, a salad with olive oil and vinegar, and *sangria* to drink made our meal a banquet. Was it starting to sprinkle? Who cares? I was warm and happy. Milagros distributed the *bocadillos*—two each for Conchita and me and one for herself.

"Are you cold, María?" I asked. "Here take my towel to put over your legs." And to my other companion, "You outdid yourself with these sandwiches, Milagros. They're delicious."

"Thank you."

The music got even better. "I didn't know Marisol sang so well. I thought she was just a pretty face."

"Oh no. She's talented," the girls agreed.

"I want to learn this song. My students would enjoy it."

"It's called '*Maruchi.*' If you have a pretty wife and want to keep her..." the girls modeled the song for me.

What an enjoyable meal! As is common in Spain, we ate the salad from the one big serving platter. The *sangria* was potent and whetted our voices, so we sang for a couple of hours. Conchita knew all of the Mexican songs including the ones sung at the California Cursillo retreats. "Where did you learn that one?" I asked her.

"An American gave me the record."

———————⊃·◆·⊂———————

67 During a subsequent trip, I called on Milagros in Salamanca. No, she had no idea that her good friend was Conchita of Garabandal. She just knew that she was special, that no one she had ever met was anything like her or even close.

"Does it have an orange label on the jacket?" I asked with a knowing grin.

"Yes."

"I think that record was made in my house. My roommate produced it."

"It's one of my favorites. I have lots of records you may borrow if you like."

"Thank you. I am always looking for good songs for my high school Spanish students." I glanced at my watch, not wanting to remind the girls to check the time. Six o'clock. It seemed impossible that the day had passed so quickly. Oh, that we would sit here till morning and begin again. It would be difficult to leave the scene of contentment and peace. But the inevitable happened.

"Shall we leave? There is Mass at 8:00 P.M. at the Iglesia de la Redención," Conchita suggested.

I paid the waiter while the girls gathered up our belongings. The rain had purified the air. Out on the Mediterranean, white sail boats "marched" south in procession towards Barcelona. Reluctantly I crossed the tracks to the train station. When the second class commuter arrived minutes later, we climbed aboard, and then sang our way to the city where we retraced the route back to Conchita's home.

There, Milagros and I waited on a street bench while Conchita went in and changed clothes. As darkness crept over the city, people came out to stroll the avenue, to meet friends, or to sit and drink at one of the outdoor cafes that dotted the promenade from the port to the *Plaza de Cataluña* and beyond. The cafes lined both sides of the avenue, but many of these served the people sitting at outdoor tables. In fact, *Las Ramblas* is one big boulevard of tables, kiosks, flower stands and small shops. I never thought of it before, but one reason the Spaniards look in such good shape is that they walk many kilometers a day—up and down the avenues.

Conchita, quite the vision herself, approached us in a print maxi dress tied at the waist with a white ribbon. "*Caramba*," I said. "How beautiful you look. Where are you going—to a party?"

"No, to Mass. I'll take your beach bags and leave them with the doorman." How thoughtful she was. Those certain of their own value

The author on flower section of Las Ramblas

are best able to attend to the needs of others."

After Mass I ran back down *Las Ramblas* and across the now bustling Plaza de Cataluña to my Continental Hotel. I quickly called to let Regina, a charming, well-educated young lady whom I had met in Garabandal, know that I would be late. When I had called to say "hello" upon arriving here in Spain's second largest and most cosmopolitan city, she had invited me for supper. Now she said that 10:00 P.M. would be fine, that her friend, Lourdes was just setting the table.

I showered and shaved. What a great day. Much of my new suntan was sand, but one layer did remain. I tarried lest the pleasures of this second party push aside the memories of the first. A short taxi ride brought me to the girls' building and the ubiquitous old elevator, to the third floor and their flat.

"Hi. You must be Lourdes."

"Hello Eddy. Regina will be right out. Sherry wine or a mixed drink before dinner?"

"Wine, *por favor.*"   There was no hurry to serve supper during Spanish summers.

Spanish Author, Mercedes Salisachs.

"We have the table set on the balcony but if you think that would be too cold we can move it in here."

"Outside is fine."

Regina soon joined us and, while her friend put the food on the table, filled me in on how the news of the Garabandal apparitions had quickly spread throughout the Region of Cataluña. "After investigating the apparitions," she said, "both an internationally known neurosurgeon and an award-winning Spanish author published

217

Neurosurgeon Doctor Puncernau with Loli, Mari Cruz and most likely his daughter.

articles on the happenings. Also, a local man filmed the 'miracle' of the visible host." Lourdes called us to the table.

"Caramba! You prepared a banquet." What a pleasure it was to dine looking out at nighttime Barcelona in the company of two attractive and attentive Spanish girls.

After dinner, Lourdes brought out a guitar, and it felt good to play for just the second time since school had ended. Both girls had beautiful voices and liked to sing even though the guitar played mostly Mexican songs.

Taxi cabs were still busy at 1:00 A.M. "The Continental Hotel, please. What a great day it has been!"

"Yeah. It's nice to be on vacation," the driver responded. Vacation? I hadn't thought of my experiences as having anything to do with a vacation.

"Good night and thanks." Tired, sleepy and happy, (sounds like some of the Seven Dwarfs) I strolled along *Las Ramblas* trying to prevent the wonderful day from slipping away.

The boy at the hotel desk handed me the key and asked, "Are you interested in an excursion tomorrow: the bullfight, Montserrat, Tibidabo or Flamenco Dancers?"

I grinned. Sir, I thought, I've just spent much of the day with one of the most beautiful and important individuals in the world and you ask me if I want to watch some ugly ladies tap and clap.

After Mass on Sunday I sat outside at a street café thinking of yesterday and of many other happy yesterdays the Garabandal visionaries helped provide these last few years. Until this week, Loli was the one I had known best.

She lacked Conchita's classic features, and standing behind the bar seemed serious and pensive. But when engaged in conversation she came alive, making it a joy to talk with her. Was it because she also sensed the presence of God in a person even though that presence and image might be dimly reflected? She knew that each of us was valuable in God's sight and, therefore, in hers.

As with Conchita, Loli cannot be unaffected by the attention lavished upon her these past ten years; however, both seem unmarred by haughtiness or pride.

Are all of the Garabandal "visionaries" special, extraordinary? Most of the time that I saw Jacinta in the village, she was shoveling cow manure into or out of the family's burro drawn cart. Much of the rest of the time, she either kept out of sight or faded into a group's background making it easy to miss her.

Bishop del Val Gallo ordaining the author's brother-in-law in 1979.

She also worked part time as a housekeeper for the Villar family in Santander, alternating with her younger sister. Carmen would come to work in the city and Jacinta would return to the village to chop wood and slosh the pigs to lighten the load for their elderly father, Simón. The Villar's daughter, Lolita, whom I had met in the village the previous summer, told me, "Jacinta is an angel. She visits the bishop (del Val Gallo) often. Sometimes she goes on her own volition and sometimes he invites her."

During my six months in the city (in 1972), I would see Jacinta at 8:00 P.M. daily Mass in the Cathedral and often afterwards strolling along the popular city sidewalks with her village friend, Alicia. Sometimes we would stop to chat. Jacinta was light-hearted and inclined to kid and joke. When I commented that they were well-dressed Spanish girls, she corrected, "*Somos montañesas*" (We are mountain girls).

One morning after an early Sunday Mass, Mr. and Mrs. Martinez, Jacinta and I sat at an outdoor café having coffee.

Jacinta with the author (later photo)

"Have you ever been in love, Eduardo?" Jacinta asked.

"Yes."

Her eyes sparkled, interested. "True love? The real thing?"

We talked about the meaning of love. Pepín (Mr. Martinez) impressed us saying that the Spanish writer Benevente defines love as, "the pronoun 'you' instead of the pronoun 'I.'"

"I only think about the happiness of those I love and don't care if it means suffering for me," added Jacinta with the nod of approval from the rest of us.

"Isn't she beautiful, such purity," *Señora* Martinez announced. Jacinta paid no attention, but I checked. Yes, she was beautiful, and how happy one feels in her presence. I wished that she would stay longer. Another coffee perhaps? Like with Conchita, this meeting reminded me that the four young Garabandal children had felt the same way when an exceptionally beautiful young lady came to spend time with them. "Don't leave so soon," they had begged. (Years later, Jacinta's husband told me that during one of those visits she learned the long *Litany of Loretto* by heart after hearing the Virgin say it.)

After a special Mass celebrating the first anniversary of his tenure as bishop, Monsignor Antonio de Val Gallo sat in front of the altar to receive all who wanted to congratulate him. I stood a couple of spaces behind Jacinta waiting as the bishop extended his hand to all who greeted him. After Jacinta did so and began to walk away, he recognized her, called her back and held her hand in his. He didn't extend anyone else this special affection.

The youngest of the four girls, Mari Cruz, moved to nearby Asturias two months before my first stay in the village. I saw her only a few times on the balcony of her parents' home or at the dances when she visited the village.

The girls don't run a popularity contest. They don't encourage people to visit Garabandal, and in the village do nothing to call attention to themselves. While I was staying at Mesón Serafín, Conchita's sister-in-law, Paquita, told me that Conchita had confided to her recently that she longed to escape from being "the one who saw the Virgin" and be just another girl.

On Monday morning I paid 2800 pesetas for a Tuesday train ticket to Amsterdam, and thus committed to leave the next day, needed to call and take leave of "just another girl." First I checked at the front desk.

"Any messages for me, Sir?"

"Yes, a Miss María González."

I called immediately but talked only with the *señora*. Conchita returned the call in the afternoon and suggested that if I was free I could come over that evening.

It was dark in the long hallway of her flat.

"*Hola,*" she greeted as I entered the sitting room.

"*Hola María.*"

"You should have been with us yesterday. We went to the bullfights but you didn't call. It was exciting. I got goose pimples (*piel de gallina*)."

After Milagros arrived we sang awhile, and then Conchita played some records for us. When she moved to the music, I told her to dance.

"No. I'm embarrassed. But when I'm alone I always dance. I can't listen to music without wanting to dance. . . . Let's go down to the street before the *señora* comes in. She will talk our ears off."

Elevators in old Spanish buildings are strange contraptions. This one, like many, only carries people up, so we walked down three flights of stairs to the street where we picked a table close to a café so the waiter wouldn't have to walk far to serve us.

"It's nice out here so I come down every evening between seven and nine."

"María, why don't you come to Salamanca and visit me?"

I tried to second the invitation, "Yes, they speak beautiful Spanish there. Does that invitation include me, Milagros? My Spanish would improve. My students will have an awful time when I return with: '*Cuando mí en Barcelona*' and '*Vino donde mí.*' They are going to learn all sorts of bad grammar." I continued feigning Conchita's bad Spanish with, "*Cuando mí en España conocí a esta chica que decía cosas como 'donde mí'*" [68]

Was Conchita attempting to help English speakers understand her by leaving out some verbs and using the objective case or possessive pronoun because they sound the same as the English, "me"? She took the kidding good-naturedly and joined in the laughter. Watching both of them, brown from the sun, now framed by their white dresses, I flattered, *"Que chicas más guapas!"*

"You never told me that I was pretty before Milagros came along."

Not long later, Conchita said she had an appointment and added, "You two continue without me. Leave your papers with me [at her place] so you won't have to go up and get them now. You can pick them up in the morning. See you tomorrow."

We watched her cross the street and enter the dark building. "Where would you like to eat, Milagros?"

The next morning I picked up my things and said good-bye to Conchita. After Mass in the Barcelona cathedral, determined to understand the negative position of the present Santander Bishop

Barcelona Cathedral

(José María Cirarda) on Garabandal, I entered the sacristy and introduced myself to a priest who had just delivered an inspiring homily on the Assumption.

"Hello. I'm from the United States and I'm interested in the reported apparitions at Garabandal."

"False. It was all a matter of hysteria."

The sacristan piped in, "Those girls are crazy."

---

68 "When me in Spain, I met this girl who would say things like, 'where me. . . .' "

222

Conchita with burro

CHAPTER NINETEEN

he big, modern ALSA bus rounded the last turns down from Labarces past Bielva then turned south at Puente de Arudo (eleven kilometers from the Atlantic Ocean) onto the recently improved, wide two-lane road that follows the Nansa River up from the coast. It runs four times that far to Polaciones but I would get off at the half way mark—Puentenansa. Small villages hang onto the hillside across the river. On this beautiful late afternoon in March, 2012, with the snow-covered Peña Sagra Ridge to the west towering 6,000 feet above sea level, with cows grazing on the spring grass on the nearer hillsides, the sun falling behind the mountains, I felt happy to be returning to Puentenansa, Cosío and "my village"— Garabandal.

Some fifteen miles to the west is the monastery of Santo Toribio, where the Christians, fleeing the Moors invading from the south, brought their relics, including the largest known portion of the true cross. An hour's drive west along the Cares River brings us to Covadonga where thirteen hundred years ago, Pelayo started the long Christian re-conquest of the Iberian Peninsula.

Santo Toribio Monastery

High up on the slopes of the western side of the Peña Sagra, five years before the discovery of America, the Blessed Virgin (*Nuestra*

Señora de la Luz) appeared to a young girl tending her sheep. Five miles into the mountains in the opposite direction visitors marvel at a recently discovered modern "wonder of the world" — the Caves of *el Soplao*.

Iglesia de San Martín, Aniezo, near Our Lady of Light hermitage.

The bus breezed through Celis (population 235), a picturesque village that won the National Prize for Embellishment in 1983, and in minutes crossed the bridge at the entrance to the town named after it, Puentenansa (Nansa [River] Bridge), the commercial and financial center for the seventeen villages of the Municipality of Rionansa. On my first visit forty three years ago, the old bus coming from the coast had stopped here to rest and take on water. This bus stopped only minutes to pick up medicine at the pharmacy to be delivered further up the valley, and to drop off three passengers.

In the early 1970's, after spending the night in a Puentenansa guesthouse, I would walk carrying a backpack and a small suitcase the mile and a half to Cosío and then hike three miles more up into the mountains following a wide burro path. For this 2012 six weeks' visit, a Puentenansa taxi carried me and a big suitcase filled with laptop, books, clothes and supplies over the same route.

Day-old calves and colts stuck close to their mothers in the fertile green fields bordering the Nansa River. In minutes we covered the kilometers through the narrow valley before turning right and through Cosío that sported new streetlights and sidewalks. We then sped up the widened "highway" to Garabandal.

Hundreds of years ago, men from the villages along the Nansa River followed this same route to graze cows in the mountains to the west of Cosío. They camped on a hillside above the spot where the Sebrando flows into the Vendul and eventually established a hamlet there— Garabandal. Later, likely seeking better farm land and access to a better water supply, they moved to settle on the plain (between the two rivers) that juts out below the eastern end of the ridge that runs perpendicular to the Peña Sagra. They named the new settlement San Sebastián. On today's maps it is San Sebastián de Garabandal (San Sebastian in the area of Garabandal) which distinguishes it from the big city of San Sebastián close to the French border.

"*La gallinera, por favor,*" I indicated, and the driver drove through the village streets to the humble hut that I have called home during my last seven or eight visits. The locals call it *la gallinera* because stonemason, Pepe, tore down an old chicken coup to make room for a small duplex. It sports no coat of arms as some of the older homes do. The earliest one on a village building displays the date 1687. Others say 1713, 1720 and 1723.

Since 1961 people have wondered, and offered reasons, why God might choose such an out-of-the-way hamlet for his important mission, a place named for the ubiquitous *garaba* bush that the men burn so the grass will grow.

Bishop Equino y Trecu, of whom there are statues inscribed *El Obispo Bueno* inside and outside the cathedral, administered the Diocese of Santander for thirty years until his death on May 7, 1961. When the apparitions started just weeks later, people speculated that their beloved, saintly bishop might have proposed his favorite village as a proper site for God's end times work.

According to the locals, during Spain's horrible civil war (1936-1939), in which ten percent of the people perished, Garabandal villagers hid priests in the hills and cared for them. The first piece of bread out of the oven was for the priests. While the customary stipend for a Mass at that time was one *peseta*, here they gave three.

Bishop Eguino's statue outside the Santander Catheral.

When they didn't have anything to eat, people from nearby villages went to *el sindicato* in Puentenansa for food. In order to punish them for being so outwardly religious, the socialists, who controlled the area, would make those from Garabandal wait till last, and go without if the food ran out.

Kelly's landlady Clementina González

It was late evening by the time I settled in. No inside heat on my side of the duplex except for a fireplace, and I had to walk outside the bedroom (the only room besides the bathroom) to enter the tiny kitchen. I tried the small, ancient refrigerator. It worked, so this year I wouldn't have to walk a hundred feet to retrieve my food stored in landlady Tina's kitchen. A pain yes, but visiting daily I had gotten to know better one of the five eyewitnesses of the first public ecstasy, and hear her relate what she had lived through during the apparitions. I unpacked my suitcase and stored my belongings. It felt good to be home.

Interior of the one room duplex (where the author lived during his last seven or eight stays in the village)

With lots of snow on the Peña Sagra ridge towering 4500 feet above the village and the wind sweeping down the mountain, it would be cold, so I bundled up with a scarf and hooded jacket before going out.

The choir directress headed for the temporary church. "Sure,

Cristina, I will sing with the group again."

"Practice for Holy Week services begins tonight at 9:00," she yelled back.

The author at choir practice for Easter Sunday

Francisco, David and five women were already warming up when I arrived and sat down on the bench. We practiced:

Siempre que digo Madre. . .

Whenever I say, "Mother,"
I find myself saying your name.
I am accustomed to fall asleep
With your name on my lips.

Viva la Virgen nuestra Patrona. . .

Long live the Virgin, our Patron
Who has her altar in our church,
And may Christ reign triumphantly
In our noble and faithful land.

*Kelly as lector at Mass in the
village church*

229

David Toribio Gonzalez working at his doorway at entrance to village

I whispered to David sitting next to me, "*Son bonitas estas canciones.*" (These are beautiful hymns.) How long have you been singing them?"

"*Desde hace más de 200 años.*" (For more than two hundred years). Tears dropped onto my song sheet as I struggled to sing with the others whose grandparents and great grandparents had sung, "We will always be your faithful children. Let us see the light of your (beautiful) eyes." I gave up attempting to sing while wondering if anyone here had ever imagined that God would answer their persistent prayers by choosing four of their village daughters to visit with his mother and gaze at her beautiful eyes as she spoke with them and smiled down at them day after day.

The next day, Holy Saturday, I strolled through the village to see who had died and what else had changed since my last visit two years

From the left: José Mari, Kelly, Tomás, Quico and Taquio (2012)

previous. Since Lino, José Mari, Taquio, Carmina, Regina, Mercedes, and the others all knew Eduardo, the Spanish-speaking American who sang in their church choir, lectured at Mass and hung out talking with them, I rehearsed their names as I walked.

While the religious customs haven't changed in forty years, the village has. A few doors from my own, AMALIA in big black letters announces a modern, three story guesthouse where the proprietors rent a dozen rooms and serve three meals a day. Amalia's sister Sari and husband own a fifty room hotel with full restaurant and bar. To spend the night here in 1970, you looked for a house with a vacant bedroom.

A few doors further down the lane, laborers worked finishing a scaffold to the roof of a house facing the main square. Marcelino, one of Pepe Diez' three sons of the Hermanos Diez Gonzalez Construction Company, yelled down, "*Hola Eduardo*," but didn't stop fitting and cementing-

The small sign says, "en vente (for sale)."

in whitish rocks on the side of the new house. Many homes now exhibit the same attractive stones. If you walk slowly and observe carefully, you might find three or four old buildings made out of rocks pasted together with patches of cement.

On the western end of the village near the start of the lane to the Pines, Paquita watered plants on the porch of "Mesón Serafín". That guest house (now closed) and the Sevillian's castle next to it were the two first "modern" residences. In the early 1970's they stood out among the village's centuries-old rows of buildings, but now they show their age compared to the Vega Hotel, a fourteen-unit condominium and new private homes.

Author distracting Paquita from work

Paquita, in whose guest house I had stayed, and taught her English in 1971, is one of some fifty whom the locals refer to as "*vecinos*" (neighbors), those who were born in the village. Most of these, some of whom now spend the winter months outside the village, are more than seventy years old. Even before the apparitions, the young people in the whole area moved out of the villages to seek easier and better paying jobs in the cities.

Many young men left to seek their fortune in Mexico.

After saying "*hola*" to my former student, I started up the rocky lane towards the cluster of pines a hundred and fifty yards up the mountain. Now, Stations of the Cross, encased in glass and cemented in rocks, line the route. Besides these, the only "apparition site" additions include: a Quonset hut style chapel in honor of St. Michael, a metal bell shaped memorial commemorating the apparitions, markings for the sites of the first apparition of the angel and of the Virgin, and the twenty mysteries of the rosary covered with glass, encased in billboard—like green frames that zigzag a kilometer up the mountain.

I have hiked many miles through the Garabandal fields and up and down the surrounding hills and mountains and even walked the pilgrim route to Santiago de Compostela, but not many walks are as challenging as this climb to the Pines. The witnesses to the ecstasies were all out of breath following the visionaries who "flew" up the lane before kneeling to pray at the Pines. After reaching the top, to catch my breath, I stood for a minute facing the nine old trees before walking to the edge of the cliff to look down at the village.

The church has been shored up at least once in my time and was then rebuilt in 2012. The Diocese approving the spending of over a third of a million Euros on a church in a little village lost in the mountains, the bishop conducting the inaugural ceremony, and the village pastor routinely including public prayers to Our Lady of Garabandal, testify that local Catholic Church officials now finally look favorably upon the apparitions.

Dr. Andrés Tuñón

In May, 2007, taking a long break from mowing the big lawn in front of his house in the village, retired kidney specialist, Doctor Andrés Tuñón told me: "While sitting on the corner of the bed visiting the bishop after I had operated on him, he said, 'I, Antonio del Val Gallo, believe in the supernatural origin of the Garabandal happenings, but as bishop I can't say that.'"

It has been a long, fascinating journey for me since first hearing, "We don't know whether it was due to God or the devil, but something unexplainable happened up there." Many eyewitnesses now say,

"Garabandal es muy serio." (Garabandal is very serious).

I thought of Conchita years ago at twenty-two sitting across from me in Bilbao's Restaurante Mesina knowing that she had never offended God seriously. Despite that innocence however, the Virgin had told her in 1965 that she couldn't go to heaven yet because her hands were empty of good works.

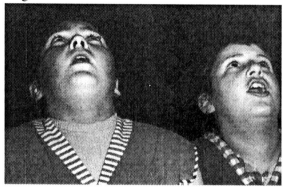

Loli and Jacinta relayed from the Virgin in 1962 that "few will see God." How can I be among them? I will love my neighbor by redoubling the effort to tell all who will listen, that God warned us over fifty years ago to be good or a great punishment would fall upon us—greater than that which reigned down on Sodom and Gomorrah.

The fog started to roll in chasing away the warm sun. Without a hiking stick and feeling more apprehensive descending than ascending, I stepped cautiously onto the flat rocks and between the jagged ones while walking back down the steep lane.

In front of his big, corner house, David sat sanding an axe handle. He returned my *"buenos días"* with his customary, *"Hola Edu."* In his mid 70's, he is one of only two village men of his generation who still work.

Thoughtful and reflective, his conversation topics, as well as his manner of expressing them, betray his "outside of the village" education. Years ago he confided that as a young man hiking (miles) through the hills, to and from the fields, he often conversed with the Lord.

During my 2010 stay we drove in his old Land Rover to visit the awesome Soplao Caves (*Cuevas de Soplao*) and afterward, at an area restaurant, enjoyed my favorite Spanish dish, roast goat. While we talked, he said that now when hiking the hills, he thinks of nothing but the happy times of the apparitions. "See you at choir tonight, David."

A modest home cooked meal followed by a siesta before the long Easter vigil services would be enough activity for one day, especially since, for the first time in fourteen stays, there was a tiny TV set in my bedroom.

For some in the village, Easter Morning starts early—when it is still night in the Cantabrian Mountains. I would try to wake up for my first Rosary at Dawn (*Rosario de Aurora*) and to make sure, I asked

The patio separating the two units of the duplex

Fátima to knock at my door in the morning on her way to the church.

The small duplex in which the author lived during his last six or seven visits.

I was already awake when I heard the clonking of wooden *albarcas* on the cement walkway outside my one room home. While dressing I heard, "*Eduardo.*" It sounded like Paquita rather than her youngest daughter. While people gathered shivering in front of the church, I asked eighty year old Tina, how long they had practiced this custom. "They were doing it at the time of our grandparents."

Five women, all about the age of the visionaries, led the procession. We walked past the old school house, past the clothes washing basin, and turned left onto the narrow cement roadway passing my duplex. I stood to the side and counted some forty villagers plus a few outsiders. We continued along past the house of the two octogenarian sisters, Clara and Milagros, while praying,"*Dios te salve María. Llena eres de gracias."* Street lights helped light the way.

Fifty years earlier the visionaries, walking through the village in ecstasy with their heads craned back and gazing into the sky, chanted the same, *"Dios te salve María. . . ."* while people, walking without street lights back in 1961 and 1962, stumbled along following them.

When God was "deciding" on a place for his mother's visit to announce the end times, he knew that those here were prepared to welcome her; for as long as anyone could remember, they had chanted the Virgin's praises along these same paths.

We turned left and headed toward the town square, veered right, past the dirt dance and bowling area, but then to my surprise, stopped in front of Conchita's vacant house, where we remained in silence for some time. Were Pili, María Jesús, Laura and the others expressing gratitude to God for his having chosen one of their playmates to announce to the world the beginning of the end times with its worldwide Warning and greatest Miracle in history?

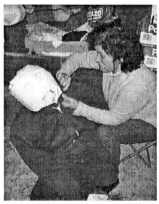

After the rosary, Laura, Paquita, Fatima, and a couple others gathered below the living quarters of a house. They invited me in. Magdalena had almost finished sewing up a stuffed effigy of Judas by the time Paquita returned with steaming hot chocolate. We talked about not wanting (or having) to go to a rest home and how much it would cost.

Magdalena sewing an effigy of Judas

Author, 1970

I wasn't quite ready for a rest home yet, but I had changed in the forty-three years since my first trip to Spain. After the eventful summer of 1971, I returned the next August on an unpaid year's leave of absence from my high school Spanish teaching position, planning to spend the first five of the fifteen free months in the Garabandal area and in the capital city, Santander, and then to return home and give lectures on the most important events in two thousand years.

On my first "looking for adventures" visit to

Spain, meeting girls had been high on the list. They would like me: I was American, spoke their language better than most foreigners, was Catholic, and had a permanent professional job. They weren't impressed.

In October 1972, I sent a postcard to Señor Gutierrez' daughter Manoli, with whom I had talked a few minutes the previous year when she had invited me to have a Rum and coke in her family's flat. She answered. A month later, living in a Santander guest house, I sat up in bed and said to myself, "I'm in love with that girl. I want to marry her."

I wanted to see her all the time but knew that 1972 Spanish customs suggested letting relationships develop slowly. When I called once a week to ask the girl of my dreams out, she would say, "My mother wants to know if you would like to come to dinner Sunday."

"Sure", and after dinner we (not the mother) would walk to a Santander bar and restaurant with the appropriate atmosphere where I helped Manoli with Algebra lessons.

On Christmas Eve while walking miles over snow to a church outside the city, she managed to put her older sister between us most of the way. Yes, Feli knew a lot about the Basques and Spanish politics, but I was in love with her younger sister. Surprise! When saying goodnight outside the elevator on the ground floor of their building, Manoli brushed her lips over mine. For the first time I felt like more than an algebra tutor away from home in need of an invitation to dinner by a charitable mother.

Kelly with father-in-law on wedding day.

Asking parents' permission to marry a daughter is challenging enough without having to do it in a second language. While I stewed over this, Manoli said that her mother already knew and that she liked me. Now if I could just find the proper words to get started after Sunday's dinner. "Señor Gutierrez, may I marry your daughter and take her away to live in America?"

We got married in April.

Conchita's brother Serafín served as best man. We have three children and eight grandchildren.

Now here I was back in the village once again. Fourteen trips to Spain, starting back in 1969, to spend a total of some four years in this area? Yes, attempting to talk with all who would speak to me about what they had seen and heard and felt during the apparitions.

The bride's two brothers, now Salesian priests, are the last and third to last on the end. The best man, Serafín is seated in the middle.

After a late Easter Sunday Mass and burning Judas in effigy, I stopped at the bar opposite the church for a loaf of fresh bread. Forty years ago, dinner had to wait for Josefa and her burro to fetch the fresh bread five miles away in Puentenansa.

I headed for the restaurant and bar run by Loli's sister Sari, her husband, Juaquín and their three young adult children. Mari Cruz' old house was on the left separated from Sari's establishment by the road leading to the cemetery.

Mari Cruz married Ignacio Caballero in May 1970 and moved to Avilés on the coast seventy-five miles west of Garabandal. They have two boys and two girls. She saw the Virgin less than any of the others did, and as far as is known, has never retracted her statements to the Santander bishop on June 24, 1965 about being unsure if she had seen the Virgin.

She told Father Retenaga that people didn't love her the way they did the other girls because the Virgin didn't visit her as much as she did them. But she loved the Virgin the same.

Villager David Toribio Gonzalez reported to Tom Windfelder in a 2011 taped interview, that a shepherd walking through the hills outside the village had come across Mari Cruz alone in ecstasy. David surmised that the Blessed Virgin showed this consideration for her child by appearing to her privately because her parents at times wouldn't let her go with the other visionaries.

I entered the bar. A young couple speaking Spanish sat at the far end. The forty-or-so American pilgrims were already inside eating "dinner" (at 1:30 P.M.). The owners' son, my friend Allen, stood behind the bar and greeted me with his inviting, "*Hola Eduardo.*" He is an avid, accomplished fisherman and sports enthusiast with whom it is a pleasure to talk. He is American, having been born while his mother was in Massachusetts visiting her sister Loli, and expresses his opinions on the pros and cons of our two societies. He also listens and learns. He wasn't a conscientious student in the English class that his mother talked me into offering twelve years previous during my fifteen month stay in the region.

Yes, he said that I could eat in the restaurant but would have to wait an hour to be served. The forty Americans in María Sarraco's group, other visitors plus a number of the elderly villagers dining out with their visiting children and grandchildren would keep Sari, her two daughters and a couple of others hopping while cooking, serving and washing dishes. I would wait.

I told Allen to give me a *blanco* and recalled his Aunt Loli serving behind the bar in the early 70"s. She had also made me feel welcome. Allen busied himself on the computer and I took my glass of white wine to the small TV room to be alone with my thoughts.

Mari Loli moved to Massachusetts in 1972 where she married Francis LaFleur two years later. She lived with her family there and died on April 20, 2009. She is survived by her husband, a son, and two daughters.

Loli was the only "visionary" I met on my first chance visit to her  village on July 2, 1969 when she was waiting on table in her family home, bar, small store and restaurant. In photos of her around the time of the first apparitions shortly after her twelfth birthday, you would see a plump faced seven or eight year old rather than a soon to be teenager. The villagers said  that while in an ecstatic trance, she was beautiful, that she looked like an angel.

But the important transformation took longer and more effort—Loli's. She had to learn to obey her parents immediately, not to criticize her father when he told her to stand behind the bar for hours waiting on customers she couldn't understand, and to love and serve God by faith alone when his mother no longer appeared to her.

All of us suffer. Without it, it is impossible to become a saint. Few are told ahead of time—like Loli was, that they will suffer their whole lives. At the time of the ecstasies she heard her father talk with village men and others, doubting that she saw the Virgin, doubting that his daughter was telling the truth—or worse—that she might not be of sound mind.

She reported, "The Virgin has made me know when a priest is in sin. . . . She has helped me to know that he needs many prayers and sacrifices. Also, she has given me to understand the Crucifixion in the Holy Mass. I comprehend the humility, his (Jesus') sacrifice for the world. I spoke with the Virgin in a locution and asked her to give me a cross to suffer for priests." The Virgin told her at that time that she was not going to die soon that, "No. You have to remain in the world to suffer. In whatever place you will be, you will suffer." Loli did so, suffering with Lupus for many years and with pulmonary fibrosis for the last two years.[69]

It is not easy to die. Loli compared the horrifying Warning to it saying that we would rather experience the pains of death. On my own awful judgment day I will plead, "Lord, there's this friend of yours in there. You know, Loli, the Spanish girl who divides morning from afternoon by when she eats rather than by the clock. I'm a friend of hers, a foreign language teacher. May I come in and teach her English?"

Having connections might help, but there is a better way, as those, many of whom had driven all the way across Spain, were told (and disappointed to hear) on that stormy October 18, 1961, "We must make many sacrifices, do much penance, visit the Blessed Sacrament frequently, but first we must be very good."

The beautiful lady whom Loli came to call, "my mother and my best friend," who visited often, let the child hold her baby, and instructed her praying, "Santa María, . . . pray for us sinners now and at the hour of our death," would certainly hear this prayer of her favored child and have

---

69 www.garabandal.org/vigil/Vigil_1984.shtml

been near at the hour of her death.

The stools at the bar were filling up with the Americans. I paid Allen for the drink and kidded him saying that if he had worked harder in our English class, he could now expect bigger tips speaking to our countrymen in their own language. Yes, now there were empty seats in the restaurant.

At almost 3:00 P.M. I was more than ready for the meal: a colorful lettuce, tomato, and onion salad with olive oil; a thin but tasty steak; french fries; all the wine and fresh bread I wanted; and a choice of fresh fruit, pastry or ice cream for dessert. With the noise abating, I ate slowly and in peace. When taking away my dinner plate, the waitress said, "Your meal is paid for," and nodded to the couple sitting a few tables away.

The grey haired man there had left Spain to seek his fortune in the hotel business in Mexico. He lives in a suite in Santander but also owns a big, attractive stone residence in Garabandal. He was eating Easter dinner in the village's fanciest restaurant with his veterinarian daughter, Lorena. Cencio Cosío, who had stopped late at night forty years previous to pick up this stranger walking up the mountain road, was as thoughtful and generous as ever.

Out at the bar Allen was again busy, serving coffee and after dinner drinks to the partying locals and dollar spending foreigners. These pilgrims were here for only a few days while my dollars had to stretch for more than two months, so I left to get a free, more refreshing drink—the water flowing from the fountain across from Conchita's house.

The story-and-a-half building has been vacant since her mother died, and is now a mini museum with photos of Conchita and her family on the walls. A lady in the village has the key and shows the house to visitors. The cost now to buy the large beautiful field across the lane that sold for $3,500 in 1968? Well over $100,000 even with the dollar at a ten year high against the euro. Owners are almost giving away land in other Spanish villages, but not in Garabandal.

In the spring after I said good-bye in Barcelona, Conchita moved from Spain's second largest city to America's largest, New York, where she lived with Doctor Jerome Dominguez and his wife and worked as a practical nurse. On May 26, 1973, a month after I married a Spanish girl, Conchita married an American, Patrick Keena (RIP Oct. 31, 2013).

They have three daughters and a son. Conchita lives on Long Island, New York.

Even though she did it with heroic patience, style, and grace, speaking to visitors was not Conchita's favorite pastime. She told me in August 1971, "I can't have a vacation here," and left her brother and his young family and her widowed mother, after just ten days of her month's vacation, to return to anonymity in big Barcelona.

In the 1980 BBC documentary, *Garabandal After the Visions*, a very concerned Conchita says that she never thought any man would love her for who she was, thinking that men's only interest in her was that she was the girl who saw the Blessed Mother. In answer to the question, "What does your husband think about the apparitions, she answers, "I don't know. He never asks me." She then breaks into a captivating smile adding, "That's why I love him so much."

I feel certain that one reason she put up with me for a couple of days in August, 1971 was that I never asked her about the apparitions. As soon as you come near her, you feel good, special, accepted for who you are. And she knows who you are, a royal prince or princess, the son or daughter of a king, the king of kings. She treats you like royalty and you want to act that way in return.

Will Conchita be a saint? Father Laffineur said to me in 1970 that when he had told her that one day she would have the stigmata she answered, "Good, then I will know that God loves me." From better informed sources than Laffineur, on December 8, 1963 the Virgin told Conchita, "Although you will not be happy on earth, you will be happy in Heaven." Jesus told her in a locution on February 13, 1966, "I want to tell you, Conchita, that before the Miracle occurs, you will suffer much. . . .I am the one who wants all this, as I have already told you, for your sanctification."

Across from her house, a wide path leads out of the southeastern edge of the village to the fields and winter barns. It soon turns into a graded (in 2007-2008) road that separates after a mile. The right-hand branch wanders into the hills, and that to the left dips down to cross the Vendul River, zigzags up the mountain and then back down the other side to connect with the Nansa River Valley Road at La Lastra.

I had hiked both those routes many times but not today. Villagers gather in the church earlier on Sunday for the rosary and after that it would be time for me to think about supper. Chicken soup, fresh bread, wine and a couple of landlady Tina's homemade oatmeal cookies would all be dessert after the day's feasting on forty years of fond memories. While walking back through the village toward the church, I thought of the events foretold here for the future—a worldwide warning, a great miracle, a permanent sign.

Which one in this row of four residences was Jacinta's family home? Was it the first or the second? I had eaten dinner there once. Her house is still as inconspicuous as she was in the early 70's.

Jacinta and Jeff Moynihan were married here in 1976 and shortly afterward moved to California where they still live with their daughter, María. During her summer visits to Garabandal, Jacinta spends time sitting in front of the houses talking with the village women. I have never heard them say a word about apparitions.

My Spanish wife, our children and I stopped once to say hello to the Moynihan family at their California home. The two young mothers, having grown up tending cows on different sides of the Peña Sagra mountain ridge and just a year apart in age, had plenty to talk about. There was no mention of apparitions.

On June 18, 2011, Jacinta told *Diario Montañés* reporter, Nieves Bolado, "[Then] I was a child and I thought that [the Virgin coming to visit her] happened to all children."[70] She didn't consider herself special, never acted as if she were, stayed mostly out of sight, and for that reason is not mentioned more in this report.

Why those four girls? When the villagers were asked, informally by many visitors, and formally as recorded by Perez, if there was anything special about the visionaries before June 18, 1961, the answer was a unanimous "no," that they were like all the other little girls in the area. I disagree. God had his choice of anyone he wanted to help prepare his people for the end times. He chose the best. He always does. Their response to God's call in 1961 seemed similar to that of their visitor at the Annunciation—"Here we are, Lord. What do you want of us?"

While nearing the church I thought about the lessons about faith

---

70 www.eldiariomontañés.es/v/20110618/cantabria/pude-soportar-intensa-mirada-20110618.html

learned here. All of the villagers and visitors witnessed and heard the same thing. Few seem certain about the origin of the events or their importance. Faith is a supernatural gift. It is natural not to believe.

Mari Cruz' mother, Pilar, told Luis Nava, "I believe my daughter when she says that she sees the Virgin; but I'm not sure that she actually does see the Virgin."

In September of 1963, Jacinta's mother told Father Laffineur: "I certainly believe when I see an ecstasy; when the ecstasy is over, I don't believe anymore."[71]

Loli's father, Ceferino, didn't know if his daughter was seeing the Virgin. Dr. Ricardo Puncernau relates what Ceferino told him about his doubts:

> It was during the winter. There were no visitors in the village. There was a light snowstorm and it was freezing cold. About three in the morning I heard Mari Loli get up and get dressed.
>
> "Where are you going now?
>
> "The Virgin called me to the Cuadro."
>
> "You are crazy, being cold as it is."
>
> "The Virgin called me to the Cuadro. "
>
> "To see if a wolf will leap on you... Do what you want... But your mother and I won't come with you."
>
> Mari Loli finished dressing, opened the door of the house and went to the Cuadro, about 100 meters away. If I had been sure it was the Virgin, I wouldn't have left my bed ... The Virgin would have taken care of her ... But since we weren't sure, my wife and I got up and made our way to the Cuadro.
>
> We found her in the middle of a snowstorm, on her knees in a trance. It was hellish cold.
>
> Expecting to find her frozen, I chafed her cheeks. They were warm, as if she had never left the covers of her bed. [72]

⊃•◆•⊂

71 Eusebio Garcia de Pesquera, O.F.M., *She Went in Haste to the Mountain* (New York: The Workers of Our Lady of Mount Carmel, 2003), p. 430. (Published in Spain under the title *Se Fue Con Prisas a la Montaña* 1972 and 1979).
72   I bid., p. 350

I entered the little church and knelt down. What will this place be like after the events foretold by the four girls are fulfilled? They say that soon, everyone in the world will suffer a horrifying warning that will purify and prepare us for the greatest miracle in history. And then if we don't amend our lives, God will send a punishment worse than that reigned down on Sodom and Gomorrah.

It is understandable that Pilar, Simón and Cefereno, knowing the scarce formation of their young daughters, wondered how they could talk about prophecies of an eschatological nature of transcendental importance for the world, and at times even doubted that they saw the Blessed Virgin.

I am certain, and grateful, that in this time of great need, God has answered our prayer begging him to:

> Raise your hand against the heathen
> That they may realize your power. (Sirach 36 : 2).

> Give new signs and work new wonders;
> Show forth the splendor of your
> right hand and arm. (Sirach 36: 5).

"Lord, your mercy is my hope. My heart rejoices in your saving power. I will sing to the Lord for his goodness to me." And my happy heart sang out once again for God's goodness to me: my life, my faith, family, good health, and for having allowed me forty-three years ago to stumble upon this little place of happiness and hope.

Thank you, Lord for the old-age reminders that I have little time left to love and serve you. Consider this work as done for your honor and glory. May it help others sing out in thanksgiving to you for your great mercy. May my hands not be found empty on judgment day.

Matilda (with apron) and Olguita in the village c. 1962

*Father de la Riva and Ben Gómez
in front of Conchita's house*

RETURN VISIT IN 2017

t has been forty-eight years since I first traveled to Spain. After wandering and wondering if trying to find San Sebastián de Garabandal was worth the effort, I spent only two hours in the little hamlet in July of 1969. Everything looked poor and old.

The next summer the Llorente family "castle" at the foot of the rocky lane leading to the Pines stood out as the only new building in town. My housemother, Josefa, fed men working on a new place, and the next year I spent six weeks in it — Mesón Serafín. I froze even with the fireplace lit and pulled blankets up over my head trying to get warm in bed during the coldest days. My small Olivetti portable typewriter kept me company, but preferred to sleep rather than wear itself out attempting to guess the correct letter when cold fingers hit two keys at a time.

When Ben Gómez invited me to his home in Pesués, I spent a night with no indoor plumbing. Ben showed me what to do. For later visits I found places with moveable butane heaters and finally in 2012, central heat.

Visitors will now see a small village full of new houses. Many of the old ones have been torn down and replaced by impressive new stone buildings, and most of the others have been rebuilt inside and out. In March, an acquaintance said, "The highest per square meter price for property in Cantabria is Garabandal."

Luxurious new stone house behind Conchita's

Outsiders from Spain and abroad have purchased

Village entrance. Sign for Posada San Miguel in the background

The author lived in the section on the right in the 70's.

Kelly stayed in the house on the right for eight months in 1999-2000 and in the small, white addition on an earlier stay.

A rebuilt house with a Jaguar in front owned by one of a number of villagers who made money in Mexico.

Old (barn) and New (condo) on path out of the village

The "Castle" and the old and new Mesón Serafín

*Comfortable fourteen unit condo a two minute walk
from the village center*

Large building under construction: May, 2017

Road construction Puentenansa to Cosío, 2008

Fields to the south of the village

property driving prices up. Villagers have also been able to make improvements to their homes by selling plots of land. A couple of locals mentioned a moratorium on new buildings.

A few old houses remain. During this last visit, I took photos of those I had stayed in over the years. They won't be there long. Some are more primitive inside than out, with the walls blackened by smoke and soot from years of open fires in the kitchen. On an early visit I stayed in an "electrician's nightmare" with the wiring outside the walls.

The town's first guest house is now closed, but San Miguel, Amalia, Lucia, the fifty room hotel Vega, and two multi-unit condominiums have replaced it. Visitors reserve rooms on line.

In 1969 the only lines in the village were clothes lines. One home phone served the whole village, and I used it as late as 1988. For room reservations you showed up and hoped to find a vacant room in a home in

One of the few remaining unimproved houses

which a son or daughter had moved out. The cost? Mine was $2 a day for full room and board. This summer I paid 35 Euros for a room and about 10€ for a meal. The dollar at a ten year high against the euro (1€= $1.06) mitigated the price increase for the twenty-five day April 2017 stay in my favorite village.

In 1969 children filled the two-room school house, and ran playing through the dirt streets. You see very few children today, and the increase in the ages of the villagers has almost kept pace with inflation. Milagros, who spends much time outside the village, and José Mari will both be ninety-nine in December; Juan José turned ninety-eight in April; Lino

José Mari and Quico

José Mari and Quico resting

Lino outside his door

Lino with the author

*Milagros and the author
forty-five years after first meeting on
the road*

Juan José in front of his home

Kelly with Garabandal author, Fr. Ramón de la Riva 2017

Chucho moving cows through town

Visitors near Tina's duplex where the author stayed on many visits

Mercedes in front of "the castle." The small monument at the side of the gate marks the spot of the first apparition of St. Michael.

and Quico (Francisco) are only ninety-five. The men take daily walks and now stop to chat. When I first met them, they spent most of the time in the hills tending cows. Quico was also a stone mason and Juan José a construction foreman.

With older people dying and the young flocking to the cities seeking higher education and easier, better paying jobs, other small villages in the area have changed also. They are abandoned or nearly so.

Do the Garabandal villagers and those in the surrounding area believe that what happened in that little hamlet starting in 1961 was due to a special intervention between heaven and earth — was supernatural?

I heard one answer even before arriving back in the village in April 2017. After the bus had left me off in Puentenansa, at my request for a taxi, a man said, "*Te subo*. (I'll drive you up)." Thirty something Angel lifted my heavy suitcase and small backpack into the back of his SUV and we were off, heading south on the widened highway up the Nansa Valley. Minutes later, driving through Cosío on the road up to the village, he started in without invitation, "*En las montañas, una para allá y la otra para allá*. (he pointed to the hills on one side and then the other) *dos muchachas* would receive interior calls and arrive at the same instant at the designated place and fall into an ecstatic trance. The doctors came to investigate and poked pins into their eyes."

I questioned, "*Alfileres?*"

"*Si, alfileres.*"

Oh for a photo of my chauffer demonstrating how the three (sic) visionaries didn't feel anything when the doctors stuck pins into their eyes, but I just hung on and hoped that, driving as fast as he talked, he wouldn't miss the next turn and drop us into the Vendul River far below on the left.

The apparitions ended some twenty years before Angel was born, so his impressions came from others. His mother or grandmother was born in Garabandal. Although he didn't have everything straight (there were four girls, not three, and the doctors poked them with sharp objects but not in the eyes), he spoke with the same interest and certainty as did the eye-witnesses, seldom pausing for questions or comments. He seemed delighted with his report and so was I. Despite my insistence, he refused money for his generous help, and said to let him know if there was anything else he could do. Welcome back!

Fátima at home

Fátima (41), the youngest of Serafín and Paquita's three daughters, is a trusted friend whose insights I have valued, it seems, since the time she could talk. During one of our enjoyable, informative chats, she told me, "The villagers believe, but their belief is partial. They know that what they saw and heard was not natural, that it was not due to the devil, and therefore they conclude that it was from God. But they don't believe everything. There are obstacles,

Manolín

and the miracle is a big one. Few seem certain it will happen."

That's not right, I thought. If you believe, you accept the whole package. Fátima continued, "People, even some who seldom attend Mass, will go to the Pines to pray — not to the church. When they are in need, they pray to the Virgin for help. When I asked Marina what she prayed for at the Pines, she said, 'to cure my eyes.' "

I had noticed that the four-year-old wore thick glasses and sometimes a patch covering one eye. "She would have learned about the intercessory powers of the Virgin from her parents," Fatima added. "People don't talk about it because they don't understand everything; there are gaps in their belief, and they fear not being able to answer."

Over a drink in front of *la Vega* Restaurant, I asked Pepe Diaz' oldest son, Manolín, "How many villagers besides you are certain that the miracle will occur?" He answered by

Lucía and Tina outside the village church

forming his fingers into a zero. To my, "and your mother [Tina]?" he waved his hands to signify a little or maybe.

Regina outside her house

Lucia, owner of *Hospedería del Carmen*, speaks on the *YouTube* program *Pueblo de María* with exceptional insight about the importance of the apparitions. She and her husband, Doro, have invested in the village. This risk would be based on confidence that pilgrims will have a reason, the promised miracle, to flock to their village over the long term.

During one of my early visits, Juan José and Regina had a room for me. On this 2017 visit, I met the husband walking slowly close to his house. I asked about the crucifix that he had found. "Yes, it was over there while I was clearing the area to build a shed. I gave it to . . . I think it was Mercedes Salisachs. Yes, it was hers that she had lost after it was kissed by the Virgin."

He knows that the Miracle will come, but added, "I'm not sure I will

Juan José and the author

live to see it." He explained his certainty, "*Se ve más con la fe que con los ojos.* (You see more by faith than with your eyes). My father taught me that." Other villagers who observed everything now offer, "The miracle? I'll believe it when I see it."

Juan José has always talked quietly and fast. Now he stopped to rest in order to talk. He said that he had been in the service and then was a construction foreman and built his own house that he glanced at proudly. After he described Adriano's bar around the corner, I complimented his good memory. He agreed that was one thing he still had — at ninety-eight.

After God's mother took leave of the village in November 1965, it seems like Envy moved in. During my sixteen visits, it surprised me to hear some villagers talk badly about their neighbors. In a small place it would be easy to rub others the wrong way. When I accompanied Ramón Pérez interviewing villagers for his book, he always asked, "Did you know those girls before the apparitions?" Maximina answered, "Here we know everybody whether we want to or not."

A village woman says she used to believe, but not anymore because one of the visionaries wasn't friendly when she visited the village. She added, "the girls would have visions only when people gave them money, when rich people came." I questioned her on that. A few villagers seem upset (envious?) that some neighbors profit by owning guest houses, gift shops or bars. None explain how profiting now from pilgrims needing food and lodging could have caused unexplainable events in the early 1960's.

Some people outside the village expected more of the visionaries. The Puentenansa guest house owner frying my fish had fired away, scandalized because none of the girls had become nuns (See pp. 100ff.). How could they visit often and became so friendly with the Blessed Virgin that she even let them hold her baby? Weren't they just the daughters of Pilar and Ceferino and Simón? Familiarity had proved an obstacle before. "Isn't he the son of Mary and of Joseph, the carpenter? How can he be the Messiah? "

Loli coming out of a house in a trance

I thought more about what Fátima had said. Yes, there is a grade of belief. Levitating, walking on air, and reading thoughts, weren't natural. Other little girls couldn't pray in Greek with no instruction, or travel over the sharp rocks on their knees feeling no pain. Conchita, Loli, Jacinta and Mari Cruz were their daughters, nieces, and neighbors. All knew them to be truthful and knew the education they had — the same as everyone else — little. They could never make up, "The cup is overflowing. Many priests are on the way to hell . . ." If they said it was the Virgin, they must be telling the truth. Belief in this part was not a big stretch.

But there isn't this logical connection for knowing that the greatest miracle in history will take place in their little village. Certainty about things for which nature does not provide an explanation is a gift, called faith. Ninety-eight year old Juan José knows that.

A group of villagers and visitors, criticizing a recent Spanish book on Garabandal, agreed that the happenings and prophecies puzzle the author. He can't find their cause because he lacks what is needed to unlock the mystery.—faith. One said, "He just took things from the internet and then told lies in the second part."

At his presentation during the 2012 Santander book fair, when an attendee asked the source for "Many say that it is Conchita who manages an association that sells all kinds of [Garabandal] material." the author answered that he just wrote what he heard. The imperfections of the visionaries, the death of Joey Lomangino, making money by serving pilgrims, running tours to the village, and selling books all pose obstacles to understanding. Supernatural faith overcomes them, allowing us to see what can't be seen naturally, or to see more clearly what can be seen only dimly without it.

If God wants us to understand his work at this village why doesn't he make it more clear? Why does he require faith? I like it when others believe me without having to provide undeniable evidence. Is God the same? The thief on the cross thought so. His, "Remember me Lord," earned him, "Okay. I'll see you in Heaven."

"He [Jesus] wished to make himself perfectly recognizable to those who sincerely sought Him." [1] He hasn't changed. Recently in Spain's Cantabrian Mountains he gave signs that can be understood by those who seek him and not by those who do not. Mary overcame obstacles, big ones:

> She saw her Son in the Crib of Bethlehem, and believed Him the Creator of the world. She saw Him fly from Herod, and yet believed Him the King of kings. She saw Him born and believed Him Eternal. She saw Him poor and in need of food, and believed Him the Lord of the universe. She saw Him lying on straw, and believed Him Omnipotent. She observed that He

———————◦•◆•◦———————

1 Peter Kreeft, *Christianity for Modern Pagans: Pacal's Pensées Edited, Outlined and Explained*. (San Francisco: Ignatius Press 1996), pp.68-69.

did not speak, and she believed Him Infinite Wisdom. She heard Him weep, and believed Him the Joy of Paradise. Finally, she saw Him in death, despised and crucified, and, although Faith wavered in others, Mary remained firm in the belief that He was God. (Father Suarez).

The man on this work's cover, David Torribio, told me years ago, "The members of the Commission and other priests, tried to convince us that what we saw in Garabandal wasn't supernatural — that it wasn't anything. They drank in the bar with us and when they couldn't convince us, they told us that we had to obey — to stop believing."

Now years later, David speaks openly about the mysterious happenings he observed in his village. He explains how he suffered, knowing that God had mandated (implicitly in the second Message) that the good news of Garabandal be made known, but that he was taught to obey the clergy.

Some men outside the village ridiculed him if he indicated that he believed. The newspapers headlined Bishop Puchol's press notice that it was all natural, a child's game. False visionaries came to Garabandal to see visions.

Paquita
at her 81ˢᵗ birthday party

Nobody understood everything. David recalls that the four girls survived falling off the cliff on the steepest part of the hill. "How did the girls get down there?" he asks. "No one saw it. Someone brought them down . . . . It's three meters straight down." He says, "in these details, the Virgin did not want us to see everything. We saw the most important things. . . . It was the Virgin Mary who brought them down, or St. Michael. If not, it would have been impossible. I mean, we young men, had to go down the steep paths on either side!"[2]

I wanted to host a party to celebrate her mother's 81ˢᵗ birthday, so on my last full day in the village, April 24, 2017, Fátima drove Paquita and me down the hill to a new family-style restaurant in Cosío. The make-yourself-at-home welcome in that

---

2 www.garabandal.it. Feb. 25, 2017

Paquita and Fátima with the owner in front of her Cosío restaurant and bar

nearest neighbor village provided the comfortable family setting for the delicious meal that started with the best *cocido montañés* that any of the three of us had ever tasted.

After that white bean stew with ribs, Spanish chorizo, blood pudding, ample portions of shredded beef and greens, I chose poached hake for the second plate. We all enjoyed strawberries with cream for desert and Fátima and I had "*un cortado*" (syrupy coffee with a little milk) served steaming hot. Since we had a driver, I had a shot of cognac in order to soften my voice to serenade Paquita.

The cook/owner brought in red roses, and her mother, an accomplished singer, led *Feliz cumpleaños. Las Mañanitas,* often played and sung at 4:00 A.M. in Mexico to serenade girls on their birthday, followed. I missed playing the violin in our Curry/del Norte Symphony Orchestra's spring concert, so this attempt to sing a duet with a talented grandmother serenading my friend of forty-six years helped make up for that loss. I remembered some of the verses.

It took time to say good-bye to all who had served us, plus the bartender and a couple of patrons. Having lived eighty-one years in the dead end village three miles up the hill, Paquita knew them all. While waiting, I thought about asking my companions if we could stop to say hello to Sarín. I had read about her recent meeting with David Torribio:

> On seeing him she said, "Oh, Davizuco, [a diminutive for David] do you remember what happened in your village in 61?"

"Of course I remember."

"And do you still believe it?"

"Completely, Sarín. More and more every day."

The two reminisced about the happy times of many years previous. But the woman from Cosío recalled how she had suffered when her neighbors talked about the Bishop saying it could all be explained by natural causes, that it was nothing more than a child's game. She told David how she couldn't sleep and spent the whole night wondering how she could recover her certitude in the supernatural origin of what she had witnessed in Garabandal.

She knew what she would do. She would get the Virgin to prove that she was appearing. She went up alone to the village, gave Loli her medal that had already been kissed by the Virgin and then hid. She would challenge the visionary to find her, and . . . the Virgin to recognize her medal (out of thousands) as having already been kissed and therefore not kiss it again.

Loli easily located Sarín, and told her that the Virgin didn't kiss articles kissed before.[3]

The author and Sarín at her door

Paquita didn't mind leading the way when I asked to meet Sarín. The very small, shy old lady opened her door just off the main street that runs from the highway through Cosío and up to Garabandal. She and Paquita could have spent the evening on mutual friends and relatives, so Fátima, knowing my interest, asked to see Sarín's special crucifix that along with a religious medal had been kissed by the Virgin at Garabandal.

3 www.garabandal.it/es/que-es/anecdotas.

The lady cradled the treasured object in her hands. I kidded about her being known throughout the world because of the story (above) on the internet. We took photos and left.

When Fátima marveled at the way the woman had handled the crucifix with such reverence and respect, I recalled how my first friend in the area, Gabino, couldn't believe it when Serafín told him that he doubted that he could find anyone to sell him a religious article kissed by the Virgin — not at any price.

Our next stop was at Lupe's house. Neither Paquita nor her daughter protested a wish to say "hello" to my 1971 informant (See pp.60-62). Sure they knew her. "She likes to talk just like her Aunt Mercedes," Paquita said.

The author with Lupe with whom he had spoken in 1971

Lupe laughed until tears came to her eyes when she reenacted a surprised and befuddled Doctor Morales observing the visionaries in ecstasy, after his bragging that he would soon put an end to the whole affair. Lupe had carried his bags up the hill from Cosío. We took more photos and said good-bye to Lupe.

The next day I rode with Fátima sixty miles to Santander on the first leg of my journey back to Oregon. During my week there in Cantabria's largest city, I worked to find the present interest in Garabandal. Manuel, the Peruvian sacristan at Los Franciscanos Church seemed fascinated with my book and said that he would bring his wife and family to Mass the next day to talk with me. He suggested I talk with Fr. Juan José.

Others answered, "It isn't talked about." Neither the sacristan nor the lector at Mass at the Jesuit Church knew much about it. It was a non-issue. I asked them, "Would any priest, well informed about the happenings, speak in public now, or write against Garabandal and sign his name to the criticism?"

Ignacio, Kelly, Fidel outside Santa Lucía Church Santander, May 2017

"No."

I delved deeper, and on Saturday afternoon, headed for Santa Lucía Church to try to find Father Juan José. After watching me take photos, Fidel introduced himself. When I mentioned my reason for being in the area, he started right in with the details of the happenings, saying that Garabandal was the only thing his mother ever talked about. He had been to the village, but wasn't a fanatic like his mother.

I said hello to the priest walking up the steps to the Church. Yes, he was Father Juan José. On my last full day in town I got right to the point. "Are there any priests here who will now speak publically against, or sign their name to writing critically about Garabandal?"

Maybe he wasn't ready for this question and answered, "Some people talk a lot about apparitions and think they know more than the bishop." He rambled on about those who don't respond properly to apparitions. I stopped him and repeated my question to which he answered, "No."

Bishop Manuel Monge in center with Cardianal Osoro with book

My new friend, Fidel, had a special Spanish word for the priest and explained, "He will never change his mind. It's closed." I thought that it would be difficult for him not to steer his people away from Garabandal. His present pastor, Father José Olano, was, when young, sent by the bishop to Garabandal to try to dissuade the people, including David, from their interest in the apparitions. After good-bye, I walked to the cathedral to try once more to see Bishop Monge and say hello. No luck.

On trips to Spain, I often spend time in the beautiful Valley of Liébana, on the western side of the Peña Sagra from Garabandal. Friends for forty years, Daniel and Lupe, invite me to stay in their comfortable condominium in Ojedo, a kilometer outside of the Valley hub, Potes. Lupe has been my expert on Spanish affairs since the couple lived for years in Palo Alto, California starting in the early 1980's.

During one visit she recounted that when she was young, the pastor told his parishioners not to believe in Garabandal, that it was false. She remembered how much this troubled her parents and others. She expressed, and I felt, her anger and disdain for priests abusing their position. She said that if there were another civil war in Spain, the people would react the same way they did in the first, murdering the clergy.

During early stays in Santander, I alternated between three or four restaurants. Now I always eat at el Figón on Cisneros Street, a block away from City Hall and the public market. This Sunday dinner would be my last there for this trip. Friendly but efficient owner, Carlos led me to a long table with room for four on each side saying, "Sit here with your friend." Old Nícolas ate very slowly, never spoke to anyone and at times seemed to sleep.

But when one of the two men at the end of our long table asked if I liked Spain and I answered telling them of my interest

Fátima enjoying a meal at el Figón in Santander

here, Nicolás woke up saying, "Garabandal is a jewel." His mother went up there all the time. He wouldn't stop telling me about how important Garabandal was for her. Maybe if you hadn't talked in days, you would have a lot to say. Accustomed to long pauses between bites, he rambled on saying that Bishop Puchol had complained that more people were going to Garabandal than to Mass. He used "Jolín" (a mild vulgar expression) repeatedly to explain his annoyance with the early bishops' opposition to the apparitions.

We both chose lamb chops for the second plate — scrumptious, and as always, ample. I put three or four in my bag to eat for supper in Madrid. Nicolás said, "The priests were against Garabandal. They obeyed the bishop and told the people not to go to the village." I treated myself and my new old friend to a cognac.

Nicolás, Carlos, Kelly

In this unique restaurant where people talk freely with each other, I had noticed a young couple at the table near the kitchen looking at us. Counting the minutes before I had to run for the airport bus, I went over and said hello. The woman said, "There are only two types of Catholics in Spain now, *los beatos*, those of apparent faith who attend church no matter what, but don't do anything to correct clerical abuses, and those who don't go to church anymore." In this atmosphere, people would not be prone to bring up apparitions. Although it seems that people are reluctant to speak about Garabandal with each other, many admit its importance to those they don't know, like me.

IF GARABANDAL IS SO IMPORTANT, WHY ISN'T IT BETTER KNOWN?

With the exception of 1995, when many expected the great miracle, there were more visitors this year, 2017, than ever. I met people from

A family from Mexico with the author and helpful villager, Rafa

Australia, Peru, Ecuador, Mexico, Germany, Canada, France, the Philippines, Scandinavia and the U.S. Why? Everyone can now see the ecstatic marches, falls, and levitations better—on the internet—than could many of the eye-witnesses.

Individuals and groups promote Garabandal. *El Hogar de la Madre* in Cantabria; *Pueblo de María* in Argentina; *Garabandal International Australia* at www.garabandal.com.au; Deacon John DiGiglio's *What is Garabandal*; Barry Hanratty's *Garabandal Journal*; www.ourlady. com in Canada; María Sarraco and her *Vigil* at www.gargandal.org and others do great work.

I am not aware of any Catholic radio or television station, newspaper or magazine that promotes Garabandal. One journalist writes, "private revelations have a way of appearing plausible if you immerse yourself long enough in them. They seep down in subtle ways into the cracks of your mind." Another writes, "there will always be people who chase after ambulances and fire trucks, but the average Catholic, like yourself, has more sense than to gawk at visionaries who see things that aren't there." A third, ". . such a false prediction got false prophets stoned in Old Testament times." All three of these mistranslate the local church's evaluations before insulting those whose belief they don't share. A fourth writes, ". . . when the 'private revelation' is a load of bushwah like . . . . Garabandal." When I asked the program director at an influential Catholic Radio station in Southern California if I could correct its misinformation, he answered, "We steer people away from that [Garabandal]."

Many Catholic book publishers won't cover apparitions that don't have Church approval.

At a February 2003 gathering of some three thousand people in Houston, the popular speaker answered a question saying, "When the church studies it carefully and approves it, we are free to believe." After I responded that the church I belong to neither requires me to believe in approved apparitions nor forbids me to believe in unapproved ones, he answered, "Believe, yes, but not promote." Before I could say that my church doesn't say that I can't tell others about Garabandal, the microphone was removed. The thousands in the audience and others who learn only what some in the Catholic media teach on this topic, are left with the misleading answer.

Contact your Catholic or other Christian radio or TV stations and ask them to cover what the late prefect for the Congregation of the Faith Cardinal Ottaviani called, "prophecies of transcendental importance for the whole world." If they suggest you stick to approved apparitions, ask them if it was wrong for my mother to talk about Fatima when she was a young teacher in 1918 or for my grandmother, when she was a teenager, to talk about and visit Knock, Ireland close to her home before those reported apparitions were approved.

Other possible contributing causes for Garabandal's lack of popularity are: negative sounding press reports out of Santander in the 1960's; inaccurate English translations of the local bishops' Spanish statements; the ease of spreading erroneous information on blog cites; lack of interest in spiritual things in general and in mystical phenomena in particular; the new idolatry of worshipping the false God of entertainment leaving insufficient time, energy and interest to ponder heaven, hell and the end times.

Some might not have heeded Pope Clement's advice to pray, "Lord, discover to me the nothingness of earth, the greatness of heaven, the shortness of time and the length of eternity" or don't know that "Life is like a flash of lightning compared to eternity."

Many in the media seem not to know or care that if God manifests his presence in an extraordinary way, we ought to pay attention. The official Catholic Church is understandably quiet.

What has changed is not as important as what hasn't. Everything past (the unexplainable reactions of the girls) and future (the Warning, the Miracle and the permanent sign in the village), are intended to prove the authenticity and importance of the two formal messages. Only the time left to comply with these has changed; much less remains than when we were first warned.

THE VISIONARIES TODAY

Mari Cruz, the youngest of the four, but the first married, lives in Avilés, Spain with her husband Ignacio. They have four children. Jacinta has lived in Southern California with her husband, Jeff Moynihan and their daughter, María for almost forty years. She visits Garabandal in the summer with her husband and daughter. Conchita, a widow, lives in New York with an unmarried daughter. She has two other daughters, one son and fifteen grandchildren. Mari Loli died on April 20, 2009, ten days before her sixtieth birthday. She leaves a husband, Francis LeFleur and three adult children. Thinking that she might have "*enchufe*" (connections) with one who works miracles, I pray to her for help in bringing this task to a fitting end.

At Garabandal presentations, people wonder why the visionaries don't promote Garabandal and ask, "Why doesn't Conchita give talks or write?" She was the focus of attention in the village for almost ten years and outside of it after that. She has said all that is important and put that in writing. When the village pastor don Rolando's asked her to participate in the celebrations marking the 50th anniversary of the first apparitions, Conchita wrote on May 17, 2011:

I join with you in the celebration of the fiftieth anniversary of the events of Garabandal. It is for me fifty years of contemplating the most beautiful thing in the world. I give thanks to God for having been a part of those experiences, impossible to describe adequately, but which have pressed upon my soul the secure assurance of faith and hope.

I thank you, Father Rolando, for granting me the opportunity to recite the Message of Our Mother in the village yet again. *"We must make many sacrifices, perform much penance, and visit the Blessed Sacrament frequently. But first, we must lead good lives. If we do not, a chastisement will befall us. The cup is already filling up, and if we do not change, a very great chastisement will come upon us."*

She also included the second formal message and ended,

Father Rolando, there is nothing of greater importance that I can speak about than this Message of Our Mother.

In Union of Prayer,
Conchita"

The warning to change in order to avoid a horrible chastisement, occupies more than half of the lines, almost sixty percent of the message.

If the eye-witnesses could not find words to describe what they experienced, and Conchita, who lived them, calls them "impossible to describe adequately," this author, who saw nothing, can only pray that his work doesn't divert readers from the Garabandal path to happiness and hope.

How will Conchita react to being praised effusively in this work? She will hate the author. And she will immediately forgive him for making the messages she revealed, known in the best way he knows how.

271

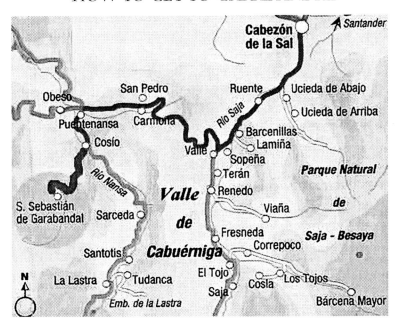

For this last visit, I flew from Seattle to Madrid and from there, on one of the five daily flights to Santander. You can book straight through to Santander – for three times the cost. Five or six Alsa busses leave Madrid Central Bus station on Avenida de las Américas each day for a five or six hour ride. You can reserve on line – in English. Buses leave the Santander Airport for the ten minute trip to the city station where a bus leaves in the afternoon for a pleasant two hour ride to Puentenansa and Cosío. At either place, ask for a taxi, or walk three miles up the hill from Cosío or a mile further from Puentenansa.

Clerk at Santander Airport with a good book

When the date of the Miracle is announced, or even after the Warning, thousands will book seats for Santander instead of visiting the Costa Brava or Costa del Sol beaches. Iberia and Alsa will reschedule those vacant planes and buses for Santander.

Will God enlighten those in charge, to make more public transportation available the rest of the way? If he doesn't have time, two trains a day leave Santander for an hour and a half ride along the Coast to Pesués, from where it's thirteen miles (a twenty-two minute drive) to Puentenansa.

Some fifteen trains daily go as far as Cabezón de la Sal. From there, it's a pleasant walk, much of it level along the Saja River, seventeen miles (a thirty-three minute drive) to Puentenansa. Extra taxis should be available in Cabezón for the miracle.

I plan to attend. Having made the long journey from home sixteen times, and traveled in and out of the village more times than one can count, I know the way. If the Warning occurs tonight, I will immediately book a flight to Madrid for late March, and reserve a flight or a bus seat to Santander. If there are enough buses to Puentenansa/Cosío you will find me on one.

My second choice is the train from Santander to Pesués. In September, 1999 I left Garabandal before dawn, walking out of the mountains with a small backpack headed for Santiago de Compostela. It was mostly downhill all the way to the Coast. Since it's up hill the other way, and my legs have eighteen years more miles on them, it will be much slower. But walking for two days up along the Nansa River, thanking the Lord for inviting me to his big party and for everything else will take half of the time. "What shall I return to the Lord for all his goodness to me?" (Psalm 116: 12). Pondering what awaits during the following days will take the rest of the time.

I will see the sick cured and the lame walk. Will God notice me among the blind, the deaf, the dumb and the lame, those with heart disease, brain tumors or terminal cancer? The tip of my numb index finger gets uncomfortable in cold weather. I will hold it up.

But there is also the "convert the sinner" issue. I won't be able to hide. Yes, it will help to witness God's omnipotent power, but that grace won't last until I die. It will remain a challenge to respond in kind for this extraordinary demonstration of his love for me. Witnessing the

Outdoor restaurants, Madrid

Outdoor portion of Santander market

Paella cooking over a fire in Barrio Pesquero, Santander.

Miracle doesn't guarantee eternal happiness. Always doing God's will does. "We have Bernadette Soubirous on the altar of sanctity because she practiced virtue to a heroic degree, not because she saw the Virgin Mary in the Grotto of Massabielle" (José María Saiz).

What if God has other plans for me, that I give my taxi seat to another, or stay behind on the road to help an elderly person? The whispers to change plans might come earlier – a prompting that requires giving up something valuable, like attending the miracle. Jesus preferred to live. His Father asked him to die. He told us to love the same way, to love one another the way he loves us, sacrificially.

Some of us have heard (possibly a legend) that Mary, knowing that the Messiah would soon come, wanted to be near and serve the one chosen to be his mother. God had different plans. Mary changed hers.

During my long-ago summers living in poor Mexican villages, there wasn't a phrase I heard more often than *"si Dios quiere."* Yes, the baby will be healthy, God willing. Yes, it will rain, *si Dios quiere.* Yes, this, and yes that, if God wills it.

Our mother taught us early, "Lord, help me to be what you want me to be, do what you want me to do and go where you want me to go." Yes, I will be present for the miracle, *si Dios quiere.* And just in case, to be prepared, I have already started, like the Three Kings before their journey, to prepare a fitting gift to present to the Lord at our meeting on the mountain.

Statue of St Michael inside the village church

APPENDIX I
SANTANDER BISHOP ON GARABANDAL

Father Antonio del Val Gallo was one of three priests on the five member Commission chosen by Bishop Fernandez to go to Garabandal and investigate the happenings. Kelly met with then Bishop del Val Gallo on January 4, 1973.

The bishop explained that the village pastor had just given the children a lesson on the guardian angels. Although he didn't say that the lesson caused the girls to see things, he gave "suggestion" as the cause of the happenings. He said, "shortly after things started, people flocked up there, and the influence of the visitors prohibited the girls from stopping the act."

He said that everything witnessed in the village was natural, that the girls were used to working hard, they knew the terrain like the back of their hand [so they could walk backwards and fall to their knees onto the rocks without it hurting them]. He said, "I was there, and it was nothing."

He explained in lengthy detail that the four Garabandal visionaries were like children who spend so much time pondering the arrival of the Three Kings bringing presents that they are convinced they see them. Kelly says that he couldn't believe he was hearing this from an educated man.

About this theory, expressed also to others, Canon Julio Porro says that the bishop was indirectly qualifying as imbeciles all those who hold the happenings to be supernatural, and that he never gave any supporting reasons for his opinion to be taken seriously. [1]

The bishop refused Kelly's request to see the report of the Commission's work. He said that it would be unfair to release things the girls said as children. At the Chancery Kelly was told that Fr. Odriozola had the report; but at the priest's office, he was told that it had burned. Others were refused the same request.

---

1 José María de Dios (pseudonym for Julio Porro), *Garabandal Hoy, ¿Mito of Misterio Divino?* (Zaragoza, EDITORIAL CÍRCULO), p. 57.

Del Val later came to believe in the apparitions, (pages 307 and 309) and as a result, lifted the ban imposed by Bishop Beitia in 1962 forbidding priests from going to the village without permission. This action fulfilled the prophesy relayed by Conchita on Christmas Day 1962, "The Bishop will receive such a proof that he will immediately afterwards decide to lift the ban." [2]

1979 INTERVIEW WITH BISHOP DEL VAL GALLO

The author, while on a year's leave from his high school Spanish teaching position and living in Santander, spoke again with Bishop del Val Gallo on June 23, 1979. He prefaced this second hour and a half meeting by expressing concern about the inadequate press coverage in Santander and abroad, and about the bishops' investigation of, and pronouncements on, Garabandal. Thus, most of his questions dealt with these issues. A report of the hour-and-a-half meeting follows.

SANTANDER BISHOPS' EVALUATION OF THE NATURE OF THE GARABANDAL EVENTS

"The American Catholic press has a difficult time reporting the Church's position on Garabandal correctly. I want to help others understand the *Official Notes* published here." I showed him and explained my article prepared for an American Catholic weekly in which I had extracted from the *Official Notes* those statements of the various bishops which evaluate the nature of the Garabandal happenings, judging that these statements would be more important for readers today than would, for example, the directives to the people of Santander during the apparitions.

Bishop del Val nodded in seeming agreement. He studied the statements which I had blocked out in the booklet, *Declaraciones Oficiales*

---

2 *Garabandal* Oct.-Dec. 1987. p. 3-4.

de la Jerarquía Sobre Garabandal. He pointed out as being the best, and a good expression of his own appraisal, the statement from Bishop Beitia's second *Nota* or Press Report. He read it. "The Commission, which is in charge of qualifying the happenings, hasn't found reasons to modify its judgment already given, stating that the supernaturalism of the phenomena that it has examined carefully is not evident."

We compared Monsignor Beitia's statements of 1962 and 1965 and he remarked, "This latter is softer, no?" The evaluation in the 1962 *Notice* could be considered the strongest against Garabandal while the 1965 evaluation, by the same man, returns to the neutral, uncertain judgment that characterized the earlier two statements by Bishop Fernandez. It is in the 1965 *Note* in which the lengthy statement of doctrinal orthodoxy appears.

"Is this [1965] statement better, more important than Bishop Puchol's [oft-quoted and misquoted] statement of 1967?" I asked.

"Yes." And he looked at Puchol's report and explained that Puchol was very much influenced by the declarations of the girls – that their declarations weighed heavily with him. (In 1973 he had told me that Bishop Puchol's conclusions were based entirely upon the girls' declarations.)

BISHOP del VAL'S PUBLISHED APRIL 1978 STATEMENT

"Could you clarify your statement on Garabandal issued by your Office of Information last April?" (The statement reporting on the Bishop's talk to the villagers in Garabandal the previous December.)

"It's ambiguous, no?" he offered. We read the article in the *Boletín Oficial Del Obispado* before he summarized, saying that it meant that his predecessors hadn't admitted the supernatural character of the Garabandal events and that he hadn't either.

"This wouldn't mean that you agree with all that your predecessors said?"

"No. Each one says it in his own way. I haven't said anything [Made any statement judging the nature of the Garabandal events or issued any directives to his people advising them what to do or not to do like his predecessors had]." He continued reading, "I was always open, in charity and without prejudice, and will always continue to being so, to consider whatever happening might occur here. But in the six years in which I have been Bishop of Santander, no new phenomenon has occurred."

"But since all of the bishops here didn't say the same thing, give the same evaluation, your statement of agreement leaves room for misinterpretation." He seemed sympathetic and repeated that for him the best statement about the nature of the events was that in Beitia's second *Notice* (quoted above).

"Is it true that Jacinta retracted her 1966 declaration of uncertainty?"

"To me, no." And he talked about the girls going through a period of denial, but later saying that they did believe, that he knew the girls, and that they were impressive and good. I recalled: (1) that Mary Loli Villar (Lolita) in whose house Jacinta was living as a housekeeper at the time, had told me that Jacinta went to see the Bishop often, both on her volition and called in by him, and (2) that in January, 1973 celebrating the first anniversary of his appointment as bishop, his people filed by to congratulate him in the Cathedral, and after Jacinta had already passed, the Bishop recognized her, called her back, greeted her affectionately and spoke with her for a moment.

PROMOTING GARABANDAL

"What is your position or attitude toward the promoting of Garabandal in America or anywhere outside this Diocese?"

"Que a cada una le dicte su conciencia." ("Let each one's conscience be his guide.")

"Is there anything in the *Official Notes* that would prohibit, or rather, advise against my promoting Garabandal?"

"No." He elaborated saying that the directives in the *Notes* were ones advising people on their behavior in Garabandal during the happenings. They were not against talking about it.

"In Cardinal Seper's letter to Archbishop Philip Hannan we read, 'Rather, the Holy See deplores the fact that certain persons and institutions persist in fomenting the movement in obvious contradiction with the dispositions of ecclesiastical authority.' Does he mean the authority of the Santander office or that of one's local bishop?"

After discussing this, he agreed that Cardinal Seper meant, or should have meant, the authority of the bishop of one's own diocese. Then, possibly realizing the very positive tone of his past few remarks, he removed his glasses, leaned across his wide desk and cautioned, "Now don't go publishing that the Bishop of Santander says that you should promote Garabandal. That is not what I am saying."

IMPRESSIVE CURES IN SANTANDER

"We've heard of two spectacular, unexpected, and unexplainable cures of a young woman here, Menchu Alvarez. After being diagnosed as incurable on two different occasions she recovered both times from the same disease after having a crucifix kissed by the Virgin at Garabandal touched to her. Have you heard of this?"

"Yes." And he mentioned that he would like to receive testimony about it from the principals involved.

"I have heard that the Santander Chancery attempted to keep the news of these two cures quiet."

Msgr. del Val said no, that neither he nor anyone in the chancery had attempted to keep the news of the cures quiet.

"Or the Garabandal Commission?" I persisted because I knew from a number of sources that after the first cure, a member of the Garabandal Commission went to the girl's father, telling him that he shouldn't talk about the cure, that it was wrong to attribute the cure to apparitions that were false. After my meeting with Msgr. del Val, I spoke with the prominent businessman, Mr. Mendiolea, Menchu's father. He told me, yes, two priests including Father Odriozola, a member of the Commission, had come to him and told him not to talk. It is difficult to believe that Msgr. del Val didn't know this. I suspect that his answer was one of the few times that he evaded the question. He answered that the Commission no longer functioned, that, in effect, there was no Commission now.

BISHOP AGAINST PRESS COVERAGE IN SANTANDER

I had noticed the tremendous change in church/press relations since my first visit in 1969. The press, previously so subservient to, and protective of, the Church, now printed insults against the Catholic faith worse than anything I've seen in America. Previously, reporters wrote what the bishop wanted about Garabandal (and other matters), but now they wrote what they wanted. During my first visits I had wanted to know which was the better of the two Santander daily papers. A well-educated newspaper distributor, with whom I chatted many times about Spanish affairs, told me that one had all of the lies of the government and the other, *El Diario Montañés,* all of the lies and cover-ups of the Church. Now, with a little prompting and help, reporters might be happy to expose the great Garabandal cover-up that had originated in the Santander Chancery. Bishop Del Val would be abreast of this changed attitude and new freedom of the press.

"Since you haven't prohibited the news of the cures from being made public, would you have anything against the newspapers carrying a report on it?"

While the Bishop had ready answers to most of my twenty questions, to this one he did not. After a long pause he said there wouldn't be any reporter in the area that could handle that task well and suggested it not be done, that it would cause many problems. One needed the help of the Holy Spirit to write well on that matter, and reporters weren't "sprinkled with the dust of the Holy Spirit."

I showed him copies of the infamous articles in the April 9, 1967 *Gaceta Ilustrada* and in the March 21, 1967 edition of *El Diario Montañés.* Both carry the by-line of the Santander reporter, Julio Poo San Román, who, when I showed him his contradictory statements, told me repeatedly that he had not written the articles, that the bishop (Puchol) had, and that the bishop had told him (at the cost of losing his job?) to sign them.

Monsignor del Val looked over the pages while I pointed out the contradictions and weaknesses. The *Gaceta* states, "And 'the Messages'? In order to 'fabricate' them they closed themselves in [a room] and made up several until they came upon the most adequate. Thus, the one of the night of October 18 was composed after having written three others before."

Santander's *El Diario Montañés* says, "In regard to the messages, Conchita wrote them alone at school, without any supernatural communication."

Santander's other daily, Alerta, reports on March 19, 1967, "A man read . . .the message that the girls had affirmed having received from the Virgin, and that they had handed to the pastor."

To explain the miracle of the angel giving communion to Conchita, the *Gaceta* says, "She made a host ... placed it on the roof of her mouth, covered everything up with a crucifix in front of her lips, went out to the street, and at the precise moment did nothing more than deposit it herself on her tongue in sight of all." *El Diario* explains it differently.

The main premise of the three page articles in the three papers is that the girls' declarations of uncertainty about having seen the Virgin explain all of the Garabandal happenings. I told Msgr. del Val that this was ludicrous, that they could retract statements, but they couldn't undo by retractions, ecstatic falls, levitations or any of the other unexplainable phenomena witnessed by countless thousands. "Who is to correct these absurdities?"

This also seemed to give him trouble. Perhaps the articles looked as foolish to him as they did to me. He did not correct, explain, or excuse them.

He finally answered, "The one who wrote them should correct them."

"This article originated in this office, from Bishop Puchol or from Puchol and Azagra" (Vicar General under Puchol).

After discussing this, he suggested that I write to the Vatican explaining the problem of the weaknesses or inaccuracies: 1) in Bishop Puchol's Note, 2) in Bishop del Val's immediate predecessor, Bishop Cirarda's 1970 letter to all the bishops in the world and 3) in the newspaper articles. I should also mention the resulting misunderstanding that these publications have caused. Monsignor suggested to whom I should write and wrote the address for me.

I asked, "Wouldn't it be better if a printed correction or update on the Garabandal investigation and the ensuing publications on it came out of this office rather than have such an article, written by some reporter who might not be too charitable, hit the newsstands?"

"No, that would cause many problems. If it were done, it would do damage to the Garabandal movement here and abroad. No, I wouldn't suggest that it be done." He didn't explain why or how it would cause damage.

I mentioned that in my opinion, Bishop Cirarda's 1970 letter to the bishops of the world was one of the main causes of the misunderstanding of the Church's position on Garabandal. We looked at some of the numerous errors, the discrepancies between statements in the original *Notes* and Cirarda's paraphrasing of them.

"Who should correct them?" I asked.

"He who wrote them."

"Father Julio Porro has extensively and pointedly criticized the Garabandal Commission's formation, investigation process, the Official Notes resulting from its recommendations, and Bishop Cirarda's letter. Has anyone refuted or even answered these criticisms?"

The Bishop pondered the question before finally picking up a copy of the Official Bulletin of the Diocese. On the back cover below the coat of arms is the motto, *Veritatem Facientes in Caritate.* He pointed to the last word, "Charity," and said that this was what was lacking in Fr. Porro's work; there were better ways of solving the problem than the way Fr. Porro chose. I observed that the Bishop picked "charity" as that which was lacking in Porro, and not "truth," which was also in the motto to be pointed out—if he had felt a need.

Bishop del Val admitted that the members of the Bishop's Investigating Commission hadn't been canonically sworn in. When I mentioned that it seemed like the Church's prescribed process for handling investigations on such matters hadn't been followed in the case of Garabandal, he didn't defend the commission's work and added that if he had been in charge he would have done some things differently. He would have, for example, removed Fr. Valentín and put in the most qualified priest in the Diocese as pastor at Garabandal. Don Valentín hadn't come to Bishop Doroteo immediately with information like he should have. The beginning was the important part. That Doroteo was an apostolic administrator, and not the one that the Curia wanted appointed, also prevented the investigation process from being handled well. They didn't give him the backing that he needed at that time.

"Since the Commission was not canonically formed, and thus was not a Tribunal of Law, it seems to me that the judgment of the Commission shouldn't have carried so much more weight than that of other qualified doctors and theologians." When he didn't disagree I continued, "Why was the Commission's judgment relied upon so extensively and exclusively?" (Canon Julio Porro reports that the Commission members never went to observe as a group, none of them went more than twice, and one never went at all.)

"Those were the men that the Bishop (Doroteo Fernandez) saw fit to rely upon."

"Isn't it true that Fr. José Olano, past pastor at Garabandal, pressured the girls into declaring to Bishop Puchol that they were uncertain about having seen the Virgin, and that Conchita's confessor at the convent in Pamplona, don Emiliano Murillo, conditioned the absolution of her sins on her denying the apparitions and even wrote her a letter reminding her of this condition while she was on summer vacation away from the convent?"

No, he hadn't heard of this pressure or coercion.

"Do you know if either of these priests has denied these serious accusations?"

"No." He hadn't heard of them denying it. As we discussed this further, Monsignor offered that there were many pressures on the girls from both sides. Many people went in there, and yes, it was probable that there were pressures on them to deny.

"Do you know of any book or pamphlet that tells the Garabandal history well—one which relates the happening accurately?"

"No." In his opinion, all of the authors, for or against Garabandal, always told the story in a partisan manner, and this interfered with the objective relating of the events, and of the proper understanding of them by the reader. He said that the author would always tend to give his own coloring to the happenings, but he didn't mention any specific errors in any books.

"Have you seen the fifty-minute movie on Garabandal that is being shown in many countries?"

"No."

"Would you like to see it?"

"Yes." And he expressed an interest on hearing that it had recently been translated into Spanish.

"Is it true that Dr. Morales has changed his mind about Garabandal from a strongly negative to a more favorable position?"

"I don't know. I would like to talk to him about it." (In 1983 Doctor Morales stated his changed position in a public statement at the Ateneo Club in downtown Santander. In his speech, he said that he now believed that the Garabandal happenings were of a supernatural origin.)

"You spoke in September 1978 and again in February 1979 with Fr. Francisco Benac who later wrote this summary of your position on Garabandal. Do you consider his report accurate?" I handed him a copy.

He looked over the nine points, confirmed that they were accurate and expanded at length on the second to the last point, saying that previous to his December (1977) visit to Garabandal, he had gone to Rome together with some twenty bishops on his *Ad Limina* visit. He had hoped that Rome would agree to cooperate in the handling of the Garabandal affair. *"Garabandal sobrepasa la capacidad de esta Diócesis de resolver."* (Garabandal is beyond the capacity of this Diocese to resolve.) He added that this was a small diocese.

It was 3:00 P.M., well past his dinner time. I felt fortunate and grateful that a bishop in a foreign country would listen patiently and answer my questions.

"After this meeting I will remember to pray more for you, Monsignor."

"Está bien." And he added that a bishop's burdens were heavy.

"You mean that you have other concerns besides Garabandal?" I kidded.

"Of course," he answered, accompanied by a big smile. I knelt for his blessing and for the second time alone in his big office listened to him call down God's blessing upon me now and forever. Bishop del Val was indeed, like some of the visionaries described him, "likeable, approachable, like a father." As I left, a young couple, perhaps with burdens heavier than my concern for accurate press coverage for Garabandal, entered.

Walking home along Santander's waterfront, I recalled that during the interview, I had thanked God for the opportunity to hear information from the Bishop, and had asked for the grace to understand it and to use it for God's honor and glory.

A member of his staff, Father José Rubio SDB, a colleague of my two Salesian brothers-in-law priests from Santander, had told me that Garabandal was a big burden for the bishop and that he would like to be relieved of that burden. May nothing in this report be used to increase it.

APPENDIX II

This article, written by the author, was originally published in the October-December 1978 edition of *Needles Magazine*.

A LESSON IN CHARITY

"This new commandment I give you, that you love one another." (JOHN 13:34)

The dining room at Mesón Serafín is a good place for meeting people. The friendly proprietor, Conchita's eldest brother, Serafín, and his wife, Paquita, who prepares and serves the meals with a motherly, concerned smile for all, are a big part of the reason. A strong common interest that visitors have in the Virgin of Mt. Carmel would be another.

I spent a month there in July of 1971, soon after the inn opened, and have spent months at that guest house on succeeding visits. Behind the bar is a big, blue guest register which is signed by visitors from many parts of the world. I will never forget some of them.

There was big red-headed Chuck from Pasadena, California, who had left his companions on the Costa Brava and ridden to Garabandal on his motorcycle. He was sitting on a bench studying his pocket dictionary and practicing "hello" and "food" in Spanish when I met him. Two days later he ran up excited. "I just talked to Conchita. I talked to her for ten minutes." In what language, Chuck? I thought.

Other visitors included: the couple on their way to Portugal, moving their children there to escape the corrupt American society; the Dutch-born couple from San Diego with their nine children; the stout German woman who carried all her belongings with her in a plastic bag because she was afraid someone would steal them; the Watsonville, California ladies, Kitty and her companion, Evy, who wouldn't visit anything in Garabandal because Kitty had dragged her around to every shrine in Europe and. . . Alfonso.

I first saw him when I entered the guesthouse for a mid-day meal.

He sat alone at one of four small tables in the dining room waiting to be served. Around fifty years old, he had little flocks of hair above the ears, a thin straggly beard, and thick glasses that hid his eyes so you couldn't see the pupils. A strange looking man indeed! I stood and watched him push his books and magazines from one corner of the table to the other. Would Paquita seat me at the table with him?

No. Soon a young clean-cut young man came through the door. Paquita, carrying in a platter of soup bowls, decided. "You speak English, Eduardo. You can sit with Fred here when the French family finishes. I think he's from your country.

Fred, from Birmingham, England, was happy to have an English-speaking companion. We talked about ourselves, the Garabandal movement, his difficulties in Spain without being able to speak Spanish, and about the odd fellow at the adjacent table. After Alfonso got up, we listened to two elderly ladies from Madrid commiserate with a third. "The nerve of that character telling you it was none of your business, and furthermore, addressing you with "tu" (the familiar form of the two Spanish "you's" that is reserved for addressing close friends, children, servants, and animals). Fred and I wondered what we would do if we ever had to sit with him.

Later Serafín filled us in. "He's a talented fellow, and his family is high up in the government of a neighboring province. He came up here during the apparitions also. Now, when he's not in Garabandal, he's in the insane asylum. Last week," Serafín continued, "he went out with me to Cabezón when I went for supplies. A Gypsy wanted to sell him a basket for one hundred pesetas ($1.75). Fonso didn't want the basket so he just gave her the money. He's crazy! Then I had to wait while he got his picture taken because he wanted a memento of himself with a beard. And worst of all, he saw this ugly king crab in a restaurant and had to buy it to give to Jacinta for her birthday. He carried the thing, dripping, through the streets, scaring the kids with it."

How do you treat such a person? At meals, Fred and I sat and observed and listened to him discuss religion and current events with other Spanish visitors. Watching him, an old song came to mind, "All the monkeys aren't in the zoo. Everyday you meet quite a few." Oh, he had talent all right—art, history, etymology. He often got on a word-root kick and then he was funny. Once I summoned courage and asked,

"Fonso, what does Garabandal mean?" He didn't hesitate a moment.

"Garabandal comes from garbanzo. There used to be garbanzo fields here. That's why sometimes you hear, 'los Garabandal' because there were two fields. Isn't that right, Serafín?

Serafín, standing by the door as he so often did while waiting to be beckoned by his customers, nodded, "Sí. Creo que sí." ("Yes. I believe so.") But Serafín seldom disagreed with anybody. And Fonso rambled on about how they quit raising garbanzos because of the difficulty in getting them to market or some such problem.

Alfonso was still in Garabandal when Joey Lomangino's American pilgrims arrived to fill up Serafín's place and most of the private residences. Perhaps he considered this onslaught of foreigners an invasion of his privacy, because later that morning, with the forty new arrivals, plus a dozen or so of us stragglers and Serafín's young family attempting to squeeze into the small dining room for Mass, Alfonso sat in the back corner puffing a cigar. About offertory time, a man approached him in halting Spanish, "Por favor, my wife is sick."

Alfonso snapped back, "Es perfume, incienso." ("It's perfume, incense.")

On Friday I left for Santander with Fred, and the next day I rejoined my wife and daughter at my in-law's house. A few days later, while re-reading previously marked passages in Father Pesquera's, *Se Fue Con Prisas a la Montaña,* in which he quotes the village pastor, don Valentín's notes for September, 1962, I came across the following:

> There is here in the village a guy who is half crazy, who does stupid things that might be judged badly by the people who come here and don't know his abnormal state. He has been a year in the insane asylum, and now he has taken a notion to stay here. He is bothersome and offensive and will have to be sent away.

> During today's ecstasy, Loli and Conchita went to the house where this crazy guy, whose name is Alfonso, was staying, and there they made the sign of the cross with the crucifix over the pillow of his bed, and on passing next to him, they gave him the crucifix to kiss a number of times, and the crazy man froze on his knees.

The page blurred before me. Alfonso, given the crucifix to kiss, shown that favor by the Blessed Virgin? Tears ran down my cheeks as I thought of the man with the thick glasses pushing his magazines back and forth across the table at Serafín's guest house. "How do you treat such a guy? Ignore him?" Fred and I had wondered. I read on about Alfonso.

> What a lesson in charity the children have given us! All of us, who had been talking about the necessity of kicking the crazy fellow out of the village, were moved by the lesson, above all the secretary to the cardinal, don Guillermo Hausschildt, who even had thought about denying him [Alfonso] Holy Communion. He said, 'It is clear that the Virgin has wished to teach us a lesson.'
>
> Conchita was asked why they had gone to where the crazy fellow was staying, and why they had repeatedly given him the crucifix to kiss, and she replied, "The Virgin told us, 'You [all] *despise him, but I love him.*'"

APPENDIX III

During one of the earliest of his fifteen visits to Cantabria, Kelly met and befriended Santander tailor, Plácido Ruiloba Arias, one of the prime witnesses of the Garabandal happenings and a prime source for articles and books on the subject. He once showed Kelly a whole room in his tailor shop used for storing audio tapes, newspaper articles, notes from the visionaries and more.

During a later visit, Placido invited the American to his flat to a gathering at which he, an auxiliary Bishop of New York, Spaniard Francisco Garmendia and a friend would listen to a fascinating tape recording made by Father Francis Benac S.J. after having interviewed Dr. Angel Alvarez and his wife, Menchu. At the end of the meeting Placido gave Kelly a copy of the tape, which the latter transcribed, translated into English and sent to the Workers of Our lady of Mt. Carmel for publication.

As far as the author knows, the story has never been published in the Santander newspapers. (Refer chap 12 page 153 and appendix IV).

TWICE CURED

Reprinted from *GARABANDAL MAGAZINE* October–December 1991

By Ed Kelly

Ever since Santander Bishop, Juan Antonio del Val, launched his new investigation of the Garabandal apparitions, there has been a great deal of interest in the outcome of this new inquiry which, from all reports, is just about complete. Among the criteria used for judging the authenticity of events such as these, are cures resulting from them. The following case bears a lot of weight in this regard since it happened right in Santander, among members of the medical profession, and consequently is well documented.

It was 1965. Menchu was just fifteen days out of the hospital where she had undergone a terrible ordeal. Now she was determined to get the most out of life, and was making the party rounds when she met the young doctor who was eventually to become her husband. Dr. Alvarez was interested in Menchu, but she cautioned him that in the hospital she had been pronounced incurable, had been given the Last Rites, but was somehow miraculously cured. He laughed it off.

"Bah! They were mistaken."

"Don't say that Angel. Some day you might have to eat those words."

THE CURE

Menchu Mendiolea was a fun-loving 18-year-old with a lively sense of humor, leading a normal life and happy finally to be out of school where she was, in her own words, a "troublemaker, a real disaster." One day upon returning to her home in Santander from Madrid, she began to feel ill. Spots had formed on her body so she went to see Doctor Tresmares. He diagnosed a disease called thrombocytopenic purpura. There was a diminution in her blood of platelets, colorless discs necessary for coagulation, so he put her on cortisone. It was serious all right, but if she followed the prescribed treatment and took good care of herself she should recover, said the doctor.

Menchu followed the doctor's orders, but saw that she was only getting worse instead of better. Hospitalized at Valdecilla, her condition became critical as she lapsed into a coma that was to last for seventeen days. Blood transfusions proved fruitless, and the hospital director informed the parents that there was nothing more they could do for her. A Carmelite priest was notified, and he administered Extreme Unction.

The day Menchu was anointed and still in the coma, a family friend brought a crucifix kissed by Our Lady at Garabandal, with the instructions that it be venerated and the intercession of the Virgin of Garabandal be sought. At the same time, a nun brought some needles from one of the pine trees at Garabandal.

When the crucifix with the instructions was given to Menchu's father, a pious man, her mother exclaimed, "Ah, Dios mío! Let's see if this is true. Let's pray."

Mr. Mendiolea then asked everyone present--their family, the group of Menchu's friends (all young people), and the Carmelite priest, who had been with Menchu every night,—to pray.

At the conclusion of the prayers, Menchu opened her eyes and began to move. The doctors were immediately called. Blood samples were taken which showed the platelets had increased. The doctors suggested she be taken home to recuperate in familiar surroundings before returning to the hospital for an operation to remove the spleen.

Eight days later, Menchu was back at Valdecilla for a checkup to see if she had enough platelets and red cells in the blood for the operation to be performed. Tests showed some 300,000 platelets and it was determined that no operation was necessary. She was cured.

TEN YEARS LATER

By 1975 the Alvarezes had two children, and Menchu was in her eighth month expecting their third, when spots again appeared all over her body. She became severely anemic and was admitted to the hospital and diagnosed as having very few platelets. The red cells were down and her anemia was more serious

It was suspected that her illness was the same as the first, but one of the problems now was to see if the pregnancy had to be terminated. It was feared that since she didn't have sufficient platelets, the placenta could become dislodged in giving birth. There could be a massive hemorrhage and more complications. They also faced the problem of delivering the baby. It was also decided to take out the spleen. The surgeons were consulted and said it was technically possible.

While the doctors were still trying to decide the best course of action, Menchu was given cortisone and blood transfusions. Then what her husband, Dr. Alvarez, had feared the most, happened. While talking with a colleague he said, "I'm afraid she hardly has any platelets left. Only 500 or so were counted. I'm afraid the placenta will become dislodged and she'll start to bleed."

The other doctor responded, "Don't worry. You can leave now, with the assurance that every precaution will be taken."

Dr. Alvarez no sooner left the hospital, than Menchu started to bleed, not much, but she started to bleed. The surgery planned for the next day had to be done at once. Platelets had to be prepared, and friends had to be contacted to donate blood. Around midnight she was moved and made ready for the operation.

In the morning, after a coagulation count was found acceptable, she was taken to the operating room where a cesarean section was performed. (A baby girl was born premature and died shortly thereafter.)

Up to this point all had gone well, but then after about an hour, Menchu took a sudden turn for the worse. Dr. Alvarez immediately informed his colleagues, the hematologists and the surgeons who had performed the operation. Menchu's condition continued to deteriorate and she went into shock. She was moved to intensive care but her condition remained serious. She went into shock again. The crisis passed, but then came the worst part, the diagnosis. Dr. Alvarez was informed that his wife had acute erythemia, the equivalent of leukemia only it involved the red cells, and thus the outcome would be fatal. Patients with this disease last no more than a couple of months or a year at the most.

GARABANDAL

Menchu had been operated on at the Residencia Cantabria but now in the post-operative state was back at Valdecilla. It was at this stage that Menchu's parents started talking about Garabandal. Not much attention had been given to the first cure, and the parents entertained thoughts that perhaps because due credit had not been given to the intervention of the Virgin of Garabandal, the disease had returned. (See chap. 12 page 153)

Dr. Alvarez had certainly not paid much attention to the first cure of his wife, but now that the situation was hopeless from a medical standpoint, he was ready to try anything, "perhaps grabbing at the last thread," as he put it.

The entire hematology team, as well as the pathologists and their assistants, and the team of Dr. Garcia Conde, head of the department of internal medicine, also a hematologist, the doctors of general surgery, and the obstetricians for the cesarean section plus the lab technicians were involved in the case. Every attempt was made to see that perhaps some other diagnosis could be given. But the consensus of the doctors was the same—acute erythemia.

The family decided to invoke the Virgin of Carmel of Garabandal. A medal kissed by Our Lady had been sent through Jacinta, one of the seers. Dr. Alvarez didn't give it much importance, but began to think to himself, "If this is true then perhaps there is a way . . . or maybe it's nothing at all."

Everyone started to pray, including Dr. Alvarez who had not practiced his religion since he was a schoolboy. One day while they were praying, Dr. Alvarez suddenly got the urge to go to Garabandal, even though he didn't know where it was. He asked his brother-in-law if he knew how to get there. When he answered, yes, Dr. Alvarez responded, "Well, I want to go."

UNUSUAL CONFIDENCE

Before making the trip, an interesting thing happened. Dr. Alvarez recalled his conversation with his colleagues:

> I spoke with a good friend of mine, Dr. Garijo, the chief of section, and said something like, "I don't know why but this [invoking the Virgin of Garabandal] is going to change everything; there is going to be a change for the better." Dr. Garijo responded, "Oh, if that were only true!"
>
> I asked him what he would think if it did happen and he said, "Well, either we've made a mistake [in our diagnosis] or it would be a miracle."
>
> It couldn't have been more than five minutes after this conversation took place when Dr. Zubizarreta, the chief of service, came by and Garijo said to him, "Listen to what our friend is saying," and he told him of my contention. I then told them both that very soon they would be in for a surprise, and I remember being very certain and calm despite the fact that this was no joking matter.
>
> Then Zubizarreta put his hand on my shoulder and said, "Well, it's good that you have high hopes, but it's my duty to remind you again that your wife's situation is very bad and that there is nothing we can do for her." I answered, "Yes, yes, but it's my duty to tell you that I believe there is going to be a great change. What would you say to that, Zubizarreta?" And he said, "Chico (my young friend), that would be a miracle." I responded, "I believe you're going to have to sign your name to that statement." And I said it smiling and confidently.

THE TRIP TO GARABANDAL

On December 7, 1975, Dr. Alvarez and Javier, his brother-in-law, left for Garabandal. It was a cold, icy day, so cold that the doctor had trouble starting the car. Menchu knew nothing of all this.

When they arrived in Garabandal, Javier went into a little cafe to have some breakfast, but the doctor wasn't interested in eating and went straight up to the Pines. There he was most impressed to find, at 10:00 o'clock in the morning on this bitterly cold day, a man kneeling motionless in prayer, with his arms outstretched in the form of a cross.

Dr. Alvarez began praying the rosary as best he could. He didn't have the beads and had forgotten the mysteries so just counted off the ten Hail Mary's of each decade on his fingers. When he finished, he went down to the village, picked up Javier and went to the car for the drive back to Santander. As they were driving down the mountain, he said to Javier, "Menchu is cured." (In the 1978 interview, Father Benac asked him, "What did you feel up there to say such a thing?" Instead of answering, he buried his face in his hands and started to weep. The tape recorder was turned off momentarily to respect his emotion and secret.) Javier just looked at him as if to say, 'This guy must be crazy. Perhaps living through this crisis was starting to affect his way of thinking.'

They arrived back at Valdecilla, but Dr. Alvarez didn't say anything to anyone. Every day Menchu was given a spinal tap so he wanted to wait until the following day to see the results. He was convinced the blood count would be good. On the previous day, tests showed 500 to 1,000 platelets.

December 8th, feast of the Immaculate Conception, is a national holiday in Spain, and Dr. Alvarez couldn't find anyone at the hospital. Finally he went to the cafeteria. There, he met the hematologist who was on duty. Confidently he asked, "And the analysis of my wife, what did it show?"

"Oh, yes. She is doing very well indeed. She has some 30,000 platelets."

Dr. Alvarez said he was expecting that, but wanted them to confirm it. With acute erythemia there are malignant cells, but from the moment the cure took effect they started to diminish; the platelets went up, and

298

"amen" the cancer was finished. He remembered the reaction of his colleagues.

Then I went to talk to [Dr.] Zubizarreta, the chief of hematology and said, "What do you say now?" He shrugged his shoulders not knowing what to say, and stammered, "Well, well I, I don't know what to say to you; if it weren't your wife . . . "

They had analyzed the spleen and the blood, first the pathologist and then the hematologists, and both of them, by different means, arrived at the same conclusion—acute erythremia. People must realize that all of these were my colleagues who went to great lengths for Menchu, that is, they all had analyzed her carefully, doing everything to avoid coming to the conclusion that it was erythremia, but that was the verdict. Now, seeing her well perplexed them. I told them over and over again, "Don't worry, you weren't mistaken; what happened was that 'somebody' wanted to change the development of the case and that's it; it's that simple."

Dr. Alvarez changed a great deal after his wife's cure, returning to the practice of his faith and reciting the rosary every day. Menchu for her part has been to Garabandal to give thanks on more than one occasion, although she knows very little about the events and never became involved in any way. The times she has gone up to Garabandal were only to pray and then leave. She never met any of the seers or ever sat down to talk with anyone.

When Menchu and Dr. Alvarez first became serious about each other (after Menchu's first cure), she gave him a medal kissed by Our Lady at Garabandal. At the time, he wore it only to please her. He is still wearing it today.

APPENDIX IV
CATHOLIC CHURCH AUTHORITIES LOOK
FAVORABLY ON GARABANDAL

Nine Bishops or Apostolic Administrators of the Diocese of Santander have issued a total of twelve statements on Garabandal that have been made public. The first six and the eighth were given as press notices in the local newspapers, the seventh as a letter to all the bishops of the world, and the last four as personal letters that the bishops later duplicated and sent to others who sought information.

Present bishop Manuel Monge (2015 -) sent a letter to José María Rovira on June 24, 2015. He writes, *"Todos los obispos de la Diocesis, desde 1961 al 2015, afirmaron que no constaba . . . "* (All the bishops . . . stated that the supernaturalism of the apparitions wasn't evident . . .).

His letter is very similar to the one that Bishop Vilaplana (1991-2006) sent to Garabandal author, Ramón Pérez on June 8, 1993.[1] Bishop Zamora (2007 – 2014) sent a copy of this to the author on May 7, 2008 saying that his position was the same as Vilaplana's. Bishop Monge makes one significant change from the letter of these two predecessors. He omits the clause, "the question [of Garabandal] that I consider ended."

In February 2007, Santander Apostolic Administrator, Archbishop Carlos Osoro (in August of 2014 appointed Archbishop of Madrid and more recently made a cardinal), in a letter to a Spanish woman gave the most positive of all of the statements on Garabandal. He writes that he has authorized priests to go to the village and celebrate Mass there at any time and to administer the Sacrament of Reconciliation to all. He adds, "I respect the apparitions and have known of authentic conversions."

In a letter dated May 7, 2007, the Archbishop wrote a letter to Kelly expressing the same sentiments. Since Kelly did not ask him his position on Garabandal, he reasons that Osoro used the opportunity to make his very favorable opinions on the apparitions better known.

——◦•◆•◦——

1 An English translation of Bishop José Vilaplana's letter can be found at www.ewtn.com/library/BISHOPS/GARABAND.2006.

In 1979 Bishop del Val Gallo (1972-1991) told the author that the best appraisal of the events, and a good expression of his own, was Bishop Beitia's statement of 1965. Beitia wrote, "*No consta de la sobrenaturalidad* ... (It isn't certain if the apparitions are of supernatural origin.)" This is a neutral position and the one that is given on all reported apparitions until a definitive "yes" or "no" decision is reached.

Beitia (1962- 965) included in his communication, "We haven't found material for condemnatory ecclesiastical censure, either in the doctrine or in the spiritual recommendations that have been divulged on this occasion. They simply repeat the current doctrine of the Church in these matters." No bishop has reversed that judgment.

Bishops Puchol Montis (1965-1967) and José María Cirarda (1968-1971) issued negative communications on Garabandal in 1967, 1968 and 1970. Cirarda, who, the locals said, took putting an end to Garabandal as the prime objective of his tenure, included in his letter to all bishops, Beitia's statement of doctrinal orthodoxy.

All of the public statements, (except those of Puchol, who based his evaluation entirely on the declarations of the visionaries, and Osoro who seemingly based his most positive opinion on all the information available) were based entirely on the information supplied by the five official investigating doctors and priests. Thus, the "All of the bishops stated that the supernatural nature of the apparitions was not evident," should not lead readers to infer that these evaluations were based upon all of the information available. They were not.

The first seven official statements, along with letters from the Vatican, are included in the booklet, *Declaraciones Oficiales de la Jerarquía Sobre Garabandal*. It can be read online, but published in 1970, it is outdated.

The Catholic Church permitting devotions at a sight is an indication that she looks favorably towards a reported apparition there. In January 1987, Bishop del Val instructed Garabandal pastor, Father Jaime Gómez Gonzalez, to allow priests to celebrate Mass there. Along with allowing devotions, this action lifted the 1962 ban placed on priests going to Garabandal without the express permission of the local chancery, and also fulfilled the prophesy given years earlier that a future bishop would lift the ban.

Since 2007, devotions have not only been permitted, but the pastor, Father Rolando Cabeza Fuentes, has been leading the way. Because

Rolando is the dean of the *Virgen de la Barquera* area, and in close contact with his bishop (He mentioned this often), it seems that his actions reflect the present more positive attitude of the Diocese.

On Holy Saturday 2007, Rolando started including in the Litany of Loreto the invocation, "*Reina de Garabandal.*" A couple of weeks later, when he led the Rosary on his knees at the Pines, a place of significance during the apparitions, he again prayed, "Queen of Garabandal," during the litany.

In May 2010, Kelly was present when Don Rolando conducted a service on the first anniversary of Mary Loli's death. Father said at the opening "Let us pray, that at her death she was greeted by the Blessed Virgin who visited her many times here." Kelly, who attends Mass daily while in the village, does not consider Don Rolando a sentimental man, but says that that morning he had difficulty holding back the tears. Another Mass attendee said that Father did not hold back the tears. [2]

On June 18, 2011, don Rolando celebrated the fiftieth anniversary of the first reported appearance of the angel with a Mass outside the village church. On July 2, after an all night exposition and adoration of the Blessed Sacrament, he celebrated the fiftieth anniversary of the first reported visit of the Blessed Virgin Mary with a Mass that started with a hymn of his own composing:

Donde en julio la Virgen María bajó	Where in July The Virgin Mary came down
De los cielos a Garabandal.	From the heavens to Garabandal.
La Virgen María, madre de Cristo,	The Virgin Mary, mother of Christ,
Ha puesto su trono en Garabandal.	Has put her throne in Garabandal.

For the second time in two weeks, he devoted the homily to the reported apparitions. He said that what happened in Garabandal fifty years ago, and has brought over four million pilgrims to the village, wasn't a child's game (Bishop Puchol Montis' judgment in March 1967). He expressed hope that Garabandal would become a school of prayer, encouraged Garabandal devotees to be Christians with candles lit in the

---

2 The author attended daily and Sunday Mass in the village, with Don Rolando presiding, in the spring of 2007, 2008, 2010 and 2012 and during September of 2015.

world, read the second message (given by the angel), and stressed the always discreet behavior of the visionaries. Some of the old Garabandal promoters present in the village cried, not expecting such positive remarks from the church before the miracle. [3]

Given the official "not certain" judgment of the present Santander bishop and the majority of his predecessors, and Rome's, "We leave it in the hands of the local bishop," to get a better idea of the attitude of the Catholic Church on Garabandal, it helps to consider what influential Church members and men of science have said or done.

Pope Paul VI

Jesuit Father Xavier Escalada reports that during a papal audience, when he complained about much opposition to his promoting Garabandal, the Pope cut him short saying, "Tell them that it is the Pope himself who tells you to make the account of Garabandal known."

This same priest reports in the *Legión Blanca,* that Pope Paul VI said to him on November 7, 1968, "Garabandal is the most beautiful human story since the coming of Our Lord Jesus Christ into the world; it is like the second coming of the Blessed Virgin to earth." [4]

On January 12, 1966 Conchita was called to Rome by the then pro-prefect of the Congregation for the Doctrine of Faith, Cardinal Ottaviani. Conchita asked to see the Pope. During that meeting the Pope told her, **"Conchita, I bless you and with me the whole world blesses you."** [5]

On December 12, 1970, he gave his apostolic blessing to Father Verfaille, S.D.B. and to his Marial Garabandal Center collaborators in Lubumbasi Republic of Zaire. [6]

On May 19, 1971, Paul VI gave his blessing to María C. Saraco, Director of St. Michael's Garabandal Center in Pasadena, California saying, "We ask the Lord to sustain you, and through your apostolate of prayer, to grant increased holiness in the Church and especially in the hearts of priests." Mrs. Saraco, in presenting to the Holy Father a rosary,

———————◦•◦———————

3 Synopsis/commentary on the homily sent from eye-witness, Fatima Gonzalez Cuenca. The song can be heard on http://es.gloria.tv/?media=171814.

4 María Josefa Villa De Gallego, *Los Pinos De Garabandal Iluminarán Al Mundo,* (Barcelona: Ediciones Rondas, 1994), P. 248.

5 María Josefa de Gallego, *Los Milagros o Favores de Nuestra Madre de Garabandal.* (Santander: 2002) p. 222

6 Porro, *Garabandal Hoy,* p. 67.

carefully explained that . . . attached to the rosary was an object kissed by the Blessed Virgin during her appearances there. The Holy Father, after hearing this and accepting the rosary, took Mrs. Saraco's hands in his with great affection, saying, "Thank you, thank you very much." *The Vigil* carries two photographs of the Pope conversing with Mrs. Saraco. [7]

In August 1965, Pope Paul VI suspended audiences for two weeks to read, study, and meditate on Conchita's *Diary* and Father Laffineur's *The Star on the Mountain*. Shortly later, on October 14, 1965, he abolished Canon 1399 which had prohibited the right to publish certain books such as those dealing with reported apparitions without an *Imprimatur* or a *Nihil Obstat* or other permission. [8]

Saint John Paul II

In *Garabandal Journal* one reads, "There is a book on Garabandal, written by Albrecht Weber in 1993, entitled *Garabandal Der Zeigefinger Gottes* (Garabandal the Finger of God), of which a first edition copy was presented to Pope John Paul II. The Pope asked his secretary, Father (now Cardinal) Stanislaus Dziwisz, to write to the author. In the subsequent printing (2000) of the book, on page 19, a portion of the message is reprinted as follows:

> May God reward you for everything, especially for the deep love with which you are making known the events connected with Garabandal more widely known. May the messages of the Mother of God find an entrance into the hearts before it is too late. As an expression of his joy and gratitude the Holy Father gives you his apostolic blessing.

Accompanying this letter [from Dziwisz], was a greeting by the Pope in his own handwriting. In regard to it, Weber states, "From the attached greeting in the pope's own handwriting, it is clear how deep an interest he has in the events of Garabandal, and how anxious he is that they should be made known in a credible way." [9]

A group of pilgrims from Santander was in a room with other small groups to meet the Pope. When he greeted this group he exclaimed,

---

7 *The Vigil*, (St Michael's Garabandal Center: Pasadena).
8 Gallego, *Los Milagros*, pp.220-221
9 Barry Hanratty, *Garabandal Journal* July-August, 2002

"Oh Santander: *La Bien Aparecida* (Patron of the Diocese), *Santo Toribio* (where the largest portion of the True Cross is housed) and *San Sebastián de Garabandal*." [10]

A photo of John Paul II meeting with Loli and her family can be seen on websites and in Garabandal journals.

Cardinal Ottaviani

In August 1979, author Ramón Pérez told Kelly, "We [he and companion, Jacques Serre] just talked with Jacinta. She told us about her visit with Cardinal Ottaviani in 1975. She said that the Cardinal told her, 'Jacinta, the Vatican has absolutely nothing against Garabandal, but since it involves prophecies of an eschatological nature [dealing with the final events in the history of the world] of transcendental importance for the whole world, don't expect that we pronounce on it quickly.' " The Vatican Secretary of State wrote similar words on April 23, 1969 to English Archbishop Fitzgerald. [11]

The Cardinal also told Jacinta at that time, "We must pray that the Church recognize the importance of the apparitions of San Sebastian de Garabandal." [12]

"On that same day..., **Cardinal Philippe**, who was meeting with some bishops, on hearing of the presence of Jacinta, told them, 'I am going to leave you for a few minutes to say hello to one of the visionaries of the Apparitions of San Sebastian de Garabandal in Spain.' On taking leave of Jacinta he said, 'I bless you in the name of the Virgin Mary, and I am with you completely.'

'And with this I understood,' says Jacinta, 'that he was convinced that the apparitions were of the Virgin Mary; we exchanged many observations about this.' " [13]

Before these meetings, the popes and cardinals would have been well informed about Garabandal through the many books that authors had sent to the Vatican and through the information supplied by the Santander bishops. It is difficult to imagine that there would be such interest by popes

---

10 Gallego, *Los Pinos*, p.252
11 Porro, *Garabandal Hoy*, p. 104
12 Gallego, *Los Pinos*, p. 249.
13 Ibid., 249-250. (also on web sites)

and cardinals at the Vatican in teenagers from rural Spain were there not some compelling reason.

Cardinal Rozales of the Philippines baptized Conchita's youngest daughter.

Bishop Antonio del Val Gallo (1972-1991). In a conversation with the bishop, Ramón Pérez said, "You don't have to answer this, but what do you think? If Garabandal were just another apparition with a request for prayer and sacrifice and not one with important prophecies for the world, then it would have been approved long ago." Bishop del Val answered, *"No está mal. No está mal."* ("Not bad. Not bad.") Kelly has a tape of Perez's account of that meeting.

The bishop agreed to be interviewed for the video, *Garabandal, The Eyewitnesses*. In that video, he says nothing negative about Garabandal.

This bishop was photographed numerous times with the visionaries and their families, and would have known that these would be publicized. The photos appear in *Garabandal Magazine*, Lindenhurst New York, and in *The Vigil*, Pasadena, California.

He gave Conchita the go-ahead to participate in the British Broadcasting Company film, *Garabandal, After the Visions*. (See Mother Theresa below.)

In 1982, Bishop del Val told his doctor that he believed that Garabandal was supernatural. (See Dr. Tuñón below.)

He commissioned a second study of Garabandal in 1986 whose work, it has been said, he financed personally.

In January 1987, Bishop del Val lifted the 1962 ban placed on priests going to Garabandal without the express permission of the Santander Chancery.

The Bishop received for personal interviews: Father Benac in '78 and '79, Kelly in '73 and '79, Ramón Pérez in '79, María Sarraco, Michael Tubberly and most likely others. Jacinta visited him often. It is doubtful that Bishop del Val, or any bishop, would devote such time to a topic he considered unimportant, "a child's game," according to Bishop Puchol.

Bishop José Vilaplana (1992-2007) appears with Jacinta and her family in an August 1992 photograph in *The Vigil*.

Monsignor Joao Venancio, Bishop of Leira-Fatima, told Father Alfred

Combe, "The Message given by the Blessed Virgin Mary at Garabandal is the same that she gave at Fatima, adapted for our time . . ." [14]   Bishop Venancio knew Conchita, and when he spent time visiting her in New York, she gave him a special ring that he wore along with his Episcopal ring.

Father Valentín Marichalar, pastor of Garabandal during the apparitions, taught the four girls, heard their confessions and kept a diary of the happenings. He said that he didn't believe at the beginning, but did so after receiving the specific proof that he had asked of the Blessed Virgin Mary.

Father Francis Benac S.J., a Spaniard, devoted much of the last thirty years of his life spreading the Messages of Garabandal throughout India and in other countries.

Father Lucio Rodrigo S.J., a confessor and counselor for Conchita, and rector emeritus of the Pontifical University of Comillas, said that he received a personal and unequivocal proof of the authenticity of the Garabandal apparitions.

Father Santiago Gamende, confessor and canon at the Santander Cathedral told Kelly that when he was a young priest, the bishop gave him the dossier on Garabandal and asked him to study it and give his opinion. Since Santiago had never had an ecstasy, in order to better judge, he thought it wise to attempt a self-induced trance. That night he heard God tell him, "Go to the Bishop and tell him that Garabandal is true." His mother came in from the next room to see what was the matter. He said, "In the morning the sheets were wet from sweat, ringing wet, not just damp."

Santiago was in no way a Garabandal promoter or even follower. His name doesn't appear in any of the many books or articles written on Garabandal. Besides a, "How's your Garabandal work going?" this account of the self-induced trance was the only thing he ever said to Kelly about Garabandal in thirty-nine years.

Father Luís Retenaga, prefect of the Seminary at San Sebastián, writes:

> The girls are in possession of a very profound knowledge of the

---

14   Gallego, *Los Pinos*, p.63

things of God and of His plans for man's salvation. Their spiritual life is very intense although, lacking as they do both education and culture, they cannot convey to us the rich experiences of their souls. In the same way that many of Christ's contemporaries were unable to discern His infinite sanctity which was masked by naturalness and simplicity, so today there are many who cannot see the supernatural riches of these girls' souls, because everything is masked likewise by naturalness and simplicity. [15]

Doctor Andrés García de Tuñón, a retired Santander kidney specialist, became a believer in Garabandal as of result of Menchu Mediolea's cure. In May 2008, he told Kelly, "I was sitting on the corner of the bishop's bed visiting him after I had operated on him (1982). He told me, 'I, Anotnio del Val Gallo, believe in the supernatural origin of Garabandal, but as bishop I can't say that.' "

Doctor Luís Morales, a member of the Bishop's commission and prime mover against the validity of the apparitions, in a well-publicized address on May 30, 1983 before a packed house at Santander's largest and most prestigious lecture hall, declared that he now knew the Garabandal events were of supernatural origin. [16]

Dr. Ricardo Puncernau was the director of Neurological Services at the University Clinic for General Pathology at Barcelona and assistant professor of the medical faculty. After performing extensive tests of many kinds on the girls for twelve days, [work that put that of the official commission to shame] he concluded, "we do not find any natural scientific explanation which would explain the affair as a whole." [17] He adds, "The parapsychological phenomena at Garabandal are so important in quality and quantity that they can be considered as landmarks in the history of parapsychology." [18]

Dr. Apostolides, the chief of staff of the Pediatrics Service in the Central Hospital of Troyes, France, met Loli, Jacinta, and Conchita in the village in 1965 after the apparitions had been going on for more than four years.

<hr>

15 From a paper with heading *Rentería*, 19 Aug. 1964
16 Christopher Morris, "Why a New Investigation?" *Garabandal Magazine* 1989, p.8.
17 Ramón Pérez, *The Village Speaks* (Lindenhurst: The Workers of Our Lady of Mount Carmel, Inc. Fourth Edition, 2002), p.90-91.
18 Gallego, *Los Pinos*, P. 230.

Later he learned that psychiatrist, Dr. Morales of Santander Commission, had called these children hysterical and victims of hallucination and imagination caused by the great poverty and isolation of any out-of-the-way village, far from the city.

Apotolides says that pediatricians can detect this "disease" immediately, and that his impression of these three girls was the opposite. Given that they had been the center of attention by countless thousands for four years, he found their modesty, kindness, simplicity, and lack of any affectation to be miraculous. He adds, "that even if the numerous trances were simulated, and more so if they resulted from natural nervous phenomena, it is still a greater miracle that these girls have remained unchanged." [19]

Doctor Celestino Ortiz Pérez is a Santander pediatrician. After spending fifty-two days in the village at the time of the ecstasies, he concluded, "I can find no explanation which could present as natural events, phenomena which, according to our present knowledge, escape all natural reality." [20]

"At a study session, a group of French doctors concluded that the Garabandal apparitions are the product of a power absolutely beyond human capabilities." [21]

Saint Teresa of Calcutta is the Godmother of Conchita's youngest daughter.

While she was at her convent in Tijuana, Mexico not long before her death, the future saint asked Jacinta, who lives in Oxnard, California two hundred miles north, to come and visit her. Mother Teresa told Jacinta, "How fortunate and happy you must feel, for all the graces you have received from the Blessed Virgin . . . Jacinta, you are a chosen soul."

In 1980, Conchita Gonzalez Keena agreed to be filmed and interviewed by the British Broadcasting Corporation for a documentary entitled, *Garabandal, After the Visions.* The day before the scheduled filming, with the BBC director and crew ready to shoot, Conchita, with family and a friend, stopped at the convent of the Missionaries of Charity in the South Bronx to ask the Sisters to pray for the success of the film. [22]

<hr>

19 Laffineur, *Star on the Mountain*, p. 139-140.
20 Pérez, *El Pueblo Habla*, p. 91.
21 Ibid., p. 92
22 "Garabandal—After the Visions." Editorial. *Garabandal*, Jan-Mar 1984: 3-7.

The sisters were happy to see Conchita, whom they knew. The driver for the group and editor of *Garabandal Journal*, Barry Hanratty, relates, "We visited for a short time when the door from the waiting room to the convent opened, and, to our utter surprise, Mother Teresa came walking toward us . . . Mother greeted us warmly, especially Conchita since they were friends."

Conchita explained about the film and that the bishop had given permission. Seeing Conchita still reluctant, Mother Teresa advised her to call the Bishop again. Conchita phoned the Bishop saying, "Mother Teresa asked me to ask you if I can make this film . . ." He responded, "Of course, you can do the film for that reason [the honor and glory of God]." He also requested that Conchita send to him Mother's written message so he could keep it as a souvenir.

Before Mother Teresa left the New York area, she called Conchita and told her that she had been praying for the intention of the film. [23]

In a letter dated November 10, 1987, Mother Teresa wrote to the Santander Bishop and said that from the beginning she felt that the Garabandal events were authentic. She asked him to send her the names of all of the priests in his diocese because she wished to offer the spiritual help of one of her sisters individually for each one of them.

Bishop del Val accepted gratefully. The letter of invitation from Mother Teresa, Msgr. del Val's moving answer of acceptance, and his letter to his priests about both, can be read in *Los Milagros o Favores de Nuestra Madre de Garabandal*. [24]

Given Mother Teresa's interest in Garabandal and her friendship with two of the visionaries, it is difficult to think it a coincidence that she chose the diocese in which the village lies for this singular favor.

Reports of **Saint Pio's** belief in the importance of Garabandal are numerous. The following are from the Spring 1975 edition of *Needles*:

> 1) When a group of Spaniards asked Padre Pio about Garabandal, he answered, "Are you still asking about that? How long do you expect her to appear there? She has been appearing for eight months already!"

---

23 *Garabandal Journal*, March-April 2004, p.14.
24 Gallego, *Los Milagros*, p.110-112.

2) Conchita reports about her January 1966 meeting with Padre Pio, "He took the crucifix kissed by Our Lady and placed it in the palm of his left hand, over the stigmata. Then he took my hand and placed it in his palm, closing his fingers over my hand, and with his right hand he blessed my hand and the cross."

3) In October 1968, Conchita received a telegram from Padre Pio's Capuchin brother, Fr. Pellegrino, asking her to come to Lourdes. She left the same night. Pellegrino gave her a letter that he had written at Saint Pio's request and a piece of the veil that had covered his face after his death. The letter says, "I pray to the Most Holy Virgin to comfort you and guide you always towards sanctity, and I bless you with all my heart."

4) Conchita asked, "How is it that the Virgin told me that Father Pio is supposed to see the miracle, and he has died?" Father Pellegrino answered that Padre Pio told him that he saw the miracle before he died.

5) On March 3, 1962, Conchita received an unsigned letter, written in Italian but with no return address. When Conchita showed her the letter, the Virgin told her that it was from Padre Pio. It says:
Dear little girls,
At nine this morning the Blessed Virgin Mary spoke to me about you dear little girls, of your visions, and she has told me to tell you, **"Blessed children of San Sebastián de Garabandal, I promise that I will be with you until the end of your lives, and you will be with me until the end of the world and then united with me in the joy of paradise."**

Saint Pio continues:

They [people] don't believe in you or in your talks with the lady in white, but they will believe when it is too late. [25]

Some others who have expressed a favorable opinion on Garabandal include: Archbishops Cardinal Carlos Osoro Sierra (Madrid); Manuel Lopez (Mexico); Philip Hannan (New Orleans); Bishops Francisco Garmendia (New York); Paolo María Hnilica S.J. (Vatican); Roman Danylac (Canada);

———————⊃•◆•⊂———————

25 HYPERLINK "http://www.virgendegarabandal.net/mita73.htm"

Priests

Venerable Fr. Ciszek S.J.; Royo Marín O.P. (Spain); Marcelino Andreu S.J. (Taiwan); Luís Andreu S.J. (Spain); Ramón Andreu S.J. (Los Angeles); Felix Corta S.J. (Bilbao); José M. Alba Cereceda S.J. (Barcelona); Felix Larrazábal O.J.M. (Jerez de la Frontera); Alfredo Combe (France); M.L. Guérard de Lauriers O.P. (France); Angel María Rojas S..J. (Madrid); Justo A. Lofeudo (Argentina) and Gabriele Amorth SSP. (Rome).

Doctors

Jerome Domínguez (New York); Jean Caux, faculty of Medicine (Paris); Serge Fournier (France); Honorio Sanjuan Nadal (Barcelona); Angel Alvarez (Santander). In his book, *El Pueblo Habla*, Ramón Pérez gives a detailed account of the studies and conclusions of seven doctors, all of whom have stated or implied that no natural explanation for the observed phenomena has been found. [26]

Priests who have promoted Garabandal and authored books on it include: Fathers Joseph Pelletier, President of Assumption College (Massachusetts); M. Laffineur (Belgium), an official investigator of the apparitions at Beauraing and Banneux; Francios Turner O.P. (France); José Ramón Garcia de la Riva, pastor (Spain); Canon Julio Porro (Tarragona); Eusebio Pesquera, O.F.M.CAP (Spain); José Luís Saavedra (Madrid).

"In addition to Saint Teresa of Calcutta and Saint Pio, there are one Blessed and four other persons whose causes have been introduced, who have given testimony in favor of Garabandal: Blessed Madre María Maravillas de Jesús (d. 1974) who was beatified by Pope Paul II on May 10, 1998; Madre Esperanza de Jesús (1903-1983), foundress of the Apostles of Divine Mercy, whose Cause was introduced in 1988; Marthe Robin (+1981), foundress of the Foyers de Charité and a stigmatist whose Cause was introduced in 1991; Venerable Padre Manuel García Nieto, confessor to Conchita (+1974); Symphorose Chopin (1924-1983) whose cause was introduced in the diocese of Versailles, France, in 2000." [27]

One can disagree with the opinion of all of the above, but given their positions in the Church or in medicine, their prudence and wisdom, and the saintly lives of many of them, the list of those expressing favorable

---

26 Perez, *El Pueblo Habla*, pp. 184-189.
27 Barry Hanratty, "Saint Maravillas de Jesús," *Garabandal Journal*, January-February, 2003, p.6.

opinions seems noteworthy, especially when juxtaposed against the lack of anyone who will now testify against Garabandal. During Kelly's Spanish visits in 2010, 2012 and 2017, he spent time asking if there were any priests or doctors who would speak out publicly now against, or sign their names to writings criticizing Garabandal. Nobody knew of any.

PERSONAL

None of Kelly's Spanish priest friends ever said or even hinted that his interest in Garabandal might be dangerous to his faith or to that of others to whom he told the story. The priest who married Kelly, his wife's uncle, **Father Antonio de la Madrid**, was a seminary professor and translator of books of the Old Testament. **Father Santiago** was Kelly's wife's spiritual director, counseled the couple before marriage, preached at their wedding, and spoke with the author during the latter's visits to Santander as late as 2010.

Father José Rubio, S.D.B. in 1979 held the position of Diocesan Superintendent of Santander Catholic Schools with an office in the Chancery. He was a confrere of Kelly's wife's two brothers, Antonio and Santos. When taking Antonio to meet the Bishop before Antonio's ordination, he invited the American brother-in-law to go along. He explained how the Garabandal affair was a heavy burden to the Bishop.

Bishop del Val Gallo (1972-1991) spoke with Kelly about the reported apparitions for three hours in the bishop's office.

These scholarly clergymen were qualified to warn of any danger connected with promoting Garabandal. None of them ever did. Because of their love and concern for the author and his family, one would have expected them to do so — if they had a reason.

NEGATIVE OPINIONS

In the early years after the first reported apparitions, Santander bishops: Beitia, Puchol, Cirarda and del Val Gallo; commissioners: Father Odriozola and doctors Morales and Piñal; and priests: José Olano Ortiz, Amador Fernandez Gonzalez and Emiliano Murillo spoke or wrote against Garabandal. Beitia later changed to the neutral, *"no consta"* evaluation, Morales publicly stated his belief that Garabandal was of supernatural origin and del Val's later words and actions demonstrated his belief.

Father Odriozola, one of the two main movers (with Morales) on the Investigating Commission, stated publicly "Unfortunately, everything about Garabandal is a totally false myth." [28]

During the first third of a three-hour 1973 meeting, Father repeatedly answered with something that had nothing to do with Kelly's questions. "Is it true, Padre, that the Commissioners pressured the girls into denying?"

"People gave Conchita nice clothes."

He also corrected Kelly's "*negaciones*," saying, "The girls didn't deny seeing the Virgin, they made statements of uncertainty."

Only after the subject was diverted from Garabandal, did Odriozola ask his visitor's name and education, and invite him to sit down "and talk."

Father Amador Fernandez was chosen as the substitute for Fr. Valentín as pastor of the village for a few months starting on August 22, 1961. After witnessing Conchita in ecstasy on December 8, he stated, "There is nothing supernatural. . .I think that it is a matter of a psychic sickness." When he was asked about the nature of the sickness he said he didn't know what class of sickness it was. In the sermon that day he called the parishioners hypocritical and superstitious.[29]

Father José Olano was pastor of Santa Lucía Parish in Santander when Kelly spoke with him in June of 2000. He said that Conchita had told him recently that she maintained her position that she had expressed to him in the 60's, that she was uncertain if the Virgin had appeared to her or not. He neither elaborated nor expressed much interest in the subject.

Father Emiliano Murillo, Conchita's confessor while she was at the Pamplona convent, not only denied her absolution if she didn't deny the Garabandal apparitions, but also wrote her a letter during her summer

---

28 José María de Diós (Julio Porro), *Las Apariciones de Garabaandal. ¿Sin Interés?* (Zaragoza, 1972), p 311.

29 Ibid., p. 315

vacation reminding her that he had conditioned the absolution of her sins on her having to deny the apparitions." [30]

Author, Ramón Pérez states that he had no intention to search out those who were "for" or reject those who were "against" the authenticity of the apparitions. He writes that only three out of the forty-eight villagers with whom he spoke indicated that they did not believe it was supernatural. All three of these refused to have their opinions tape-recorded. He quotes Mari Cruz' mother, "Everything was a hoax. The children arranged everything and the witnesses in the village were deceived on account of their religious and intellectual ignorance."

He comments, "Her arguments, like those of the two others, lacked precise details and were not convincing." [31]

Since April 25, 1970 there have been no public negative statements by any Santander church official or, to Kelly's knowledge, by anyone who has studied the case.

THE INVESTIGATIONS

From the beginning there has been much confusion about the Catholic Church's rulings on the reported apparitions. The poor work and lack of systematic reporting of results by the Bishop Fernandez appointed Commission started the confusion.

Canon Julio Porro points out that the members of the Commission changed their minds about the causes of the observed phenomena and disagreed with each other. Morales gave as his final diagnosis, "reactions due to mental or emotional disorders." Del Val Gallo opined that it was "suggestion" like that of children when expecting the Three Wise Men. Porro expresses doubt that Del Val would have said this if he had been working under a canonical commission and sworn to tell the truth.[32]

In September 1972, when discussing the Garabandal investigations, a professor at the Santander Diocesan seminary at Cueto told Kelly, "People in positions can't always tell the truth."

---

30 *Garabandal Hoy* p. 94
31 Pérez, *El Pueblo Habla*, pp.193-194
32 Porro, *Las Apariciones*, p. 310-311.

On September 2, 1972, after hearing the author's confession at the Jesuit Church in that city, ninety year old Father Cobo S.J. said,"sure, they were forced confessions [those given by the visionaries to Bishop Puchol and others]"

On October 19 of that year, Kelly took the wobbly narrow gauge train to Bilbao to try to find the girl he had met the previous year and would later marry. While there, he dropped in on Father Felix Corta S.J., who had made an early study of Garabandal. He said, "The visionaries were subjected to horrible pressures by everybody — the bishop, members of the Commission, priests sent there [Garabandal]. They had no spiritual direction. A good priest, well versed in theology, mysticism, should have been sent there."

The author knows of no one close to the situation who claims that the investigation of the apparitions was done well or even according to the Church's guidelines. Commissioner, Fr. Francisco Odriozola told Kelly that the members were not sworn in as is required by Church law. Due to that omission, the Bishops' evaluations and directives do not have the force of law.

Prime mover of the bishop's investigating commission, Doctor Luis Morales, admitted to Jesús Hoyos, a reporter for *Alerta*, that there wasn't any commission or formal investigation; it was a sham.[33]

At a May 2, 1979 meeting at the Santander Chancery, Vicar General, Father Agapito Amieva Mier, told Kelly and his Salesian priest brother-in-law, "The Commission did its work lightly and without seriousness."

As a young priest commission member, del Val Gallo resigned after two months because he did not agree with the methods of the commission.[34] As bishop, he instituted a new commission in 1986. Both actions evidence that he did not consider the work of the first commission adequate. He mentioned weaknesses to Kelly (Appendix I).

One member of the second commission, from the sociology department of the University of Alcalá de Henares in Madrid, Montaña (most likely one of two synonyms along with Valmadian), wrote on December 29, 2008:

———⊂•◆•⊂———

33 Gallego, *Los Milagros*, p. 45
34 *Garabandal* , The Workers of Our Lady of Mount Carmel, New York, Jan-March 1989, "Why a new Investigation" Christopher Morris, p.7

The first thing that surprised me about the affair was the ignorance about the topic on the part of those of us who were going to take part . . .We were informing ourselves [about the nature of our task] while we worked. . . I refused to sign the final conclusions of the study based upon the data collected, because they didn't correspond with the truth of what was observed.

On his first of three visits, he spent days interviewing eye-witnesses. He castigates the original commissioners for their work, or lack of it writing, "I have reliable evidence that there was an authentic conspiricy against the Garabandandal happenings to discredit them . . . including making judgments without evidence on the part of a group of people [original commissioners] who ought to have been procescuted or at least some of them expelled from their mission." [35]

In September 2014 he wrote:

The official position of the Chancery was one of authentic persecution, and not only on the part of a single bishop, but of a number of them . . . Various individuals named themselves as part of an imaginary commissión that, representing the Santander Chancery, submitted the oldest of the vissionaries, Conchita, to all kinds of absurd and ridiculous tests . . . including visits to diviners, fortunetellers and others of that ilk. They threatened her and her family if she wouldn't deny. Pure mafia style moral gangsterism. [36]

In mid March, 2017 the author wrote to Bishop Monge asking to see the reports made by the two Investigating Commissions, saying that he did not want to disseminate false information. He followed a month later with an e-mail but received no answer. At the reception desk on March 24, the Santander Chancellor, Father Isidro Pérez López told him, "no, you aren't allowed to see the Commissions' reports."

Read more on this investigation and how anxious the villagers were to talk (after waiting twenty-five years) and what they would have told these commissioners in "Garabandal's New Investigation" by Kelly in the magazine *Garabandal*, January-March, 1989.

<hr />

35 www.foros.catholic.net/viewtopic.php?p=793598&sid=83327d03603ee2cc7fdd9d1
9a5570b2c"
36 www.Hispanismo.org/literatura/12770-garabandal.html"

Father Julio Porro Cardeñoso, a canon from the Spanish Diocese of Tarragona, is the one, in the opinion of the author, who has done the most work in appraising the local church's work on the apparitions. He devotes much in four books pointing out in great detail the many contradictions and weaknesses in the Bishops' official statements, and the poor work of the Commission on whose study the statements were based.

Bishop Cirarda, who wrote to all the bishops in the world that there wasn't much interest in the apparitions in his own Diocese, denied Porro permission to speak there. In August 1979, Kelly spent an afternoon in his home, during which lengthy, informative meeting, he told the American that Bishop Cirarda, in whose Santander Diocese a Father José Pérez had caused a scandal by impregnating a girl, appealed to the Cardinal of Tarragona to forbid Porro from writing more (against Cirarda). To which request the venerable Cardinal answered the young bishop, *"Cuídate tú de Pepe Pérez pero no te metas con los míos.* (You take care of Pepe [diminutive of José] Pérez but don't meddle with my priests."

Father Porro's: *Dios en la Sombra; Las Apariciones de Garabandal ¿Sin Interés?; Garabandal Hoy, ¿Mito o Misterio Divino?* and *El Gran Portento de Garabandal,* are good sources (in Spanish only) on the Santander Catholic Church's early reaction to Garabandal.

It remains for a future work in English to provide a comprehensive account of the Church's study of Garabandal, her public pronouncements on it, and the significance of these pronouncements.

THE PRESS

Reporters in and outside of Spain have not written accurately about the Church's pronouncements.

Because, up until 1975, the Catholic Church controlled much of the press in Spain and influenced the rest of it, reporters wrote what the local bishops wanted published and refrained from writing what they didn't want known about Garabandal. Page five of the Santander daily *Alerta* of March 19, 1967 is revealing. The first paragraph of the article, *Nunca Hubo Apariciones Milagrosas en Garabandal (There Never*

Were Miraculous Apparitions in Garabandal) starts by saying that the newspaper, in compliance with the Diocesan recommendations, has maintained silence about the supposed miracles of Garabandal (See also Appendices I and III).

But, "Yesterday afternoon, *el excelentísimo y reverendísimo* doctor Puchol Montis, bishop of Santander, assembled the members of the press, radio and television to make known an official note, that appeared in the *Diocesan Bulletin* that clarifies and puts an end to all of the speculations that have been disseminated about this subject."

The article without bye-line continues, "Respecting the authority of the bishops who have successively led the diocese of Santander in recent years, *Alerta* has refrained—as our readers can confirm—from giving publicity to this affair of San Sebastián de Garabandal, today formally declared false and without [any] foundation."

The Spanish press was submissive and quiet about anything positive, including the unexplainable cures of Santander resident, Menchu Mendiolea, but when the "visionaries" told the Bishop that they were not certain if they had seen the Virgin, the press gave this full coverage.

The Catholic media outside Spain has not been careful either, often representing the Santander bishops' "*no consta*" statements as definitively negative instead of neutral.

For example, three Catholic groups in the United States with widespread following issued a copy of the letter that Bishop José Vilaplana sent to Garabandal author Ramón Pérez in June 1993. They incorrectly give, "All the bishops . . . agreed that there was no supernatural validity for the apparitions" as the translation for, "*Todos los obispos . . . afirmaron que no constaba la sobrenaturalidad de dichas apariciones . . .*" They also misspell "Vilaplana" three times, miss two out of five letters in his predecessor's name and give 1996 instead of 1993 as the issue date of the letter. [37]

The Catholic Church classifies reported apparitions in the following three ways:

<hr/>

1) *Constat de supernaturalitate* — It is certain that the events are of supernatural origin.

2) *Non-constat de supernaturalitate* — It is not certain that the events are of supernatural origin.

3) *Constat de non supernaturalitate* — It is certain that the events are not of supernatural origin.

Bishop Puchol Montis gave a negative sounding *Nota Oficial* in 1967. Puchol, as Bishop del Val Gallo admitted to Kelly in 1973, and as is stated in the qualifying introductory phrase, based his judgment entirely on the statements of uncertainty by the "visionaries" of whether they had seen the Virgin or not.

Puchol wrote, "From the declarations of the visionaries it results: 1) That there has been no apparition . . . 2) That there has not been any message . . . 3) That all of the happenings in that locality have a natural explanation."

This judgment is scoffed at by countless eye-witnesses, and discounted by others, including apparently all of the Santander bishops after Puchol's successor, Cirarda. How does one undo or nullify by a statement, the naturally unexplainable trances, ecstatic marches, reading of minds, levitations, praying in Greek and Latin without any preparation? Puchol never responded to requests for an answer.

All together, the twelve statements on Garabandal issued by the Santander bishops contain fourteen neutral "*no consta*" clauses and only one "*consta de la no*" (definitively negative) statement. The latter was used by Bishop Cirarda in his 1970 letter when summarizing the now disregarded statement of Bishop Puchol Montis. Despite this written evidence, many Catholic publications still report the bishops' statements as if they were the third (not supernatural) category.

Kelly claims that his second year Spanish students know the difference between putting the "no" after, and putting it before the verb. It is the difference between, "I'm certain (sure) that my mother (or God's) did not visit Garabandal" and "I'm not certain (sure) if my mother (or God's) visited Garabandal or not." The bishops, basing their statements on the Commission's recommendations, used the impersonal, "It isn't certain," structure.

GUIDELINES

Five articles, *Apariciones y Revelaciones Privadas* by José María Saiz, one of three priests on the original Commission, were published in *Alerta* in July of 1961 to guide readers to a proper understanding of the events that "were turning Santander on its head." Excerpts follow:

> When one of these presumed preternatural happenings breaks onto the scene, few are able to situate themselves on an even keel on the balance of equilibrium. . . The majority fall into one of the two extremes, into skepticism or into facile credulity.

> The Church speaks with relative ease when the absence of the supernatural is manifest. On the other hand, for positive affirmation, its reserve is much greater . . .

> The Church, . . . acts with such an extreme prudence that many of the faithful judge it excessive. Its distrust seems to reflect a negation of the supernatural. In reality it is different. The Church doesn't put limits on the power of God to intervene in the history of each day in new and disconcerting ways. The Church believes in the positive personal action of God in our world in extraordinary ways.

> Man always feels an irresistible attraction towards the unusual and the marvelous and he trembles with seductive vibrations confronted by the possibility of an experimental contact with persons from the celestial world. . . [but] Those who might think that they run only on the impulse of faith, might reflect on the abandonment of Christ in the tabernacle and suspicions will arise in them of whether or not their tremblings proceed exclusively from their faith.

> That which gives us worth before God is supernatural love with all its derivations and consequences. If this is lacking, apparitions, revelations and all the rest don't count before God. The Church conforms its judgment with God's. For the canonization of the saints it prescinds from the exciting charisms and pays attention to the virtues. We have St. Bernadette on the altars because she practiced virtue to a heroic degree, not because she saw the Blessed Virgin in the Grotto of Massabielle.

THE MEANING AND RELEVANCE OF THE CATHOLIC CHURCH'S TEACHING ON GARABANDAL

According to the decree issued by the Sacred Congregation for Rites on November 29, 1931, the Church doesn't judge supernatural charisms. "When the Church approves private revelations, apparitions and visions, it limits itself to testifying with its approbation, that in them there isn't anything contrary to faith and customs and therefore, these can be believed according to human faith without danger of error." [38]

From Kelly's experience promoting Garabandal, it seems that many infer from the Church's approval of an apparition more than she intends, and from lack of approval, a negativity that the Church doesn't intend.

The Catholic Church does not require its members to believe in approved apparitions nor forbid them believing in unapproved ones. Detractors teach that it isn't necessary to believe in any unapproved apparitions. Kelly does not agree. There is a difference between obligation and necessity. If God intervenes with his children in an extraordinary way (apparitions), it is logical to believe that he thinks we need his special help. Yes, we can ignore his warnings, but we do so at our own peril. Although the church doesn't oblige members to believe in apparitions, God obliges us to seek and follow the truth. The church confirms the truth.

It is Kelly's understanding that his certainty that Garabandal is God's work, is of the same nature as his certainty about other religious truths (e.g., that God exists, that there is eternal life). Father Tenant Wright S.J., answering for the Theology Department of Santa Clara University, agreed without qualification. Father Kevin Joyce PhD., Diocese of San José, said that the only difference was that in the former case new evidence could be found while in the latter, not.

God can do anything. He can grant the certainty that Garabandal is his special work, of extreme importance, and that he desires that it be made known. Kelly says that when he first heard a villager erupt in anger against the prohibitions put on her village, he thought, "What happened here is important. It is too much for my finite mind to understand. I will

---

38 Porro, *Garabandal Hoy*, p. 47.

pray and keep my eyes and ears open." As a child he learned "God can neither deceive nor be deceived." He has done neither so far.

Detractors accuse promoters of disobedience if they disagree with the Commissions' evaluations.

In 1982, Antonio del Val expressed his belief in Garabandal to Doctor Tuñón but explained that as bishop he couldn't say that.

In admirable prudence, he knew the bishop was held to higher standards than he was as an individual. Do detractors fault him for disagreeing with his bishop?

All outside of the Diocese owe the Santander bishops respect, but not obedience. That is owed to one's own bishop. A bishop might direct his priests not to allow a talk on Garabandal in his parish, but it is difficult to imagine a bishop telling people not to tell friends or neighbors about Garabandal or not to give a lecture on it at the public library. Bishops did that in Spain until some forty years ago but not in America.

Detractors might be thinking of prudence when they accuse of disobedience. Yes, one needs to be prudent about Garabandal and in all matters, including rejecting it and especially before speaking against it. All must seek the truth and not disseminate error.

Those who say or write that the Church judges that Garabandal is not supernatural are incorrect. They are teaching something that is not true. They are very imprudent.

"If it is from God, you will not be able to stop them [those who make known what they have seen and heard and felt]. You may even find yourselves fighting against God"(Acts 5:39).

SOURCES CONSULTED

English

Garcia de Pesquera, Eusebio, O.F.M., CAP. *She Went in Haste to the Mountain*. Lindenhurst: The Workers of Our Lady of Mount Carmel, 2003.

Laffineur, M. and le Pelletier, M.T. *Star on the Mountain*. Newtonville: Our Lady of Mount Carmel of Garabandal, Inc. 1968.

Pelletier, Joseph A. *Our Lady Comes to Garabandal*. New York: Workers of Our Lady of Mount Carmel De Garabandal, INC. 1971.

Perez, Ramón. *The Village Speaks*. 4th ed. Lindenhurst: The Workers of Our Lady of Mount Carmel. 2002.

Van Zeller, Dom Hubert. *Ideas for Prayer*. Springfield: Templegate. 1966.

Kreeft, Peter. *Christianity for Modern Pagans: Pacal's Penseés Edited, Outlined and Explained*. San Francisco: Ignatius Press, 1996.

Pelletier, Joseph A. *God Speaks at Garabandal*. Worcester: Assumption, 1970.

_____. *Our Lady Comes to Garabandal*. 7th ed. New York: Workers of Our Lady, 1971.

Sanchez-Ventura y Pascual, F. *The Apparitions of Garabandal*. 7 ed. Trans. A. de Bertodano. Detroit: San Miquel, 1973.

Turner, François. *Our Lady Teaaches at Garabandal*. 4 ed. Lindenhurst: Workers of Our Lady, 2002.

Spanish

Gonzalez, Conchita. *Diario de Conchita*. OFFSET e IMPRENTA, Domingo Savio. 37-12-81-37-42-42 Mexico.

Dr. Gobelas. [Father Eusebio García de Pesquera], *Se Fue con Prisas a la Montaña*. Zaragoza: Octavio y Féliz, S.A. 1972.

_____. *Se Fue con Prisas a la Montaña*, Vol. 3. Zaragoza: Octavio y Féliz. 1974.

José María de Dios. [Father Julio Porro Cardeñoso], *Dios en la*

Sombra. Zaragoza: Editorial Círculo. 1967.

_____. *El Gran Portento de Garabandal.* Zaragoza: Editorial Círculo. 1969.

_____. *Garabandal Hoy. Mito o Misterio Divino?* Zaragoza: Editorial Círculo. 1975.

_____. *Las Apariciones de Garabandal Sin Interés?* Zaragoza: Editorial Círculo, 1975.

Laffireur-Noseda, M., and le Pelletier M.T. *La Estrella en la Montaña.* Tielt (Bélgica): Editorial Lannoo. 1970.

Obispado de Santander. *Boletín Oficial Del Obispado,* Junio 1978. Santander: HH. Trinitarias. 1978.

Declaraciones Oficiales de la Jerarquía Sobre Garabandal. Santander: Arts Gráficas Bedia. 1970.

Pérez, Ramón. *Garabandal el pueblo habla.* Industrias Gráficas Grupo Centro. S.A. 1991. Edición en lengua española ampliada y actualizada sobre la 3ª edición francesa, publicada por Edicones Résiac, Montsurs. 1977.

Puncernau, Doctor Ricardo. *Fenómenos Parapsicológicos de Garabandal Quince Años Después.* Barcelona: Librería San Miguel. 1974.

De Santiago, A.M. Garabandal 67 Crónica Espiritual de un Año. Zaragoza: Editorial Círculo. 1968.

Villa de Gallego, María Josefa. Los Milagros o Favores de Nuestra Madre de Garabandal. Santander: Edificio Interfacultativo. 2002.

_____. *Los Pinos de Garabandal Iluminarán al Mundo.* Barcelona: Ediciones Rondas. 1994.

Roman-Bocabeille, Christiane. *El Misterio de las Apariciones de Garabandal.* Barcelona: Ramón Sopena, 1984.

Saavedra, José Luis. *Garabandal Mensaje De Esperansa.* 3 ed. Santander: Van Keerbrergen, 2017.

Sanchez-Ventura y Pascual, F. *El Interrogante De Garabandal, Las Apariciones no Son Un Mito.* 5 ed. Zaragoza: Editorial Círculo, 1968

Lanús, Santiago. *Madre de Dios y Madre Nuestra.* Madrid: S.L. Gaudete, 2013.

Spanish newspapers

Alerta, Santander, Spain.

Diario Montañés, Santander, Spain.

Por Que, Barcelona, Spain.

¿Que Pasa? Madrid, Spain.

Web sites

Hogar de la Madre, www.garabandal.it/es/que-es/anecdotas, Feb.25, 2017

PHOTO ACKNOWLEDGMENTS

p.12 Map. garabandal.org

p14   Pesués Train Station 1969

p. 19 Loli and her father. www.whatisgarabandal.wordpress. com/2010/06/ Also St. Joseph Publications

p. 21   SAN SEBASTIAN DE GARABANDAL.   WETO Albrecht Weber, Meersberg/Garabandal

p. 23   Running of Bulls Pamplona.   Fotos Gonzalez, Pamplona

p. 30   Conchita at Her Window. www.whatisgarabandal.wordpress. com/1987/page/6/

p. 48 Conchita at her door. www.whatisgarabandal.blogspot.

com/2007_09_01_archive.html

p. 61   Cosio bridge over the Vendul.   www.cantabriarural.com

p. 78   Sari, Loli, and their mother, Julia.   St Michael's Garabandal Center for Our Lady of Carmel Inc.   http://www.garabandal.org/vigil/Loli_Ma.shtml.   Oct.,Nov., Dec. 1972.

p. 80   Carmona.   Fidel.   www.fotoscantabria.com

p. 96   Caracoles.   Nacho Facello.   https://commons.wikimedia.org/wiki/File%3ACaracoles_servidos_en_Barcelona_-_nachof.jpg   June. 22, 2010.

p. 110 Bishop Puchol Montis.   www.whatisgarabandal.files.wordpress.com/2010/12/priest_participants_13.jpg

p. 127 Puente en el Núcleo de Cosío.   info@valledelanansa.org valledelanansa.org/pdi/cosio-rionansa.   .

p. 140 SAN S. DE GARABANDAL (Santander) Iglesia.   Foto: Bustamonte Hurtado – Torrelavega.

p. 149 San Vicente de la Barquera.   Tania Astuy,   www.fotoscantabria.com/pueblo11.san.vicente.barquera.cantabria.htm.

p. 150 Pontifical University of Comillas.   www.wikimedia.org/wiki/File:Universidad_Pontificia_de_Comillas.jpg

p. 150   Conchita with Fr. Lucio Rodrigo. www.whatisgarabandal.wordpress.com/category/uncategorized/page/163/

p. 151 Fr. L. Rodrigo.   www.whatisgarabandal.wordpress.com/tag/lucio-rodrigo.

p. 154 Painting of the Garabandal Virgin.
http://www virgendegarabandal.net/netindexuno.htm

p. 155 Entrada del Palacio de Sobrellano.   Francisco Tazón Vega. www.rutasporcantabria.com.

p. 155 La mar, la costa y los Picos de Europa. (bottom photo) Fidel, www.fotoscantabria.com.

p. 156 Bisonte de Altamira. Ramessos. December 25, 2008. National Museum and Research Center of Altamira.   commons.wikimedia.org/wiki/File:AltamiraBison.jpg.

p. 157   Cocido Montañés.   http://www.eldiariomontanes.es/cantabria/201511/23/cocido-montanes-embajador-gastronomia-20151123121531.html

p. 163 Conchita. www.novacastalia.blogspot.com/2015/04/os-avisos-de-nossa-senhora-guerra.html   Also St. Joseph Publications

p. 165 Fr. J. Pelletier. www.whatisgarabandal.blogspot.com/2009/07/rev-fr-joseph-alfred-pelletier-1912.html

p. 171 Maximina. https://whatisgarabandal.wordpress.com/2008/11/

p. 175. Kelly with Conchita at her door. M. Warren W. Palm Beach, Florida.

p. 205 Iglesia de San Nicolás (Bilbao). Zarateman. www.commons.wikimedia.org/wiki/File:Bilbao_-_Iglesia_de_San_Nicol%C3%A1s_17.jpg.

p. 213 Las Ramblas

p. 217 Mercedes Salisachs. St. Michael's Garabandal Center for Our Lady of Carmel. September 29, 1978. www.garabandal.org/News/Loli_Interview_1978.shtml

p. 272 Map. forosdelavirgen.org/

The photos of the visionaries at the time of the apparitions (1961-1965) both in ecstasy and natural, and the following are used thanks to St. Joseph Publications. www.stjosephpublications.com.

p. 18 Rocky lane

p. 42 María ringing the bell

p. 46 Conchita with Fr. Laffineur

p. 48 Conchita alone (top) Conchita at her door (bottom)

p. 84 Father de la Riva

p. 88 Fathers Andreu on the road to the village

p.100 Conchita at 19 or 20.

p. 101 Aniceta

p. 107 People crowding the lane

p. 112 Three photos Fathers Ramón and Luís Andreu

p. 153 Fr. Odriozola

p. 174 Margarita Huerta

All of the other photos were taken by the author or if the author is in the photo, taken with the author's camera and permission or request.

Ed Kelly is a retired high school and college Spanish teacher who lives in Brookings, Oregon where he plays in the local symphony orchestra, acts in local theater, fishes in the nearby Pacific Ocean and writes and speaks on the reported apparitions at Garabandal.

Because he has written many articles for Garabandal journals, he is widely recognized as an expert on the happenings, especially in the area of special interest to him — the local church's investigation and evaluation of the apparitions.

This first book, *A Walk to Garabandal*, is a detailed account of his life in the village, starting just three and a half years after the last reported apparition. Because he has spent some four years total in the area, everyone in the small village knows the Spanish speaking American who now serves as a lector and sings in the church choir when in the village.

He has spoken with four of the five members of the Bishops' Investigating Commission, (Fr. Saiz had died before Kelly arrived), spoken twice with Santander Bishop del Val Gallo, and received letters stating their position on the apparitions from two of that bishops successors.